MOVIES
AS ARTIFACTS

MOVIES AS ARTIFACTS

CULTURAL CRITICISM OF POPULAR FILM

EDITED BY MICHAEL T. MARSDEN, JOHN G. NACHBAR,
AND SAM L. GROGG, JR.

NELSON-HALL 𝑛𝒽 CHICAGO

Visual Studies Workshop
Research Center
Rochester, N.Y.

V. S.W.
Gift of publisher
May 2, 1984

LIBRARY OF CONGRESS CATALOGING IN PUBLICATION DATA
Main entry under title:

Movies as artifacts.

   Articles originally published in the Journal
of popular film.
   Bibliography: p.
   1. Moving-pictures—United States—Addresses,
essays, lectures.   2. Moving-picture plays—
History and criticism—Addresses, essays, lectures.
3. Moving-picture industry—United States—Addresses, essays, lectures.   I. Marsden, Michael T.
II. Nachbar, John G.   III. Grogg, Sam L.   IV. Journal of popular film.
PN1993.5.U6M67   791.43'75   82-6300
ISBN 0-88229-453-9 (cloth)   AACR2
ISBN 0-88229-803-8 (paper)

Copyright © 1982 by Michael T. Marsden, John G. Nachbar and Sam L. Grogg

Manufactured in the United States of America

10 9 8 7 6 5 4 3 2 1

The paper in this book is pH neutral (acid-free).

CONTENTS

ACKNOWLEDGMENTS

We, the editors, would like to thank the authors whose work has appeared in the pages of the *Journal of Popular Film and Television* since 1972. Their rich and varied contributions have made *JPF* viable and vital.

We would also like to thank Ray B. Browne, Director of the Center for the Study of Popular Culture. He fanned the sparks of our ideas into a good, strong fire.

And we would like to thank our families, who allow us to be who we are.

CONTRIBUTING AUTHORS

Ralph Brauer is a writer who lives in Anoka, Minnesota. He has written articles
on film for the *Journal of Popular Film and Television* and a book on
television Westerns entitled, *The Horse, the Gun, the Piece of Property.*
James Damico is a playwright whose *Trial of A. Lincoln* toured the United
States in a production starring Henry Fonda and Billy Dee Williams.
Damico also co-authored the pilot for the television series "Love American Style." He is preparing a book on *film noir.*
Walter Evans teaches at Augusta College in Augusta, Georgia. He has published
fiction and essays in *Kansas Quarterly,* the *Journal of Popular Culture,* and
elsewhere. A more comprehensive theory of monster movies by Mr. Evans
appears in the *Journal of Popular Film* 4:2 (1975), pp. 124–42.
*Sam L. Grogg, Jr. is executive director of the Dallas-based USA Film Festival
and president of Media Development Associates, a Los Angeles based arts
management and public relations consulting firm. He is a consulting editor
for the *Journal of Popular Film and Television.*
Garth Jowett is a faculty member in the Communications School of the University of Houston. He is the author of *Film: The Democratic Art* and the
general editor of a series of film books published by Arno Press.
Stuart M. Kaminsky teaches film courses at Northwestern University. He is the
author of *Don Siegel: Director, American Film Genres, Clint Eastwood,*
and a number of other books. He is a frequent contributor to such publica-

tions as *Take One, Cinefantastique, The Velvet Light Trap,* and *Film-maker's Newsletter.*

Larry Landrum teaches courses in literature and popular culture at Michigan State University. He is bibliographer for the *Journal of Popular Film and Television* and the Popular Culture Association. He is presently completing a bibliography in book form on American popular culture.

Frank McConnell teaches English and film at Northwestern University. He is the author of *The Spoken Seen: Film and the Romantic Imagination.*

*Michael T. Marsden is an associate professor of popular culture at Bowling Green State University, where he is co-editor of the *Journal of Popular Film and Television* and director of the interdepartmental doctoral program in American Culture.

Brian Murphy teaches at Oakland University in Rochester, Michigan.

*John G. Nachbar is an associate professor of popular culture at Bowling Green State University, where he is also co-editor of the *Journal of Popular Film and Television* and director of the interdepartmental Film Studies Program.

Thomas H. Pauly teaches at the University of Delaware and is the author of numerous articles on American literature, popular culture, and film.

Gene D. Phillips, S.J. teaches literature and film at Loyola University in Chicago. He is the author of *The Movie Makers: Artists in an Industry, Graham Greene: The Films of His Fiction,* and *Stanley Kubrick: A Film Odyssey.*

Calvin Pryluck teaches courses in media at the University of North Carolina, Chapel Hill. He has published articles on the formal characteristics of film and related sign systems.

Brian Rose teaches media studies at Brooklyn College. He is a syndicated film and television critic for the Susquehanna broadcasting stations.

Charles S. Rutherford teaches at the University of Maryland, where his primary teaching and publishing interests are in Old and Middle English literature.

Timothy E. Scheurer teaches courses in writing, literature, and popular culture at Franklin University in Columbus, Ohio. He is a member of the Advisory Board of the *Journal of Popular Film and Television.* Mr. Scheurer is currently completing a study of the ballad opera and composes music in his spare time.

Joseph W. Slade is director of communications and chairman of the department of media arts at Long Island University's Brooklyn Center and is the editor

---

*The three editors of this volume co-founded the *Journal of Popular Film* in 1971 at the Center for the Study of Popular Culture at Bowling Green State University. Its title and scope were changed to the *Journal of Popular Film and Television* in 1980 and it is now published by Heldref Publications, Inc.

of the *Markham Review*. He is currently at work on a history of the stag film for the Institute for Sex Research.

Julian Smith teaches literature and film at the University of Florida. He has published articles in over twenty journals and is the author of *Looking Away: Hollywood and Vietnam*.

Vivian C. Sobchack is an associate editor of the *Journal of Popular Film and Television*. She is a faculty member at the Univeristy of California, Santa Cruz. Her articles have appeared in *American Quarterly*, the *Journal of Popular Film* and *Literature/Film Quarterly* and she is the author of *The Limits of Infinity: A Critical Study of Image and Sound in the American Science Fiction Film* and co-author of *An Introduction to Film*.

Alice Sodowsky, Roland Sadowsky, and Stephen Witte wrote their article while doing graduate work at Oklahoma State University.

Maurice Yacowar teaches film and drama at Brock University. He is author of *Hitchcock's British Films: A Critical Study* and *Tennessee Williams and Film*.

John Yates has contributed several essays to the *Journal of Popular Film*.

Movies are the mirrors by which the American culture surveys its mottled complexion. Palmolive beauty may show up in *The Sound of Music* or disgusting blemishes may call attention to themselves in *Midnight Cowboy*. The *Journal of Popular Film* encourages a close look at these mirror images, however distorted, keeping in mind the idea that a movie says as much about its audience as it contributes to the development of its art form. Rather than stand in awe of the personal beliefs of Bergman, Antonioni, or Fellini, the *Journal* intends to explore the public visions of John Ford, Frank Capra, Arthur Penn, and all of the many others. The purpose is to present material which treats films because of their popularity, not in spite of it. The *Journal of Popular Film* does not ignore the unalterable fact that the box-office, the American public, has determined the developmental thrust of its films. The millions of popcorn munching moviegoers must be brought back into the study of film. They are its life-blood. Without them, movies can only wither and die.

The above editorial comment appeared as the "First Frame" in the first issue of the *Journal of Popular Film*.

INTRODUCTION

MOVIES AND AUDIENCES: A REASONABLE APPROACH FOR AMERICAN FILM CRITICISM

SAM L. GROGG, JR., AND JOHN G. NACHBAR

I have been on this pitch for quite a long time, and now I should like to inquire why we as the nation that produces the movies should never have developed any sound school of movie criticism. That we haven't is obvious; read your papers.

—Otis Ferguson

During the last quarter-century, movie criticism has flourished in books and periodicals, on radio and TV. Film reviewers take up columns of space in most newspapers, collections of reviews dot the bookstands, and the rigid, gray faces of critics wedge themselves between the weather and sports on local and network television. But critical attitudes, apparatuses, and methodologies for the evaluation and analysis of popular movies are just as chaotic today as they were in 1942 when Otis Ferguson, film critic for *New Republic,* made the above inquiry. The nation that makes the movies has yet to develop a solid school of movie criticism.

Contemporary American film criticism is a dappled complex of discordant attitudes and principles. The discipline, if it merits such a decisive label, em-

1

braces the adamant elitism of John Simon, the whimsical cynicism of Rex Reed, the cryptic banality of Gene Shalit, the indignant tirades against the movie industry and audiences of Pauline Kael, and the controversial auteurism of Andrew Sarris. As David Denby puts it in his perceptive introduction to a collection of film criticism, *Awake In The Dark,* "American film criticism is strikingly anti-theoretical, empirical, descriptive, pragmatic, local, and spontaneous." [1]

Behind Denby's comment is qualified admiration. And indeed, it would be foolish to argue that the subjective approach employed by American film critics has not produced valuable and perceptive movie commentary. A reading of Robert Warshow's *The Immediate Experience,* the late 1970s articles by British writer Robin Wood, or the reviews of Otis Ferguson, himself, powerfully illustrate the value of a personal, impressionistic approach to film analysis. The problem is in the limitations of the guidance which an individual sensitivity can provide. We may be awed by the poetic skill with which a critic guides our perceptions of a film or group of films, but what do we do next? Subjective criticism is rarely useful beyond the subject at hand. Only scant attention has been paid to the foundations of the critical process. Making aesthetic pronouncements has taken the time of most of our film critics. Only a few have publicly considered why they do what they do; and, when these few thinkers do glance at their personal critical credos, their looks often only muddy the already cloudy situation.

A few years ago, Dwight Macdonald, one of our nation's more monolithic film critics, attempted to assess his critical stance in the introduction to a collection of his writings: *Dwight Macdonald on Movies* (1969). [2] The look may or may not have blinded his filmic perception, but it does give an insight into the critical mind-set of too many of America's film reviewers.

Macdonald sketches the "rules of thumb" he follows as: (1) Did it (the film) change the way you look at things? and (2) Did you find more (or less) in it the second, third, nth time? Such arbitrary terminology fits the spirit of these catch-all principles. But Macdonald does go on to elaborate and add credence to his aesthetic with reference to the traditionally sound rules of shape, form, consistency, rhythm, and climax, all supposedly legitimate by their allusion to reverential Aristotelian precepts.

Aristotle, though, never got to the movies; such an appeal to his authority may have less validity than Macdonald would hope. The security of such a position comes with the general activity of our critics, who have repeatedly sorted the art of the twentieth century into ancient categories. Rather than focus on the nature of the American film as the true progenitor of its critical assessment, the movie critics have tended to settle for a prefabricated veneer of traditionalism to explain away their activities.

When Macdonald directly faces his critical rationale, abandoning the Aristotelian refuge, he must admit its lack of foundation: "I know something about the cinema after forty years; and, being a congenital critic, I know what I like and why. But I can't explain the *why* except in terms of the specific work under consideration, on which I'm copious enough. The general theory, the larger view, the gestalt—these have always eluded me. Whether this gap in my critical armor be called an idiosyncrasy, or, less charitably, a personal failing, it has always been most definitely there."

Unable to hold firmly a notion of the *why* behind his judgments, Macdonald resorts to a simple credo of, "I know what I like." It is this self-centered attitude that characterizes American film criticism. Richard Schickel, for example, in a rebuttal to a review of his 1972 collection of criticism, *Second Sight,* angrily announced: "All I do know is what I like at any given moment in time. All I try to do is put that down in plain English" (*Variety,* April 19, 1972, p. 24). Schickel's words, like Macdonald's, could probably be justified as mere slips of the critical tongue. But, in the quiet of contemplation and assessment, those words, "I know what I like," echo as the vastly insufficient rule by which many critics operate and by which they have always operated. The slogan may serve well for the brilliant and the perceptive. Unfortunately, it also serves the shoddy and the unimaginative—the majority of those writing about the movies in this country. "I know what I like" has long served as the touchstone for the origin and development of film criticism in America.

Early film critics were unavoidably handicapped. They came to the movies out of diverse backgrounds. They had been interested in painting, drama, literature, music, psychology, sociology, etc.; and the filmic medium provided shelter for all. Sergei Eisenstein, speaking of the parallel genesis of the Soviet cinema, described the situation with these words:

> It is interesting to retrace the different paths of today's cinema workers to their creative beginnings, which together compose the multi-colored background of the Soviet cinema. . . . We pitched our tents and dragged into camp our experiences in varied fields. Private activities, accidental past professions, unguessed crafts, unsuspected eruditions—all were pooled and went into the building of something that had, as yet, no written traditions, no exact stylistic requirements, nor even formulated demands. (*Film Form,* 1949)[3]

The beginnings were confusing, spattered with half-baked ideas of the nature of film and its potential. Because of this, the infant film critics and theorists relied more on their already developed talents than upon an intrinsic understanding of the new cinematic medium. Our first critics knew only what they liked, and their estimations of the movies reflected their biases.

In 1915, Vachel Lindsay gave the motion picture its first aesthetic with *The*

Art of the Moving Picture. But rather than a poetic for film study, the work creeps into a poem of Lindsay. Insight turns to a self-indulgent eulogy:

> It has come then, this new weapon of men, and the face of the whole earth changes. In after centuries its beginning will indeed be remembered. It has come, this new weapon of men, and by faith and a study of the signs we proclaim it will go on and on in immemorial wonder.[4]

It is this type of awe-filled evocation that characterizes Lindsay's book and overshadows his often perceptive critical ideas. Lindsay felt the film deserved the attention and protection afforded to the greatest of art forms, and his comments were designed more for the establishment of film museums than for understanding and evaluation of the form itself.

A year after Lindsay's publication, Hugo Münsterberg, an eminent psychologist and a friend of William James, offered his estimation of the American film with *The Photoplay: A Psychological Study*. In a particularly clinical fashion, Münsterberg examines the primal nature of the film and its viewers. So clinical, in fact, is his treatise, that he feels obligated to warn the novice reader away from one chapter in the book with the note: "Readers who have no technical interest in physiological psychology may omit Chapter 3 and turn directly to Chapter 4 on Attention."[5] Unfortunately, even those who dismiss the third chapter find the reading unbearably technical.

Münsterberg's analysis, though supposedly objective because of its scientific nature, suffers from the same naive enthusiasm that mars Lindsay's work. Near his conclusion, Münsterberg ecstatically remarks, "Yes, it is a new art—and this is why it has such a fascination for the psychologist who in a world of ready-made arts, each with a history of centuries, suddenly finds a new form still underdeveloped and hardly understood."[6] Münsterberg delights in his cinematic innocence and happily jumps to play with the movies and their audience. But the novelty and lack of tradition that Münsterberg sees as a blessing has a corresponding evil. The film may give psychologists a chance to observe firsthand the growth of an art form, but it also provides a convenient receptacle for their already formulated theories. Münsterberg presents his evaluation of the cinema in terms of his own psychological expertise, which may or may not speak to the true nature of the American film.

In the beginning as now, it boiled down to Macdonald's words, "I know what I like." The pioneers of film criticism simply knew what they liked. Lindsay liked great art, and he loved to write poetry. Münsterberg liked psychology, and his mouth watered over the experimental possibilities offered by the novelty of the movies. When the two men came to the cinema, they brought their tastes with them, and the movies never had a chance. But a proper aesthetic of any art form must start from what the art is, not what it can or should be. Criticism of American movies can begin in only one place—the movies themselves. The critic must know the nature of the object of his criticism.

It is surely no secret that the movies were born at the height of the industrial and social revolutions of the late nineteenth and early twentieth centuries. The machine had given the worker more leisure time, and he took the time to demand his rights. One of those rights was the right to entertainment, which had been reserved, for the most part, for the wealthy of the elite culture. Expense kept all but the wealthy out of the legitimate theater. Only the grossest and most mottled types of entertainment were accessible to the common man. The motion picture changed all that. It didn't depend on the verbal ability of its viewers, and it was cheap.

By 1910, ten to twenty million men, women, and children were visiting the movie nickelodeons each week. The people demanded movies, and the industry feverishly expanded to meet the demands. The new art depended on the whim of the expanding marketplace. Artistic integrity took a backseat to a salable product, and what sold was what pleased the taste of the lowbrow mass audience.

Millions fell in love with the Victorian ideal of American womanhood, Lillian Gish. They gasped at the exploits of William S. Hart, who kept the alluring experience of the Old West alive in spite of civilization. And they laughed, cried, and conquered along with Charlie Chaplin, who was a little guy like them. The lifeblood of the new art was (and still is) the common experience of the American people. It provided material for the fledgling directors, and it sold the tickets that gave the industry the breath to thrive. American movies became the province of artists with sweeping public visions, men like D. W. Griffith, John Ford, and Frank Capra. They did not foster the growth of the artistically self-conscious, like the skilled European directors Jean Renoir, Ingmar Bergman, or Federico Fellini. To view an American film is to witness the dreams, values, and fears of the American people, to feel the pulse of American culture.

But the communally oriented vitality of the movies brought harsh comments from the early critics who were disciplined not to accept the new art's base nature. In his *A History of the Movies,*[7] Benjamin Hampton recounts that the early detractors called the movies the "plaything for children of all ages," the "cheap show for cheap people," and the "flimsy amusement for the mob." The movies' connection with the people rendered the form unfit for sophisticated critical attention. The people's art was, for the critical establishment, the rabble's art. Only on the narrowest of artistic terms did the critics approach the movies. A critical snobbishness forced the early reviewers into the "I know what I like" syndrome. On their own court and with their own rules, the critics felt more comfortable and could ignore the clamoring masses outside the gates.

The proper critical mind-set regarding any art form should be born of the art form itself. Aristotle, among others, demonstrated criticism should grow out of, and be dependent upon, the nature of its object. The critic must begin with an observation of the true nature of the art form and work to his conclusions and judgments from that essential estimation. Such an attitude does not exclude praise of a self-conscious artist like Robert Altman, but it places his work in an appropriate perspective in reference to the definitive nature of the art form with which he is working. This attitude does not attempt to be exclusive or to set up restrictive standards, but to categorize and treat the art form on its own terms. Criticism then becomes not a question of which is better, *Gone with the Wind* or *Citizen Kane,* but of what they are and where they fit in the overall spectrum of American filmic art.

If the clamor of our critics is ever to provide insight, it must be stimulated by a grasp of the essential relationship of American movies with the mass American audience of moviegoers. The elemental nature of our movies is grounded in the people. The critic must throw out his credo of ''I know what I like'' and consider closely ''what *they* like.''

Above the cacophony of voices in American movie criticism during the last half century or so have been heard the sweet songs of critics and historians who have recognized the essential relationship between movies and moviegoers. Although they have been in the minority of those writing about movies, these audience-based film critics have emerged, not surprisingly, to be among the few writers whose ideas about films remain valuable reading decades later. Hampton's *A History of the Movies,* for example, was centered on the business, rather than on the art, of making movies. Hampton, himself a Hollywood wheeler-dealer of sorts, recognized the central interest of Hollywood producers was box office and, therefore, the goodwill of the paying public. No doubt because he was so realistic in assessing the essence of American movies, Hampton's book remains in print and is often quoted, more than forty-five years after its initial publication.

In 1939, another important history of American film was first published— Lewis Jacobs' *Rise of the American Film.* Unlike Hampton, Jacobs' main interest was in the movies themselves; but, like Hampton, Jacobs realized films were as much a business and a reflector of public taste as they were an art:

. . . movies from their beginning presented more than cheap entertainment. From the onset . . . they were three things: a commodity, a craft, and a social force. These different aspects of the new medium were to affect the course, character, and development of one another. Being a commodity, the movie depended for its existence primarily on the money it made; as a potential art, it demanded new techniques; as a social force, it was to represent both business and art, with an influence proportional to its own genius and vitality.[8]

With such an all-inclusive and balanced viewpoint, Jacobs' history is still read annually by thousands of American film students. Some of his ideas and facts have been disproved, but Jacobs' refusal to remove the artistic from the business or cultural elements of film makes his history almost as useful now as it was in 1939.

During the succeeding years, other film writers began to apply their own methods to the cultural study of movies. The results continued to be memorable. Parker Tyler used emerging concepts of myth and Freudian psychology in such books as *Magic and Myth in the Movies* (1947) to suggest what Walt Disney cartoons and other popular films suggested about audiences of the 1940s.[9] In 1950, Martha Wolfenstein and Nathan Leites applied modern psychological theories to groups of movies in *Movies: A Psychological Study*.[10] Also during this period, in 1947, Siegfried Kracauer published the most famous and controversial study of the decade, *From Caligari to Hitler*.[11] "It is my contention," Kracauer stated in his preface, "that, through an analysis of the German films, deep psychological dispositions predominant in Germany from 1918 to 1933 can be exposed—dispositions which influenced the course of events during that time. . . ."

Perhaps because the 1960s were a period of exceptional sociopolitical concern, books conceived during the 1960s and published in the 1970s have resulted in a decade when the study of film as a medium– audience relationship has come fully to life. "The movies were meaningful because they depicted things lost or things desired," Andrew Bergman wrote in his study of 1930s movies, *We're in the Money;*[12] and he went on to show how popular movies revealed the souls of Depression moviegoers, including changing attitudes toward F.D.R., the federal government, and the American Dream. Michael Wood, in a more informal approach, studied audience values and attitudes in 1940s and 1950s movies in *America in the Movies* (1975).[13] Several film books of the 1970s deal with audience attitudes suggested by screen stereotypes. Notable contributions to film scholarship have been made, for example, by Molly Haskell's study of women in film, *From Reverence to Rape* (1974),[14] and by Thomas Cripps' history of black stereotypes in *Slow Fade to Black* (1977).[15]

Three recent histories of film all emphasize cultural perspectives. Garth Jowett in *Film: The Democratic Art* has produced the definitive social history to date of American moviegoing.[16] Jowett details who went to the movies during particular times and describes the pressures that audiences have traditionally exerted on Hollywood. Robert Sklar's *Movie-Made America* (1975)

combines a knowledge of the social conditions of various historical periods
with perceptive insights into films released during those periods.[17] Thomas
Bohn and Richard Stromgren's *Light and Shadows* (1978) is an almost up-to-
date textbook history.[18] Its method, however, is a return to the proven successful idea of Lewis Jacobs to discuss film business and audience as well as film
art.

As the above brief survey of criticism shows, there never has been any
"school" of American cultural film criticism. Nor is one needed now. Cultural
criticism began too practical for narrow categorization, and it remains so. The
study of film's relationship to its audience has never found a specific acceptable
method which a large group of critics would be willing to accept. Film analysts
are trained in a large number of disciplines and as a result have absorbed
myriad methodologies. All of these are applied to the serious study of movies.
All of them, in the hands of the imaginative, sensitive, and intelligent, can be
used successfully.

What is needed, then, is not a revolution of the means of perceiving what is
on the screen. Rather, what is needed is the continuation of a growing trend
about how the movies themselves are perceived. American movies have always
been commercial products made to appeal to the desires and tastes of a mass
audience. Isn't it reasonable, therefore, for us to consider their importance from
this perspective? And isn't it reasonable to expect critics we admire to do the
same?

NOTES

1. David Denby, Introduction to *Awake in the Dark* (New York: Vintage Books, 1977), p. xvii.
2. Dwight Macdonald, *Dwight Macdonald on Movies* (Englewood Cliffs, N.J.: Prentice-Hall, 1969).
3. Sergei Eisenstein, *Film Form* (New York: Harcourt Brace, 1949), p. 3.
4. Vachel Lindsay, *The Art of the Moving Picture* (New York: Liveright, 1970), p. 317.
5. Hugo Münsterberg, *The Film: A Psychological Study* (New York: Dover, 1970), p. 18.
6. Münsterberg, p. 100.
7. Benjamin Hampton, *A History of the Movies* (New York: Covici, Friede, 1931).
8. Lewis Jacobs, *The Rise of the American Film* (New York: Teachers College Press, 1968), p. 21.
9. Parker Tyler, *Magic and Myth of the Movies* (New York: Simon and Schuster, 1970).
10. Martha Wolfenstein and Nathan Leites, *Movies: A Psychological Study* (New York: Atheneum, 1970).
11. Siegfried Kracauer, *From Caligari to Hitler* (Princeton: Princeton University Press, 1947).

12. Andrew Bergman, *We're in the Money* (New York: New York University Press, 1971).
13. Michael Wood, *America in the Movies* (New York: Basic Books, 1975).
14. Molly Haskell, *From Reverence to Rape* (New York: Holt, Rinehart and Winston, 1974).
15. Thomas Cripps, *Slow Fade to Black* (New York: Oxford University Press, 1977).
16. Garth Jowett, *Film: The Democratic Art* (Boston: Little, Brown, 1976).
17. Robert Sklar, *Movie-Made America: A Cultural History of American Movies* (New York: Random House, 1975).
18. Thomas W. Bohn and Richard L. Stromgren, *Light and Shadows,* 2nd ed., (Sherman Oaks, Calif.: Alfred Publishing Co., 1978).

ONE/MOVIES AND THEIR AUDIENCES

Movies were not truly born until they recognized their audience. The scientists and inventors who toyed with the moving image in the nineteenth century thought it was at least an amusing parlor trick, at most an instrument for improved scientific observation and record. But the entrepreneurs of the last decade of the nineteenth century seized on the new illusion and decided it might be of interest far beyond the confines of the sitting room or the magician's routine.

The great influx of immigrants into America during the 1880s through the early 1900s helped create a need for a cheap and simple entertainment form. Movies caught the imagination of these new Americans and became their art. As the complexion and nature of the audience changed over the years, so did the movies. But never have the movies and their audience pulled very far apart.

This chapter traces the relationship between the moviegoers and the movies since the first one-reelers. The articles here give a picture of who went and who goes to movies and how these people provide a basic key to understanding popular film in America.

In his essay on the nickelodeon movie audience, Garth S. Jowett outlines why the most important group of initial moviegoers was the urban poor. Moving beyond the usual argument that the poor attended early, one-reel movies just because the movies were cheap, Jowett demonstrates that other factors, such as increasing leisure time and the extension of theater melodrama to the screen, were also important in the dramatic rise of the movies as a mass entertainment form.

Ralph Brauer's article on the relationship between 1930s movies and their audiences is based on a working method different from that of Jowett's essay. Whereas Jowett relies on the careful gathering of sociological data for his conclusions, Brauer, who writes fiction, prefers to base his conclusions on impressions and instincts. The result is an unusual essay evoking largely through imagery and metaphor what it must have been like to experience the movies during the Great Depression.

The breakdown of the quarter-century-old studio system during the late 1940s and early 1950s forced radical changes in the way movies were produced. Calvin Pryluck points out in his essay on the film industry, 1945–1969, that changes in the structure of the industry led directly to changes in the movies themselves. Whereas earlier films were characterized by assembly-line uniformity, more recent movies reveal a "boom or bust" industrial philosophy. Brian Rose's study of 1970s movies, based for the most part on box-office figures compiled by *Variety*, verifies Pryluck's thesis. Even though 1970s Hollywood was in a boom era, the industry, as Rose points out, because of the need to create blockbuster hits, remains in a continuous state of uncertainty. Together, these four articles demonstrate a rich variety of ways to study audiences and film eras. From Jowett's statistics to Pryluck's box-office data, from Brauer's political analogies to Rose's discussion of marketing techniques, the methods seem endless and the conclusions endlessly fascinating.

The First Motion Picture Audiences

GARTH S. JOWETT

The exact composition and nature of the first motion picture audiences has always been something of an historical mystery. While the classic histories of the movies all attempt to describe the initial devotees of the new entertainment, they are seldom able to go beyond a cursory analysis of the type found in Benjamin Hampton's *A History of the Movies* (1931), where the author noted that, "A new class of amusement buyer sprang into existence as quickly and apparently as magically as screen pictures themselves appeared."[1] Only Lewis Jacobs in his seminal work, *The Rise of the American Film* (1939) goes into the kind of detail which is useful to film and social historians.[2]

The question remains—who was this audience, and where did they come from? And why were they attracted to this new entertainment form in such vast numbers in such a short period of time? Only now are some of these answers beginning to appear, as film and social historians start to piece together the early years of the motion picture industry. It is becoming more and more obvious that the movies were no idle innovation, arriving at a propitious time, but that they answered a deep social and cultural need of the American people. The work in this area has just begun, and only by continuing such research can we hope to reconstruct the dimensions of the social impact of the motion picture on American society in the last seventy years.

RECREATION AND ENTERTAINMENT AT THE TURN OF THE CENTURY

A major aspect of the immense social and cultural changes taking place in America in the period after the Civil War was a growing interest and participation in new forms of recreation and entertainment. Eventually these new "mass" recreational forms would alter the pattern of American social and cultural life away from an emphasis on local interests and activities to a more national level of participation, with which we are so familiar today. The rapid influx of immigrants and rural Americans into the burgeoning urban centers provided the raw population base, but this alone did not account for the tremendous increase in newspaper and periodical literature readership. The circulation of daily newspapers increased 400 percent between 1870 and 1900, while the population grew only by 95 percent.[3] This discrepancy is partly accounted for by the decrease in illiteracy and by a general raising of educational standards. The aggressive tactics of the publishers, who became much more expert in gauging the tastes of their readers, was also a major factor.

However, the single most important reason favoring the growth of all recreational activity was the increase in available leisure time. The decline in the workweek of American workers meant more time for reading and other forms of self-improvement, which in turn led to greater efficiency and productivity and more available leisure hours. Thus in non-agricultural industries the workweek declined by about 10 hours between 1850 and 1900—from 66 to 56 hours. In the next four decades reductions were even sharper than in the previous half century. Between 1900 and 1940 the workweek in non-agricultural industries declined from 56 to 41 hours, with the sharpest declines occurring between 1900 and 1920, when the average workweek in non-agricultural industries dropped about 5 hours every 10 years.[4] An examination of the decrease in the workweek of certain types of workers between 1890 and 1928 indicates the amount of extra leisure time available. The increase in available

AVERAGE HOURS OF LABOR PER WEEK IN ELEVEN INDUSTRIES, 1890–1928*

INDUSTRY	AVERAGE HOURS PER WEEK		PERCENT DECREASE DURING PERIOD
	1890	1928	
Bakeries	64.7	47.4	26.7
Boot and shoe	59.5	49.1	17.5
Building	52.0	43.5	16.3
Cotton goods	62.8	53.4	14.9
Foundry and machine shops	59.8	50.4	15.7
Blast furnaces	84.6	59.8	29.3
Marble and stone	54.7	44.0	19.6
Millwork	52.0	44.8	13.8
Book and job printing	56.4	44.3	21.5
Newspaper printing	48.2	45.1	6.5
Woolen goods	58.9	49.3	16.3

*Source: Recent Social Trends, p. 828

leisure time would encourage the creation and usage of all recreational forms, especially commercial amusements such as the motion picture, which required a more definite and specific commitment of free time, unlike books, newspapers, or periodicals, which could be read in the home with greater ease.

Recreation of all forms took a firm hold in America in the 1890s and the newspapers of the time were also full of advertisements for summer resorts, or fashionable tours of Europe or to the American West. However, the old American ethic which praised the virtues and rewards of hard work taught so assiduously in the famous McGuffey Readers, was still much in evidence and the increased leisure time made available by the shorter workweek was seen by some as a frivolous waste of human resources. It was especially in the city that this traditional view would meet its strongest opposition, while in the rural sectors the old prejudices against amusement would continue to hold fast for some time to come. City children found outlets for their pent-up energies in the various activities created specifically for them by well-meaning social organizations conscious of their needs. The Boy Scouts, the Girl Scouts and Camp Fire Girls were all created to supply city children with some knowledge and understanding of the outdoors. Towards the end of the century, urban needs led to larger-scale planning of public parks, reaching a peak in the 1890s and resulting in such achievements as Chicago's beautiful Lincoln Park along the lake front and the metropolitan park systems of Boston, Cleveland, and other cities. Old favorites such as the circus, the theater, burlesque, vaudeville, and the melodrama continued to thrive in the growing urban environment.

These entertainment forms sometimes had a social significance which was not immediately apparent but which went deep into the social fabric of the new emerging urban culture. Albert F. McLean, in a provocative study, *American Vaudeville as Ritual,* examined this entertainment form and suggested that vaudeville was, "for at least four decades, not only a significant social institution but also a mythic enactment through ritual of the underlying aspirations of the American people."[5] Much of what McLean claims for vaudeville could be said for the movies, with the added factor that movies had a much greater audience and appealed to a wider range of immigrant groups, especially to those in the lower social-economic groups. In the final analysis the two entertainments were essentially different, in that vaudeville was a highly stylized, artificial, and ritualistic form, with recognized and repetitive actions which were expected by the audience, while the film medium relied more on elements of surprise and visual effects in an attempt to be as realistic as possible. (In time, the film audience would also come to expect certain forms of "ritual.")

The demand for urban recreational activities seemed insatiable, and sharp-witted entrepreneurs were not slow to exploit this need by supplying a myriad of entertainment forms such as the dime-museum, dance halls (which were extremely popular, but also a great source of consternation to many city authorities), shooting galleries, beer gardens, bowling alleys, billiard parlors, saloons, and other more questionable social activities. Thus, entertainment in the cities was available in many different forms; but there were still many segments of the population which were unable to partake of these amusements on a regular basis because of economic considerations, long working hours, or problems with the language. It was from this group that most of the initial adherents to the motion picture would come, for the movies could satisfy all of these problems in one way or another—they were cheap, available for the whole family, easily accessible, and needed no proficiency in the English language.

THE NEW AUDIENCE

But what was the nature of this "new" audience that so eagerly embraced this welcomed digression in their lives? Part of this answer can be found in a brief examination of the religious, social, and economic conditions of the era. The motion picture's first audience seemed to have been made up from three groups: first, those from the middle class who had never previously attended the theater or other amusements because of religious beliefs and who were now free to explore new entertainments. Benjamin Hampton, in his *A History of the Movies*, noted the motion picture was perfected at a time when "more and more people, mainly the young, broader minded and more daring than their forebears, crept through the barriers which had been erected by religious prejudice."[6] Once freed from religious strictures, this group began to enjoy theatrical presentations of local or professional repertoire groups. Among the plays which helped break down the religious objections to this type of entertainment were *Uncle Tom's Cabin* and *Ten Nights in a Bar Room*.[7] As church restrictions were relaxed, informally at first, then later by popular assent, more and more Americans began seeking new diversions, with the major criteria being moral acceptability and low cost. It was many of these same people who also welcomed the phonograph, kinetoscope parlors and arcades, and then later the dime museums, trolley rides, and amusement parks. However, most of them turned to the movies as a principal source of entertainment, slowly at first, and then with an increasing fervor which caught the whole country by surprise.

The second group of early movie adherents came from those middle and upper working class patrons of the live theater, especially the fans of the popular melodramas. They grabbed hold of the movies as a new source of

theatrical experience because the live theater was unable to fill the entertainment void created by the alteration in social and cultural conditions. Nicholas
Vardac, in his book *From Stage to Screen,* has shown how the audience's
desire for "pictorial realism" had created a demand favorable to the introduction of the motion picture, for the theater was not capable of providing the
extension to the realism already indicated on the stages of that period. The
dramatic improvement in theatrical lighting with the introduction of electricity
also helped to destroy many illusionary effects. Only the movies, with their
realistic illusion of depth, could continue the evolutionary process begun with
the increasing attempts at realism in the melodrama.[8]

Then too, as a commercial offering, the theater suffered from the many
serious deficiencies found in the majority of provincial theaters, which were not
technically equipped to handle the very complex machinery used for the realistic productions in New York or other large Eastern cities. Most towns with a
population of below 10,000 possessed inadequate equipment for the presentation of road shows which might have competed with the realism and sensationalism available in the motion picture melodrama. In *Middletown,* the Lynds
point out how meager were the offerings of the provincial theaters in the 1890s:

> Like the automobile, the motion picture is more to Middletown than
> simply a new way of doing an old thing; it has added new dimensions to
> the city's leisure. To be sure, the spectacle-watching habit was strong
> upon Middletown in the nineties. Whenever they had a chance people
> turned out to a "show," but chances were relatively fewer. Fourteen
> times during January, 1890, for instance, the Opera House was opened
> by performances ranging from *Uncle Tom's Cabin* to *The Black Crook,*
> before the paper announced that "there will not be any more attractions at
> the Opera House for nearly two weeks." In July there were no "attrac-
> tions"; a half dozen were scattered through August and September; there
> were twelve in October. [In a footnote, Lynd adds that there were less
> than 125 performances, including matinees, for the entire year.][9]

By 1923, however, there were nine motion picture theaters in Middletown,*
operating from 1 to 11 p.m. seven days a week, summer and winter, with a
total of over 300 cinematic performances available to the residents every week
of the year. It is clear therefore that by the time of the introduction of the film
as a commercial entertainment, the extensive provincial audiences were being
offered nothing more than conventional staging, while the more "realistic"
productions were limited in circulation to a few large Eastern cities. This is

---

*"Middletown" was, of course, the city of Muncie, Indiana.

The Comet Theatre in New York City, circa 1910.

further evidenced by the remarkable growth in the number of motion picture houses in those outlying areas once they had been spawned and found acceptance in their urban birthplace.

In the cities, the live theater, although a very popular and well-publicized entertainment, was still not capable of reaching all the people. Benjamin Hampton estimated that "perhaps a million, possibly two million, people were regular patrons of the various forms of theater entertainment—opera, spoken drama, musical comedy, vaudeville, and burlesque—and perhaps another million enjoyed the stage occasionally. . . . However, ninety percent of the American population was not reached by any method of story-telling and character delineation by play-acting."[10]

A special study commissioned by the Twentieth Century Club of Boston on "The Amusement Situation in the City of Boston" in 1909 supported Hampton's contention that the live theater did not reach as many people as the movies later did.[11] The exhaustive survey indicated that in 1909 the weekly seating capacity (calculated by multiplying the theater's seating capacity by the number of weekly performances) of the various segments of the entertainment industry was as follows:

SEATING IN BOSTON PLACES OF AMUSEMENT, 1909

AMUSEMENT	WEEKLY SEATING CAPACITY
Opera	13,590
First class theaters	111,568
Popular theater	17,811
Stock house	21,756
Vaudeville houses	45,744
Burlesque houses	80,700
Vaudeville and moving pictures	79,362
Moving picture theaters	402,428

The population of metropolitan Boston at this time was estimated at 625,000. The study noted that, of the entertainment seating total, vaudeville and moving picture shows accounted for 85.4 percent, legitimate performances, 13.5 percent, and grand opera, 1.1 percent. The average attendance prices were:

Moving-picture shows	.10
Vaudeville and moving pictures	.15
Vaudeville	.50
Regular Theater	$1.00
The Boston Opera	$2.00

The authors of this study noted with some alarm the "overwhelming preponderance of cheaper and less desirable forms of entertainment," but realistically commented that, "these theaters evidently appeal more and more strongly to their habitués. The great growth of new houses of this type indicates not only a rapidly increasing following, but also a tremendous and growing tendency toward a lower and less desirable form of recreative amusement."[12]

The relatively high cost of the theater also proved to be prohibitive to its wide acceptance and use, especially amongst the lower, working classes. The price of tickets ranged from $1.50 to $2.00 for orchestra seats to 50¢ for the gallery in metropolitan areas and $1.50 to 25¢ in smaller areas.[13] At this time the average workman's pay was approximately $2 a day, and the relatively high cost of the gallery seats could not have been a great inducement considering the noise of the gallery mob. However, after 1880, the presentation of drama and melodrama at "popular prices" in second-class theaters in the larger cities had achieved some success in attracting new groups of entertainment buyers. Many of these same companies also later toured county seats and larger provincial towns, appearing in opera houses, which we have seen remained dark between these infrequent engagements. Nevertheless, all the live theatrical entertainment available could not satisfy the special and growing needs of a very large segment of the American population.

As the moving picture evolved from its early exposure in arcades, vaudeville and "store-front" theaters, it passed into the mainstream of American life. For the price of 5¢ to 10¢ a patron could partake of an entertainment experience that was demonstrably more realistic than anything he would find on the stage. Initially, at least, this low cost was a great inducement to sampling the new entertainment and was an important reason for its quick success. However, once established as a permanent and highly desirable attraction, the price of film-going increased commensurate with the increasing length and improved quality of the product being offered.

The third and most important group which made up the first movie audiences came from the large urban working class, who seldom went anywhere near live theatrical entertainment. For them, the movies were the ideal form of recreation. Especially for the immigrant worker, the movies provided more than just a way of filling-in time, but also acted as a guide to the newcomer on the manners and customs of his new environment. It is somewhat ironic that, while the workers formed by far the largest segment of the nickelodeon audience in the early years, the owners of these establishments very quickly coveted the more prestigious middle class.[14] Russell Merritt has demonstrated that, from the first, the nickelodeon "catered to him [the worker] through necessity, not through choice. The blue-collar worker and his family may have supported the nickelodeon. The scandal was that no one connected with the movies much wanted his support—least of all the immigrant film exhibitors who were working their way out of the slums."[15] However, whether he liked it or not, the exhibitor had to contend with the worker, and especially the immigrant, as the backbone of his support.

There is no doubt that the movies were indeed an important factor in the social life of the urban working class, and this is graphically confirmed in the following extracts taken from one of the studies forming the *Pittsburgh Survey,* an in-depth social study of the workers in that city done in 1907–1909. One researcher reported:

[We walked] among the crowd of pleasure-seekers on Fifth Avenue, and watched the men and women packed thick at the entrance of every picture show. My companion and I bought tickets for one of the five cent shows. Our way was barred by a sign, "Performance now going on." As we stood near the door, the crowd of people waiting to enter filled the long vestibule and even part of the sidewalk. They were determined to be amused, and this was one of the things labeled, "Amusement." They were hot and tired and irritable, but willing to wait until long after our enthusiasm was dampened, and we had left them standing in line for their chance to go in.

It was an incident not without significance, this eagerness with which they turned toward leisure after a working week of unmeaning hours. . . .[16]

The lack of available recreational opportunities for many workers is amply demonstrated in the findings of the *Pittsburgh Survey*. Discussing the role of recreation in the lives of working women, the *Survey* pointed out that, of the 22,185 working women surveyed in Pittsburgh in 1907, only 258, less than 2 percent, were in touch with a center for social development and recreation.[17] While the importance of the motion picture in filling this "leisure gap" was obvious even then to the social workers involved in doing the survey, they were still somewhat skeptical about its ultimate value. The report continued: "Nickel-odeons and dance halls and skating rinks are in no sense inherently bad, but so long as those maintained for profit are the only relief for nervous weariness and the desire for stimulation, we may well reckon leisure a thing spent, not used."[18]

A few of the reasons for the immense popularity of the "movies" have already been suggested, but the extra relief they provided in a dreary, work-laden life must be emphasized. The *Survey* research only alluded to this when it continued: "In so far as hours of work tend to dull and stupefy the worker, they are longer than the community can afford. Dulled senses demand powerful stimuli; exhaustion of the vital forces leads to a desire for crude, for violent excitation. . . . Craving for excitement is the last symptom of a starved imagination. . . ."[19] However, the fact that some forms of recreational stimuli were needed was not lost on the social workers; their only doubts concerned the medium's social utility. The report continued: "Any excitation, destructive or not, is acceptable, if only it be strong; the effect of it is to create a desire for stronger stimulation. Roller-skating rinks, dance halls, questionable cafes, may figure only temporarily in the worker's life or, by increasing the demand for excitement, may lead to sexual license."[20] It was becoming ominously clear: the motion picture, although a major source of entertainment and recreation for a large portion of the working class was already being classified as "destructive," "unsocial," "wasteful," and the cause of "sexual license."

The whole problem of leisure and recreation was of great concern to the newly emerging professional social workers, who were anxious that all Americans made maximum use of their spare time in constructive ways. Unfortunately, the movies' origins as an adjunct of both vaudeville and the rather "seamy" arcades had saddled it with an unsavory reputation. While there certainly were unscrupulous motion picture house operators, and store-front theaters that were both unsanitary and morally unsafe, by far the majority of nickelodeons provided their ever-increasing clientele with a form of recreation and entertainment which was vastly superior in "moral tone" and low cost to that available in many other urban leisure activities, such as saloons, vaudeville, or burlesque.

In many working-class districts, the motion picture was the *only* source of amusement available and certainly the only form of public amusement which many working-class families could afford to attend together as a family unit. In a survey of the mill town of Homestead, one reasearcher reported:

> Practically the only public amusements in Homestead, during my stay there, were the nickelodeons and skating rinks. Six of the former, all on Eighth Avenue, sent out their penetrating music all evening and most of the afternoon. There was one ten-cent vaudeville house, but others charge five cents for a show consisting of songs, moving pictures, etc., which lasts fifteen minutes or so.

> The part these shows play in the life of the community is really surprising. Not only were no other theatrical performances given in Homestead, but even those in Pittsburgh, because of the time and expense involved in getting there, were often out of the reach of working men and their families. . . . Many people, therefore, find in the nickelodeons their only relaxation. Men on their way from work stop for a few minutes to see something of life outside the alteration of mill and home; the shopper rests while she enjoys the music, poor though it be, and the children are always begging for five cents to go to the nickelodeon. In the evening, the family often go together for a little treat. . . . In many ways, this form of amusement is desirable. What it ordinarily offers does not educate but does give pleasure. . . . As the nickelodeon seems to have met a real need in the mill towns, one must wish that it might offer them a better quality of entertainment.[21]

The expense of entertainment was therefore a major consideration for most working-class families, and the study indicated that, with a weekly budget of between $12 and $15, the average allowed for "sundries" was $1.23. The social worker commented, "we see how small an amount can be free at this and lower levels for what could be called amusements. Ten cents a week for the nickelodeon or for candy, a car ride to the country once in a while—these are the possibilities which seem open to mothers and children depending on a day laborer's pay."[22]

It was, however, the lack of alternative recreational opportunities which was the major factor accounting for the popularity of the motion picture amongst the entire urban working-class population, of which the immigrants were, of course, a significant segment. We have already noted the relatively high cost of other forms of commercial amusements and the expense and other difficulties encountered in attending the live theater. Alternative forms of recreation were either too expensive or not widely available in the working-class districts of cities. Very few public playgrounds were in existence at this time, and by 1910 the playground movement had just begun to make a little headway.[23] The report on "Recreation" in the U.S. government study *Recent Social Trends* noted that, in 1910, only 17.6 percent of the playgrounds reported were operating on a year-round schedule, and that organized playground activities formed only a small part of the regular recreational program of the urban community.[24] It is little wonder therefore that the motion picture appealed to the working class, and especially the children with time on their hands. The new medium of entertainment had no difficulty in finding a ready-made and eager audience amongst this segment of the urban population.

NOTES

1. Benjamin Hampton, *A History of the Movies* (New York: Covici-Friede Publishers, 1931), p. 17.
2. While very little work has been done in this area of film studies in recent years, an important article on this topic has recently been published. See Russell Merritt, "Nickelodeon Theaters: Building an Audience for the Movies," *AFI Report,* May, 1973, pp. 4– 8. For a more extended examination of the factors surrounding the introduction of the motion picture into America see Garth Jowett, "Media Power and Social Control: The Motion Picture in America, 1896– 1936" (unpublished Ph.D. thesis, University of Pennsylvania, 1972).
3. Edwin Emery, *The Press in America* (Englewood Cliffs: Prentice-Hall, 1962), p. 346.
4. This summary is taken from Joseph S. Zeisel, "The Workweek in American Industry, 1850– 1956," in Eric Larrabee and Rolf Meyersohn eds., *Mass Leisure* (Glencoe: Free Press, 1958), pp. 145– 53.
5. Albert F. McLean, *American Vaudeville as Ritual* (Lexington: University of Kentucky Press, 1965), p. 2.
6. Hampton, p. 15.
7. "Uncle Tom's Cabin" was one of the many theatrical presentations which found its way into film scripts, thus creating a further bond of continuity. For a detailed examination of the career of this play as a motion picture see, William L. Slout, " 'Uncle Tom's Cabin' in American Film History," *The Journal of Popular Film,* Vol. II, No. 2 (Spring, 1973), pp. 137– 52.
8. The best treatments of the melodrama are Frank Rahill, *The World of Melodrama* (University Park: Pennsylvania State University Press, 1967); and Nicholas Vardac, *From Stage to Screen* (Cambridge: Harvard University Press, 1949). See also John L. Fell, "Dissolves by Candlelight," *Film Quarterly,* Vol. XXIII, No. 3, 1970, pp. 22– 34.
9. Robert S. Lynd and Helen Merrell Lynd, *Middletown* (New York: Harcourt, Brace and World, 1929), p. 263.

10. Hampton, p. 14.
11. *The Amusement Situation in the City of Boston,* a report prepared by the Drama Committee of the Twentieth Century Club, Boston, 1910, pp. 10–11.
12. *Ibid.,* pp. 6–7.
13. Hampton, p. 14.
14. Merritt cites a Russell Sage Study which indicated that seventy-eight percent of the audience in New York nickelodeons were members of the "working Class." See Merritt, p. 5.
15. *Ibid.,* p. 5.
16. Elizabeth Beardsley Butler, *Women and the Trades: Pittsburgh 1907–08* (New York: Charities Publication Committee, 1909), p. 333.
17. *Ibid.,* p. 332.
18. *Ibid.,* p. 333.
19. *Ibid.,* p. 356.
20. *Ibid.,* p. 356.
21. Margaret F. Byington, *Homestead: The Households of a Mill Town* (New York: Charities Publications Committee, 1910), pp. 110–11.
22. *Ibid.,* p. 89.
23. *Recent Social Trends in the United States* (New York: McGraw-Hill Book Company, 1933), p. 916.
24. *Ibid.,* p. 917.

When the Lights Went Out—Hollywood, the Depression, and the Thirties

RALPH A. BRAUER

Now gather round me people, let me tell you true facts,
Now gather round me people, let me tell you true facts,
That tough luck has struck me and the rats is sleepin in my hat.
—Blind Lemon Jefferson
"Tin-Cup Blues"

It was a split thing. They were cursing Roosevelt for the intrusion into their lives. At the same time they were living off it. Main Street still has this fix.
—Ed Paulsen in
Studs Terkel's *Hard Times*

Rows. Rows. Lines. That's the mental picture many people have of the 1930s. Sometimes the rows were geometrically perfect, as if choreographed by the army or Busby Berkeley (as some of them were). Sometimes they wound sinuously, like Harlow posed on a bed in draping silk. Sometimes they were bunched chaotically, as if threatening to erupt, the way the brooding Okies threaten to erupt in *The Grapes of Wrath* (1939). Rows: breadlines with beaten people whose drooping heads avoid the camera, or the lines of robust CCC workers planting trees and smiling.

What intrigues so many people about those rows is the question of what was going on in the minds of those who stood in the soup lines or waited outside factory gates for the job that never came or stood in lines while working for the CCC and the WPA. The predominant belief has been to assume that what all those people had on their minds was escape—booze, drugs, radio, the movies, even suicide, the ultimate escape.

This image of those rows of people indulging themselves in the delusions of escape is a painful and unfortunately stereotyped image which has come to color all perceptions of the films of the 1930s. The reality of the complex thoughts of people faced with desperate times, alternately burdened and soothed by elements in their cultural psyches, ranging from Puritan/Protestant attitudes toward work and misfortune to America's mythic individualism, is a little more difficult to unravel. Harvey Swados remarks that Louis Adamic "found, in his stint as a caseworker among New York families on relief, that some families were knit more closely together by their common suffering, while others were so devastated by economic catastrophe that they were torn apart and often destroyed by illness, desertion, and disappearance."[1] Swados's point is that the Depression produced a whole variety of contradictory reactions in people.

The Depression also brought out a variety of social contradictions. It was a time in which the head of President Hoover's Organization on Unemployment Relief could seriously advocate giving free movie tickets to the poor but could not consider giving them government-sponsored jobs. Such a time produced a film (*Stand Up and Cheer*, 1934) which advocated the appointment of a Secretary of Amusement who would help people sing and dance their way through the Depression—an absurd scheme by today's standards. Escapism? Who was the escapist—Secretary Gifford (who, after all, had been president of AT&T) or Warner Brothers?

Contradictions, not escapism, that's what you get both in the lives of people who suffered through the 1930s and in the movies that for a few hours each week relieved their suffering. Read Pauline Kael's memories in Studs Terkel's *Hard Times,* and then at random read a half-dozen other memories. They will tell you more about the psychology of people in the Depression than all those facile theories about the movies as escapism. Those rows of people who sat in the darkness viewing the screen had more on their minds than escaping. Their reactions were as varied as those of the people on the outside: laughing, leering, booing, cheering, surreptitiously reaching a hand inside a blouse, kissing, sleeping, sitting stoically. That was the audience, and to a large extent those were the films.

Those who occupied the rows in 1933 were fewer than those who had occupied the rows in 1930. Attendance dropped from 90 million per week in 1930 to 60 million per week in 1932 and 1933. Five thousand movie houses closed down. In order to lure folks back into the theaters, various solutions were tried. Theaters cut ticket prices by as much as twenty-five cents. They showed double features—booking two movies together, showing them one right after the other—sometimes for the price of one. When that didn't work, they tried gimmicks. There were the "give aways" in which theaters gave away glasses and china and there were "bank nights" which were nothing more than get-money-quick lotteries that offered to lucky patrons prizes ranging from a few dollars to a hundred dollars.

The attendance figures, despite their decline, still are startling. Bank nights and free dishes aside, people still went to the movies. If one figures the total population in the early '30s was around 122 million, then the 60 million per week moviegoers represented, on a pure numbers basis, about one-half of the population. Now admittedly, some of those people who attended movies were repeaters. A 1936 *Fortune* survey found that 13 percent went more than once a week, while 24.9 percent went at least once a week and an additional 12.1 percent went more than once a month. If we use these *Fortune* figures as a way of extrapolating back to 1932, we can estimate that as much as one-third of the population went to the movies at least once a week at a time when the unemployment rate reached 25 percent of the work force (12 million in 1933).[2]

The intriguing question about all those statistics and all those rows of moviegoers is what is the relationship between the one-third who went to the movies and the one-fourth who were out of work? Statistics of that sort are hard to find, and where the facts are marginal, stereotyped images take over. The stereotype of the typical Depression movie watcher is a down-and-out person who is so poor that he or she ironically spends money to sleep in a theater because there was no other warm place to sleep. This image of people sleeping in theaters is now an accepted part of Depression folklore. In contrast to this myth the only real index we have of who the moviegoers were in the Depression is Warner and Lunt's 1935 Yankee City study, which is cited in Garth Jowett's book, *Film: The Democratic Art*. According to Warner and Lunt, movie attendance in 1935 in Yankee City (Newburyport, Massachusetts) was highest among the lower-middle and upper-lower classes (34.16 percent and

34.4 percent, respectively). Yet, though attendance among lower-lower-class people was only 14 percent, they tended to go more often: their average weekly attendance frequency was the highest (2.65 times per week as compared to 2.43 and 2.3 times per week for the upper-lower and lower-middle classes).

The Yankee City study, then, bolsters an obvious supposition about the Depression moviegoer—which is that the 25 percent who were out of work were probably not among the one-third who attended once a week (especially if we extrapolate the 1935 figures, when unemployment was 10 million, back to 1933).[3] It also uncovers an intriguing look at those who did go. In all probability those faces sitting in the rows were people who were just getting by as marginal members of the work force and who no doubt lived in daily fear that tomorrow they might join the 25 percent who were out of work. The movies these people paid to see, the stars who were the top box-office draws, are about as close a look as we will ever have at the collective dreams and nightmares of those who stood on the edge of the abyss and peered down into the darkness of the Depression.

In effect, those films constitute a part of what might be called a "popular New Deal" that coincided with the governmental New Deal. The popular New Deal dealt not so much with economic issues, such as whether to stimulate the economy through a more liberal monetary policy or higher taxes on corporations, but rather with how people felt about themselves and their institutions. Oral histories such as Studs Terkel's *Hard Times* give us some insights into the popular New Deal through the reminiscences of people who lived through the Depression. However, the insights of oral history are necessarily fragmented, individualistic, and fraught with all the problems that occur when people try to remember what happened and, more importantly, how they felt decades ago. In Terkel's book, we can see the popular New Deal from the perspective of the individual, just as memoirs like Raymond Moley's provide an individual view of the governmental New Deal. To complement this individualistic approach, one needs the insight into the popular New Deal that can be found in the popular arts. The films of the '30s provide an insight into the collective mind of the popular New Deal the same way government documents are an insight into the collective mind of the governmental New Deal.

Wading into the popular New Deal we must remind ourselves of a remark Raymond Moley made about the political New Deal: "The New Deal was not of one piece. . . . It was . . . a loose collection of many ideas—some new, most borrowed from the past—with plenty of improvisations and compromises."[4] For the popular New Deal, perhaps even more than for the political New Deal, there was an immense variety of expression and opinion ranging from Shirley Temple to gangsters, monsters, and prostitutes. All of these reflect aspects of the collective vision of those who sat in the rows.

Taking a lead from Moley and from historians of the political New Deal we can, though, see a crucial watershed in the popular New Deal just as we can see a division of the political New Deal into what have come to be called the First and Second New Deals.[5] If there is a time that stands out as a crucial watershed in the consciousness of those citizens, it is the years 1934 and 1935. In 1934, Shirley Temple made her first appearance among the top ten box-office stars, making it to eighth place. The next year she was to rocket to the number one spot, a position she would hold through 1938 to be replaced in 1939 by another child star, Mickey Rooney. The Oscars of 1934 were virtually swept by Frank Capra's *It Happened One Night,* with a special award going to Shirley Temple. Unemployment first began to drop in 1934, after reaching its height in 1932 and 1933. Also in 1934, the censorship of the Legion of Decency resulted in the creation of the Production Code Administration—a move which was to have as great an effect on film content for the next twenty years as the New Deal would have on governmental policy and organization.

History books have traditionally talked about the New Deal and the 1930s as a time in which liberalism rode high. Yet looking over these events, it appears that 1934 marked a conservative counterrevolution of immense importance for the popular New Deal. It was certainly not a visible counterrevolution, at least not in terms of any of the direct political acts one associates with this phenomenon. There were no conservative purges of liberal revolutionaries, no armed conflicts between leftists and rightists. Rather, the 1934–35 counterrevolution in the popular New Deal was a counterrevolution in consciousness.[6] It marked the victory of conservative values over some of the revolutionary values of the preceding years. It is the time when the shape and meaning of those rows became apparent. Instead of rows of churning masses, those rows became orderly. Our Marx, Groucho, gave way to the "screwball comedies" of middle-class citizens. If we recall our typical Depression moviegoer—that person teetering on the edge of unemployment—then the change in consciousness represented by the 1934–35 counterrevolution becomes even more significant, for it is that marginal group which has always provided the "swing vote" in any time of great social change. In France in 1789 and Russia in 1917, it cast its lot with the revolutionaries, ushering in a period of radical social change. In America in 1934, it cast its lot with the counterrevolution. Standing in their orderly rows, our moviegoers of 1934 dramatically mark a line across the history of the 1930s. On one side of the line lie the early '30s—the depth of the Depression with its films of violence, sexual freedom, and social consciousness. On the other side stand Shirley Temple, Frank Capra, and "screwball" comedy. The primary documents we have of how the "swing vote" moved from the chaotic and conflicting implications of the early '30s to the "normalcy" of the late '30s are the movies and movie stars, with whom those people most identified.

Jean Harlow and Clark Gable in *Red Dust* (1932).

Before Shirley Temple and Clark Gable ruled as the number one and two box-office stars from 1935 to 1938, the top draws were Marie Dressler and Will Rogers. Both Dressler and Rogers personified Everyman. Neither of them was glamorous; both of them seemed to have an earthy quality of having experienced enough to be skeptical about everything. Rogers' homespun humor pricked the pretensions of the smug and self-righteous and more often than not revealed an insightful social commentary about American society in the early '30s. If Rogers can be said to have had a vision of America, it was an abiding faith in popular democracy coupled with a healthy dislike for technocrats, bureaucrats, media "tastemakers," and other assorted folks who were for planning and centralized control by self-styled "experts."

Rogers' vision has been called an agrarian vision, similar in many ways to the vision of the twelve Southerners who wrote an agrarian critique of modern society in *I'll Take My Stand*.[7] As it appears in Rogers' films of the early '30s, the agrarian vision is complex and two-edged. In *David Harum* (1934), Rogers plays a benevolent banker who ministers to the inhabitants of a small town called Homeville. *David Harum* draws an explicit contrast between the effects of the 1893 depression on the big city and the small town. Under the benevolent wing of banker Harum, the citizens of Homeville weather the depression, in contrast to the panic that affects the city. The agrarianism of *David Harum* grows out of the contrast between the city and Homeville. In Homeville are all of the nostalgic stereotypes we have of the small town: neighborly, simple, down-to-earth, helpful, happy people, close to nature and without the obsessive drives and problems associated with the big city. The double-edged sword of this agrarian vision in *David Harum* is the same double-edged sword one finds in *I'll Take My Stand,* for there is in this nostalgic vision also a very pointed critique of much of modern society. The friendliness and understanding of Rogers' banker Harum is contrasted with the big city banker, General Woolsey. The General (the significance of the title is obvious) runs his bank just like all the big bureaucracies we have come to fear and despise. The big city bank is the embryo of our modern banks, whose computers make many mistakes which prove impossible to correct. There is in *David Harum* an implicit critique of the centralization, impersonalization, and bureaucratization of much of the modern world, which parallels the Southerners' critique of positivism—their term for the social-science-oriented, behavioralistic, statistical impulse in modern thought that they felt was threatening to eclipse the humanistic vision of man as a free creative individual. As Allen Tate was to put it in a later essay, "the trouble ultimately goes back to the beginnings of finance capitalism and its creature, machine production."[8]

If Rogers and *David Harum* share an agrarian ideology with *I'll Take My Stand,* they also share a characteristic of the Southern agrarians' enemy, Franklin Roosevelt, for Rogers' banker figure contains an element of benevolent paternalism that many found in FDR. Both seemed wise and yet folksy—able to talk to people. Raymond Moley remarks that Roosevelt liked to think of himself as a gentleman farmer and felt close to the soil and to nature: "He turned by nature to rural scenes." Moley believes the essential nature of the First New Deal was agrarian, "an appeal to rural elements."[9] The Second New Deal, Moley believes, was a turn away from that agrarian vision. The popular counterrevolution also moved away from Rogers' agrarianism to a different vision.

To gauge the effect of the counterrevolution it is revealing to compare Rogers' homespun populism with the populism of Longfellow Deeds and Jefferson Smith, the heroes of Frank Capra's *Mr. Deeds Goes to Town* (1936) and *Mr. Smith Goes to Washington* (1939). Capra's populism ostensibly has its roots in the same milieu as Rogers'—that small-town, pastoral haven we have come to call Middle America. Like Rogers', Capra's Middle Americans are suspicious and critical of much of the mass society of twentieth century America. As Capra himself put it in talking about the theme of *Mr. Deeds*, "It was the rebellious cry of the individual against being trampled to an ort by massiveness—mass production, mass thought, mass education, mass politics, mass wealth, mass conformity."[10] That's a phrase Will Rogers probably could have agreed with; but, if we go beyond Capra's rhetoric to look at exactly what the meaning of that phrase is, we will see how radically different was the thrust of the populism of Capra and Rogers. Perhaps the most important distinction between Capra and Rogers is that Capra's social critique centers on people, while Rogers' centers on institutions as well as people. In Rogers' mind, "The government which governs best is the government which governs least" is more than the catchy punch line of a humorous aphorism. For Capra it is not "The government which governs best governs least," but rather "The government which governs best is the one which governs most in tune with the will of the people." The villains in Capra's films are not so much modern institutions as they are individuals who have lost touch with the people. There is Senator Paine in *Mr. Smith* who has sold out to the machine of Jim Taylor, a businessman who is interested only in lining his own pockets. There are the cynics who try to take Mr. Deeds' fortune away from him by having him declared insane for proposing to spend his new inheritance on buying small farms and giving them to the poor. Jim Taylor and Deeds' cynical relatives are motivated only by self-interest and care nothing for the people. Senator Paine serves Taylor, not the popular will. It is the concept of "the popular will" which is at the heart of Capra's populism. Democracy, for Capra, is paying heed to the wishes of the majority. For all his attacking of mass this and mass that, Capra is a firm believer in the masses. His populism, with its faith in the benevolence of Middle America, is not without its fascist undertones, as critics have pointed out, and certainly it is the precursor of Richard Nixon's famous silent majority. Unlike Rogers, Capra does not criticize modern institutions. Notice how both *Deeds* and *Smith* feature benevolent authority figures in the highest offices. The judge in *Mr. Deeds* and the vice-president in *Mr. Smith* are the senior officials appearing in each film and also the most wise and benevolent. Robert Sklar probably described Capra's ideology best when he said, "He was not making a critique of the American social and economic system . . . he simply wanted more neighborly and responsible people to be at the top."[11] Capra's politics are Rooseveltian and New Deal—use the government (or money or any other handy institution) to bring about desired results in accordance with the popular will.

Will Rogers is not so easily moved by mass populism. He recognizes that people can be manipulated, as in *Judge Priest*, when he arranges the playing of "Dixie" outside a courtroom window for a Southern jury, which eventually acquits his client. Rogers plays the whole episode for humor, recognizing that patriotic balderdash can be used to manipulate people. For Capra such an implication would cut against the grain of his populism. He plays patriotic scenes straight, as in the famous sequence from *Mr. Smith* where the Congressman goes to the Lincoln Memorial.[12] Capra is at heart a believer in orderly rows. At best, orderly rows strike Rogers as humorous; at worst, they frighten and appall him. Deeds' and Smith's patriotic evocations no doubt would have brought out the best of his humor.

The contrast, then, between the adult wiseness of Rogers, the number one draw of 1934, and the childish innocence of Shirley Temple, who replaced him in 1935, is dramatic. It is a cliché by now to speak of Temple and the Depression with the phrase "A little child shall lead them." Still, the phrase rings true. She tap-danced and kidded her way through the '30s. Oh, she wasn't the complete goody-goody the legends have unfortunately painted her. As she herself sings in "Oh, My Goodness" from *Poor Little Rich Girl* (1936), "One minute you're good, and the next minute you're bad." This impish, fun-loving quality was what made people of the '30s take to her and what makes her films fun to watch today. Shirley was no skeptic like Will; she bounced and tapped her way into anything and everything from the Bengal Lancers to the plantation. She grew, in a sense, from one edge of Rogers' double-edged agrarian sword, personifying those values of innocence and simplicity, with none of the implicit social criticism one finds in Rogers. Shirley's values are nature, love, simple things, and good times. As she sings in *Rebecca of Sunnybrook Farm* (1938), "Just find Mother Nature's address and come and get your happiness." Above all, Shirley was optimistic; in fact, one of her songs was titled "Be Optimistic" (*Little Miss Broadway,* 1938). In "I Love to Walk in the Rain," she sings, "The lightning may be frightening; I love the rain so I don't care" (*Just Around the Corner,* 1938). Even the Depression cannot spoil her optimism, for, "Though you haven't any money, you can still be bright and sunny" ("Polly Wolly-Doodle," *The Littlest Rebel,* 1935). Shirley characteristically plays an orphan, a child searching for the right environment to live in or a child whose environment is threatened. This rootless innocence further dramatizes her optimism. For all her rootlessness, though, Shirley's dream world is not of a life as a free, roaming individual, but rather as a middle-class child of benevolent parents. Shirley is always escaping from freedom. She submits to authority. Even after citing all the reasons for not eating spinach in the delightful song "You've Gotta Eat Your Spinach" (*Poor Little Rich Girl*), Shirley admits that "children should not be so very bold; children should do as they are told." The popular New Deal counterrevolution moved ahead, led by a little child who believed in a world of candy canes, peppermint bays, and benevolent authority. It was a conservative dream of comfortable surroundings and submission that little Shirley hid behind those innocent eyes.

Shirley Temple in *Wee Willie Winkie* (1937).

The strong contrast between Shirley Temple and Will Rogers is further borne out by looking at the other top box-office stars before and after the counterrevolution. Drawing a line at the end of 1934, we see on the one side such female stars as Greta Garbo, Jean Harlow, Mae West, Joan Crawford, Janet Gaynor, and Norma Shearer. On the other side are Shirley Temple, Ginger Rogers, Sonja Henie, Claudette Colbert, Joan Crawford, and Jeanette MacDonald. On one side of the line are sexuality, sophistication and depth of character; on the other side are ice shows and musicals, with only Colbert and Crawford for any interest at all. With the male stars, it is the same story, although not quite as dramatically. Gable, Bing Crosby, and Joe E. Brown appear on both sides of the line.

Of all these stars who appear on both sides of the line, only Gable appears with any consistency, ranking second in '34, '36, '37, and '38. Both Colbert and Crawford drop out of the Top Ten entirely after 1936, while Joe E. Brown appears only in 1935, due no doubt to his success in *Alibi Ike* (1935), where interestingly enough he plays a rural wit. A glance at the titles of some of Colbert's pre- and post-1934 films gives some idea of the scope of the change, going from *Secrets of a Secretary* (1932), *Misleading Lady* (1932), *The Wiser Sex* (1932), and *The Torch Singer* (1933) to *She Married Her Boss* (1935), *The Bride Comes Home* (1935), and *It's a Wonderful World* (1939). Crawford goes from *Rain* (1932) to *Ice Follies* (1939). Gable is a bit more complex. Suffice it to say his pictures change from the sensuality of *Red Dust* (1932) where Jean Harlow takes her famous shower to the more tame scenes of *It Happened One Night* (1934) and *Gone with the Wind* (1939). Crosby appears only twice, in '34 and '37, going from *We're Not Dressing* (1934) to *Waikiki Wedding* (1937). Perhaps most interesting, though, in line with Moley's analysis of the First New Deal as essentially agrarian in impulse, is that earthy, agrarian stars like Will Rogers, Marie Dressler, and Wallace Beery do not appear on the Top Ten list after 1934.

The contrasts found in the stars are found in the films as well. The movies of the early '30s were perhaps as varied and intriguing as the movies produced during any other three-year period in our history. It was the era of the classic gangster and classic horror films. Two of the most insightful pieces of social realism ever made—*Wild Boys of the Road* and *I Am A Fugitive from a Chain Gang*—are early thirties films. Perhaps the greatest antiwar comedy ever made, *Duck Soup,* had to wait some thirty years before another film, *Dr. Strangelove,* approached its satire; and the liberated sexuality of the Mae West films was not equaled until the 1960s. It is difficult to draw any unified generalizations from such an incredibly varied group of films. Perhaps all we can say is that they reflect the chaos of the times. Like the varied reactions of individual people to the Depression, we have the varied reactions of Hollywood. If one cannot find a single unified theme among these films, one can still see many things in them that died after 1934–35. The counterrevolution killed those seeds that were waiting to bloom and, for them, substituted plastic flowers. Certainly there are incidents of social realism and sexuality occurring in films after 1934–35, but they are pale isolated examples lacking the vitality of blossoms grown on more fertile soil. It is the difference in the sexuality of Claudette Colbert in *It Happened One Night* and Colbert in *Cleopatra,* both released in 1934 but lying far apart in their approach. In one a glimpse of leg and separate beds, in the other more than a glimpse of a lot more than leg as Cleopatra seduces Antony accompanied by drums that punctuate the scene with the rhythms of sexual intercourse.

After the counterrevolution, the independent, sexually liberated female that Colbert plays in *Cleopatra* and which Mae West personified disappears. Before the counterrevolution many of the screen's actresses had played prostitutes. Greta Garbo made her sound debut in *Anna Christie* (1930) as a prostitute. In 1932, Marlene Dietrich *(Blonde Venus),* Harlow *(Red Dust),* and Irene Dunne *(Back Street)* all played prostitutes. After the counterrevolution the middle-class heroines of the screwball comedies replaced the prostitutes as roles for many of the top female stars. Carole Lombard and Katharine Hepburn, among others, appear as screwball heroines. Irene Dunne changes from prostitute to comedienne. The screwball comedies feature women who on the surface seem liberated but who would have blushed at the most racy of Mae West's lines. There is a lot of dialogue and action involving sex in screwball comedy, but it is quite innocent, like Cary Grant and Katharine Hepburn playing little kids in the children's playroom in *Holiday* (1938). Of the top box-office stars, only Joan Crawford and Bette Davis, who makes the top ten for the first time in 1939, appear to be really liberated women, but their roles in films like *The Women* (1939), *The Bride Wore Red* (1937), *Dangerous* (1935), and *Jezebel* (1938) lack the sexual dimension of the prostitute roles played by stars before the counterrevolution. Crawford even appeared in *Ice Follies* (1939).

There is no question that the hand of the 1934 Production Code Administration lurks very heavily in this change. Yet the code is a part of the counterrevolution, not its cause. There are many who see the code as a determined effort made by Legion of Decency types to impose their standards on the general population. The Catholic bishops of the Legion of Decency, allied with Protestant and Jewish churchmen as well as others who felt for various reasons that films of the '30s had gone too far in their portrayal of sex, crime, and social disorder, all certainly influenced Hollywood to "clean up its act" by forming the P.C.A. under Joseph Breen. However, the relative ease with which the code was instituted and the lack of wide protest by the general audience after its inception suggest that the public was closely in tune with the P.C.A. An index of public feeling about some of the early '30s films is suggested by a Dallas reviewer of *State Fair* (1933) who said, "*State Fair* . . . taught the industry that pictures concerning inland provincial characters were more appealing than penthouses and gun-spattered pavements . . . [it tapped] a forgotten public . . . [which] . . . had lost interest in crime and so-called 'smart films'."[13] In short, the code represented the wishes of Capra's Middle Americans. There were no large outcries by people with accusations of censorship after it was instituted. The creative talents of Hollywood did not rise in indignation against it. Frank Capra, for example, doesn't even mention it at all in his autobiography. The code, which received so much villification by contemporary analysts, slipped into the counterrevolutionary times of 1934–35 with relative ease.

The validity of such an interpretation can be seen by looking at changes in other films made during the '30s before and after the counterrevolution. The social realism, for example, of *Wild Boys of The Road* (1933) or *I Am a Fugitive from a Chain Gang* (1932) is of a completely different sort from that of, say, the Dead End Kids films of the late '30s—*Dead End* (1937) and *Angels with Dirty Faces* (1938). Even with its upbeat ending—"Things are going to get better all over the country," *Wild Boys* is a much more cutting and disturbing film than the Dead End Kids films. The Wild Boys represent a revolutionary force, using violence when necessary to bring about social

Marlene Dietrich in *Blonde Venus* (1932).

change. They throw rocks at the cops invading their Hooverville and appear ready to fight anyone who crosses them. The Dead End Kids, on the other hand, are critical of their lot and the system, but they are not a revolutionary force. In both *Dead End* and *Angels,* they are disturbed by their status as poor slum-dwellers yet take no concerted action to change their situation. The chief concern of these films seems to be that the kids will become gangsters, like Bogart and Cagney, out of a desire to make it big so they can wear fancy clothes like the ones Bogart shows them. The only organized response the kids seem in danger of mustering is that of organized crime. The Wild Boys, though, are quite capable of organized rebellion as they battle cops and railroad detectives to maintain their freedom. The Wild Boys in the end may believe the benevolent judge (who looks like FDR) when he tells them to go home to their families because "things will get better." They are bought off by the system, but it is an uneasy truce. The priest—who else but Pat O'Brien—convinces the Dead End Kids in *Angels* that the gangster's life is not a good one, leaving us with a much less uneasy feeling than we have from the ending of *Wild Boys.* The Kids will go straight—straight on to become comic Bowery Boys—but the Wild Boys will stay quiet only if things *do* get better. The contrast between the two groups even extends to their names. The Wild Boys are wild: like animals, they can be tamed, but like tame tigers, their docility could possibly erupt at

Humphrey Bogart and the Dead End Kids in *Dead End* (1937).

any time. The Dead End Kids, on the other hand, are kids, angels with dirty faces; clean up the faces and you reveal the angels underneath.

If the Wild Boys and Dead Enders are somewhat related, nothing after the counterrevolution approaches *Fugitive*. This oppressive, pessimistic social realist film indicts pointedly but gives no solution and no satisfaction. Muni's hissed explanation—"I steal"—at the end of the movie echoes in our ears much more than if he had cried out at the pain and injustice of it all. For Muni, unlike the Wild Boys, things will not get better. They may well get worse. There is no comfort in the system or in traditional values, and the only rows the fugitive can look forward to are the stark rows of wooden beds in the prison farm and the stark rows of striped prisoners working the roads.

The contrast one sees in the social realist films also appears in the classic gangster and horror films of the early 1930s. Both the gangsters and the monsters of this period were deviants and social outcasts. In their own ways, they represented perversions of traditional American moral and social values. Rico in *Little Caesar* (1930) and Tommy Powers in *Public Enemy* (1931) clawed unscrupulously towards success. *Dracula* (1931), *King Kong* (1932), and *The Mummy* (1931) can all be said to represent various types and degrees of sexual frustration. While the gangster pursues the dollar, the monster pursues the girl. Both gangster and monster are evidence of a deep dissatisfaction with and even fear of modern life that parallels that found in Will Rogers and the Southern agrarian manifesto, *I'll Take My Stand*. Where Rogers used humor and the twelve Southerners used historical evidence and logic to make their points, the gangster and monster movies use exaggeration and psychology. The critiques of Rogers and the Southerners represent our conscious fears and criticism of modern society, while the gangsters and monsters represent our subconscious fears. The scientist—the force of reason and progress (what the Southerners called positivism)—becomes the exaggerated mad scientist who creates the monster. The Mummy is turned loose by archeologists who, like little boys playing with matches, do not understand the implications of what they have done until it is too late. Kong is exploited by promoters and businessmen who are so blinded with greed they do not understand what they are responsible for. Rico, Tony Camonte (*Scarface*, 1932), and Tommy Powers are the mutants created by the corruption and impersonality of the modern city. They showed that "section of America to itself against the background of poolrooms, stale beer, cigarette smoke, alleys, bare electric light bulbs, cities at night."[14] Implicit in the gangsters' worship of and drive for success is a criticism of our definitions of success and of a system built upon the monetary worship of success. Implicit in the monsters' drives is a criticism of the forces which create those drives and of the repression which denies them their fulfillment.

There is a sense, too, in which both monster and gangster represent the out-groups of modern society—the disaffected, the victimized, the individual who, by virtue of what he is, is an outsider. In the monster movies, it is an impersonal society which victimizes the very personal monster. Kong is the innocent snatched from his Eden. Frankenstein's creation is an innocent persecuted by misunderstanding and conformity, befriended only by a little girl. *Freaks* (1932), perhaps the strangest of the monster movies, is a thinly veiled rebellion against all that the middle-class world represents. In these films, the audience plainly identifies with the monster. In psychological terms, the monsters personify the fears which early '30s audiences had about what society was doing to them.[15] The psychology of the gangster is similar to that of the monster. Notice how many of the gangsters are little men—Edward G. Robinson and James Cagney, for example. This physical smallness elicits the audience's sympathy, especially when viewing the gangster's early confrontations with modern civilization. The audience can understand why the gangster behaves as he does and perhaps gains some personal gratification in watching the gangster's ruthless climb to the top. Maybe that's why the conservative forces of order were so worried about the impact of the gangster film.[16]

Both the gangster and monster films of the early 1930s stand diametrically opposed to planning and centralization and certainly to orderly rows. In Little Caesar's drive to control all the rackets, in his devious planning and in his worship of money and success, we see the terror of those values. If Will Rogers' populism satirized the excess of the New Deal, Little Caesar personified them. Rico, the little Caesar, represents the possibility of a big Caesar (FDR) gone mad. The monsters are the madness that a repressed and centralized society creates.

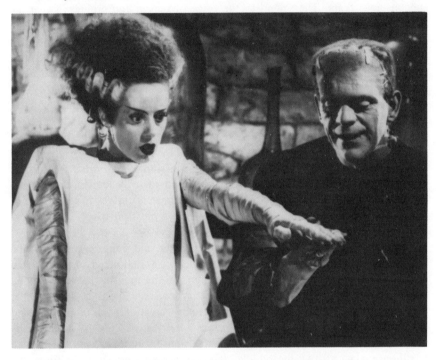

Elsa Lanchester and Boris Karloff in *The Bride of Frankenstein* (1935).

Looking at two post-counterrevolution examples of gangster and horror films, *The Roaring Twenties* (1939) and *The Bride of Frankenstein* (1935), we can see the thrust of the criticism has become mute. Cagney's 1939 gangster is driven to success not by the idea itself but by the love of a woman. Bogart's cynical gangster has none of the personality of Rico. In *The Roaring Twenties,* what social criticism that surfaces is muted and undirected. Its hero is a young establishment lawyer who gets the girl and lives in comfortable upper-middle-class surroundings. Pointedly, the hero is a government employee of a big city. He is, in short, Mr. New Deal personified. In *Little Caesar,* the good guy goes on to be a successful night-club dancer. He is comfortable and part of the establishment, but still Rico's crack about him rings in our mind: "Dancing, that's for sissies." *The Bride of Frankenstein* also defuses the criticism of the earlier movie. There is none of the innocence of the first Frankenstein monster in this sequel. By 1935, the monster has become almost a caricature of himself, with his wish to have a companion and his clumsy attempts to woo her after he is rebuffed. The bride, too, with the famous lightning streak of white hair zig-zagging across her crazily piled hairdo, seems almost a parody of a monster. Both the bride and the monster are mutant outsiders whose rejection of one another should be the stuff of tragedy, yet it inspires in us only snickers. When the bride is brought to life, looks at the monster, and screams, audiences laugh. The spell the first monster held for us has been broken. He is no longer an innocent victim of society whose rage is the product of society's conformity and impersonality. Instead, when he destroys the laboratory, his bride, and the mad scientist, he seems merely a childish person who over reacts to being jilted by his girlfriend. After the bride screams, the monster tries to be friendly towards her; but she is afraid, and the monster can only utter the melodramatic phrase of every jilted lover, "She hates me." The monster's rage in the original *Frankenstein* is a rage against society; here it is only a rage against a rather ridiculous-looking girlfriend. The counterrevolution has turned the social critique of the monster into the comedy of a jilted love affair.

In hindsight, we can see that orderly rows were perhaps what everyone was yearning for. They appear repeatedly in the films. They appear in the New Deal. For all their rhetoric to the contrary, they even appear in the dreams and rhetoric of the leftists of the time. So the rows straightened themselves up; after all, it made getting the soup a little easier, a little more orderly. Fortunately, our rows were not as perfect as those of so many other nations, which opted for totalitarian control as opposed to centralization. As Ed Paulsen put it, with us it was a split thing. Like so much else we do, we moved; but we did it grumbling all the way.

Those rows, of course, needed some direction. Like those who opted for totalitarian rows, we opted for a father figure, but our father was more benign. F.D.R. was like all those fathers Shirley Temple had or the wise judge in *Wild Boys of the Road.* Rico may have been F.D.R. gone mad; but, fortunately, we recognized the madness, its causes, its methods, its results. Those who opted for totalitarian fathers were not so fortunate. They did not recognize the madness until it had infected everyone.

In the 1930s, the lights went out in more ways than we realize. The events of the Depression itself plunged us into darkness; but then, so did the counterrevolution of the popular New Deal. Rows, rows, rows. Standing in the darkness. Mumbling, crying, shouting, silent. They prayed for the lights to come on.

They opted consciously for the conservative counterrevolution. They turned their backs on the implications of the films of the early '30s. Instead of social and sexual liberation, they chose a conservative vision. It would not be until the '60s that films would again be as open. The popular New Deal delayed that revolution for thirty years.

The audiences of the 1930s made their decision the way we all make decisions and for all the varied reasons we make them. They were not forced into it—at least not in the conspiratorial way the doctrinaire among us like to imagine people are forced to make decisions. The counterrevolution of the '30s was not a conspiracy. In literary terms, it was a tragedy, not a melodrama or an allegory. For the most human of reasons, our parents and grandparents, who were only trying to do right by themselves, and those who came after made what we now can see might well have been the wrong decisions. As in all tragedies, it was a combination of fate, circumstance, and the tragic imperfection of all of us that led them there.

NOTES

1. Harvey Swados, ed., *The American Writer and the Great Depression* (New York: Bobbs-Merrill, 1966), p. xv. Swados' anthology is a good introduction to the way writers responded to the Depression. Don Congdon's anthology, *The Thirties: A Time to Remember* (New York: Simon & Schuster, 1962), is a broader look at the whole decade and contains sections on everything from music to politics.
2. Statistics and numbers during the thirties can be slippery. Given today's arguments about the number of people unemployed, one can imagine how the same problems which prompt those arguments can play havoc with 1930s figures. The 12 million figure I used comes from Arthur Schlesinger, *The Politics of Upheaval* (Boston: Houghton-Mifflin, 1966), p. 1. The *Fortune* survey is quoted in Garth Jowett, *Film: The Democratic Art* (Boston: Little, Brown, 1976), p. 285. The 122 million population figure is based on the 1930 census.
3. Jowett's chapters on the thirties are, along with Andrew Bergman's *We're in the Money* (New York: Harper & Row, 1972), the best source for studying movies of that decade. The Yankee City study is cited on pp. 263–65. Jowett's resourcefulness and imagination in tracking down statistics of the thirties is remarkable.
4. Raymond Moley, *The First New Deal* (New York: Harcourt, Brace & World, 1966), p. xvii.
5. Moley is generally credited with being the first to look at the New Deal this way. Historians such as Schlesinger and Freidel have accepted Moley's division and bolstered it with evidence of their own.
6. The historical interpretation of the ideological underpinnings of the so-called Second New Deal of 1935 is admittedly a complex can of worms to open. In light, though, of my own theory of the ideological watershed that one can find in the

films of the '30s and Schlesinger's observation, "The year 1934 marked a watershed," in his chapter "The Ideology of the New Deal," I believe the relationship between the two watersheds bears close investigation. My idea in this essay is to throw out a new interpretation of the 1934–35 watershed based on what happens in the films. It would take another essay, at least, to discuss parallels between the popular counterrevolution and what happened in the political New Deal. Schlesinger draws the contrast between the two New Deals by saying, "The one tried to convert business through new institutions; the other tried to discipline it through new laws." My belief is that there was the potential in the First New Deal to radically alter American society, and that that potential died in 1935 due to lack of popular commitment. Schlesinger points out the ideas of the First New Deal also changed within the Roosevelt Administration, due to several factors. What needs to be done is to examine more closely the parallels between the popular and governmental watersheds to determine why there is this shift occurring quite closely in time in both areas. Who is reacting to whom? (The popular watershed actually begins in 1934, so was the 1935 governmental watershed a reaction to it?) Was there some sort of simultaneous change? If so, why?

7. Peter C. Rollins, "Will Rogers: Symbolic Man and Film Image," *Journal of Popular Film* 2:4, pp. 323–53. Rollins' article is an excellent discussion of Rogers' film persona.

8. Allen Tate, *Collected Essays* (Denver: Allan Swallow, 1959), p. 267.

9. Moley, pp. 524–25.

10. Frank Capra, *The Name Above the Title* (New York: Bantam, 1971), p. 206.

11. Robert Sklar, *Movie-Made America* (New York: Random House, 1975), p. 210.

12. In this light compare Capra's little-boy, gosh-golly experience of going to Washington for the first time with the worldly skepticism one finds in Rogers' descriptions of the Capitol.

13. Rollins, p. 337. Garth Jowett's chapter on the code is the most up-to-date assessment of its inception and results. See his chapter 10, "The Motion Picture Controlled."

14. Museum of Modern Art Film Library Program Notes, Series 4, No. 8. Quoted in Lewis Jacobs, *The Rise of the American Film* (New York: Teachers College Press, Columbia University, 1968), p. 510.

15. Walter Evans, "Monster Movies: A Sexual Theory," *Journal of Popular Film* 2:4, pp. 353–66, advances a similar interpretation of the monster. Evans, however, looks only at the sexual dimension, whereas I would argue that the monsters' psychological appeal is much broader.

16. Some scare stories in newspapers at the time the gangster film was most popular told of teenagers who were adopting Rico's mannerisms and even some of his tactics. Interestingly enough, kids today still like to run around mimicking Edward G. Robinson's and James Cagney's gangster accents.

Front Office, Box Office, and Artistic Freedom: An Aspect of the Film Industry 1945–1969

CALVIN PRYLUCK

A common view of the film industry has it that, in the early days, moguls forced their hirelings to conform to the boss's ideas about the world; according to this view, the demise of the Big Studios was followed by a period of unfettered artistic freedom. A close look at the film industry in the period of transition between 1945 and 1969 suggests that there is an element of truth in this view. But this element of truth is suffused by another set of facts which indicate that the freedom of both Big Studio tycoons and contemporary film-makers is limited by institutional constraints.

Within the constraints, there are obvious differences between a Bogdano-vich, a Schary, and a Mayer, but it is incomplete to emphasize the foibles of individuals without trying to understand the constraints under which they were and are forced to operate.

The story begins with the earliest attempts at including production, distribu-tion, and exhibition under one financial mantle. By the end of the silent period, this economic integration had been more-or-less completed. In the thirties, the film industry in the United States was controlled by five fully integrated or-ganizations: Paramount, Loew's (MGM), Twentieth Century-Fox, Warner Brothers, and RKO; two partially integrated producer-distributors: Columbia and Universal; and one distributor: United Artists. Between them, these eight companies controlled most of the important theaters and produced the over-whelming majority of films. These circumstances were to continue through the end of World War II although the government had pressed various antitrust proceedings against producer-distributor combinations starting as early as 1921.[1]

One way or another the government attempted to mitigate various aspects of monopolistic practices until, in 1938, the Justice Department filed a legal blockbuster which came to be known as the *Paramount* case. The intricate maneuverings on both industry and government sides are unimportant to the present story; the result of the case is central. Eleven years after the case was first filed, and following Supreme Court decisions, the process of divorcement between production and exhibition was undertaken. Under divorcement decrees, production and exhibition became independent operations; no company could perform both functions.

Previously, there was a steady flow of products between the studios, the distributors, and theaters guaranteeing an outlet for the productions of the eight affiliated companies and guaranteeing a continuing supply of films to the theaters. In the process of divorcement, between 1949 and 1953, theaters previously owned by producer-distributors were sold to independent corporations which could follow their own economic best interests instead of being subordinated to the overall control of a corporation which also included production facilities.

It is one of the ironies of which history is full that two industry-shaking crises occurred contemporaneously; the period of divorcement is precisely the period of the development of a nationwide television industry offering a competing form of mass entertainment. During the period 1929–1945, the expenditures for motion picture admissions accounted for an average of 21.2 percent of recreation expenditures; during the same period, comparable expenditures for home entertainment equalled 12.7 percent. By 1949, well before the completion of divorcement, home entertainment and motion picture admissions had reversed their relative standings; home entertainment expenditures accounted for 24.3 percent of recreation expenditures, while motion picture admissions accounted for only 12.1 percent.[2] In short, the public was using a more dominant share of its discretionary income for home entertainment, rather than motion picture admissions. Moreover, this trend has continued to the contemporary period with home entertainment accounting for increasingly larger shares of recreation expenditures, while motion picture admissions' share was becoming decreasingly smaller.[3]

Prior to 1945, the motion picture industry had been structured to produce, distribute, and exhibit films which would receive about a fifth of the recreation expenditures. This orderly flow of income was disrupted by competing forms of recreation at the same time that studios could no longer depend on any kind of guaranteed income supplied by affiliated theaters nor could theaters depend on a guaranteed supply of films to exhibit. Open market competition for films had been introduced at a time when the whole market was shrinking.

In succeeding years, total motion picture receipts continued to decline, as did the share of recreation expenditures. During the same period, an anomalous situation began to develop. Some films were earning more money than any individual pictures had earned previously. In 1953, when the motion picture share of recreation expenditures declined to a then low of nine percent,[4] *The Robe,* a DeMille-like spectacle, earned more money than had any previous production with the exceptions of *Gone with the Wind* and *The Birth of a Nation.*[5]

Jean Simmons and Richard Burton in *The Robe* (1953).

Examination of a listing of pictures with high earnings between 1945 and 1969 demonstrates that *The Robe* was not an isolated instance. Using an arbitrary cutoff point, a list of all pictures earning more than ten million dollars in distributor's gross was drawn from *Variety's* roguishly titled "All Time Box Office Champs," an annual listing of all titles which attained a distributor's gross of more than four million dollars.[6] The sample is thus a complete list of the extremely successful pictures in the United States market during this period.

To level out the effect of inflation in comparing earnings across years, a consumer price index adjusted for each year was applied to the distributor's gross earnings reported in *Variety*. This adjustment used two different bases — ten million 1945 dollars and ten million 1970 dollars.[7] There are thus three overlapping samples; in increasing order of size they are:

Reduced sample: films grossing the equivalent of ten million 1945 dollars

Regular sample: films grossing ten million actual dollars

Expanded sample: films grossing the equivalent of ten million 1970 dollars

The number of films in each sample is shown in Table 1. Regardless of the base on which the sample is constructed, there is a prominent increase in phenomenal grossing films in each succeeding five-year period. The only ex-

TABLE 1: NUMBER OF HIGH GROSSING FILMS BY FIVE YEAR PERIODS*

	REDUCED SAMPLE[a]		REGULAR SAMPLE[b]		EXPANDED SAMPLE[c]	
	N	%	N	%	N	%
1945–1949	-0-	0.0	3	3.7	19	13.0
1950–1954	2	7.1	6	7.3	12	8.2
1955–1959	5	17.9	11	13.4	28	19.2
1960–1964	9	32.1	21	25.6	37	25.3
1965–1969	12	42.9	41	50.0	50	34.2
TOTAL	28	100.0	82	100.0	146	100.0

a. Films grossing more than the equivalent of ten million 1945 dollars
b. Films grossing ten million actual dollars
c. Films grossing more than the equivalent of ten million 1970 dollars

*Source: based on *Variety,* January 6, 1971, pp. 12, 34, 36

ception to this pattern is in the expanded sample for the pre-divorcement years of 1945– 1949. The majority of films accounting for this single deviation were films released during or before 1947, that is, under the old integrated production/distribution/exhibition system during the best box office years ever.

The general pattern of pre-divorcement production organizations is clear from these and additional data on overall film supply. It was apparently the policy of integrated production organizations to release a fixed supply of films. The average number of films released by major companies in the prewar years 1929– 1941 was 362 pictures per year. In only two of these years was there a slightly more than 10 percent deviation from the average. In five of these years, the percentage deviation was less than 1 percent; and in three of these years, the number of productions was exactly 362. The pattern is essentially the same for either all releases by majors or only major releases produced in the United States. [8]

The old system was based on a smooth flow of product from the studio to the theater, with relatively fixed amounts of playing time in a certain number of theaters for each picture. This even flow of films from the major studios was integral to the production/distribution/exhibition system that had been built up. What was required by the system as organized was only a moderate number of highly successful pictures, no more in any one year than in any others. It is probably the case that, in planning for a year's production, there was a certain amount of leeway allowed for some number of pictures which would have more lengthy playing time than customary. This might account for the pre-1947 bulge. But too many pictures playing for extended time would cause problems.

For theaters, it was relatively unimportant which film was playing, so long as they had some kind of product to display profitably. From the production side, however, an even flow of films in release was crucial. They had built up a factory system geared to produce about 350 films per year plus or minus about 10 percent. There was an investment in physical plant and personnel which was based on this assumption. The necessity of recovering the money invested in unreleased films was a further consideration.

The several considerations of plant, personnel, and finance were the impetus for maintaining a more-or-less steady flow of pictures from the studios. The integrated corporations were protected from outright losses on a single film by the system of block booking and guaranteed playing time; what they could not afford were too many pictures which preempted screen time through extended engagements. This kind of success was too erratic and when it happened with too many pictures at the same time, it clogged the pipelines.

The increase in distributor's grosses for individual pictures since 1950 might be accounted for in a number of ways that stem from independent economic determination by distributors and exhibitors. Successful pictures may be subject to longer engagements in particular theaters; or the picture might be shown in more theaters; or the percentage of admissions that are forwarded to the distributor as rental might be higher than usual for successful pictures; or the price of admission might be raised. Whatever combinations of these factors are operative in given circumstances, the results are the same. Increasingly, few pictures preempt larger shares of a shrinking total of motion picture admissions.

The process of extended play and expanded engagements is related to a shortage of product,[9] which seems to be in part the result of a change in the utilization of production facilities. The ownership of studios and location equipment has become independent of the actual production of films for television or theaters. Producers for the current market no longer have to produce theatrical films on a regular basis in order to cover the overhead of physical production facilities. These facilities are now rented as needed. There is no economic imperative to produce films for theaters.

A shortage of pictures of proven profitability is entailed by a general shortage of product. Under these conditions, exhibitors may hold over a picture, instead of playing one of the limited alternatives whose profitability is problematic, if there is some reason—even vague—to believe that there is any kind of profit in an extended showing. This situation could lead to a paradoxical shortage of screen time through preempting playing time in a period when product is in short supply.

These tendencies introduce a boom-or-bust principle into production; showings that are only marginally profitable for exhibitors can cumulate into a jackpot for the distributor and producer. There is now a continuing thrust on the part of motion picture producers to break into the magic circle of jackpot pictures. One can get very rich very quickly with one picture in the phenomenal grossing category. Moreover, even if one is not avaricious, it is necessary at least to be able to get enough playing time to recover costs. The rules have changed for production just as they have for exhibition. Now the impetus is to appear to stand out strikingly from the crowd where previously the impetus was to a workmanlike job along established lines.

A rationalized system like that of the Studio Years requires a product with predictable qualities and predictable performance. Phenomenal grossing pictures are unpredictable. There is no way to plan for a very popular picture— hope may spring eternal, but a rationalized system cannot depend on hope. Conservatism was built into the system; it was a conservatism which favored moderate pictures.

Pre-divorcement organization of production was a system which encouraged each successive Betty Grable picture to be only slightly different from previous ones. Instead of "boy meets girl," the next picture would be "girl meets boy." The shifting of one of the male leads in *Front Page* to a female character in *My Girl Friday* is the kind of daring innovation found in pre-divorcement film production.

In contrast to the ponderous studio system, contemporary film production is a volatile system which emphasizes the novel and the unusual. Now the first picture might be "boy meets boy" and the succeeding one "boy meets boy— and he is naked." By stressing one kind of film over others, the contemporary process limits the kinds of films that will be made in quite the same way (if not with the same results) that an integrated organization imposed limits on the kinds of films that might be made.

The list of phenomenal grossing films in Table 2 is suggestive; just listing the fifties' titles evokes something vaguely passé.[10] The thrust for novelty did encourage one of the few genuinely new story types of the contemporary period. These films are prime examples of the contemporary production imperatives: each new film postulates situations more grotesque than the last.

Starting in 1966 with *Alfie*, several subsequent jackpot films interlarded heavy doses of comedy with more serious dramatic observation. So unusual was this approach that a critical debate was precipitated in 1967 over whether *Bonnie and Clyde* was drama or comedy. The mid-sixties seems to have been a watershed. Before this time we had, say, *Cleopatra* and *The Longest Day;* after this time we had, say, *The Graduate, Butch Cassidy,* and *Midnight Cowboy.* Numerous other films flaunted increasingly bizarre tragi-comic circumstances for their alienated anti-heroes.

TABLE 2: PICTURES GROSSING MORE THAN TEN MILLION 1945 DOLLARS
(1945– 1969)

1959 OR EARLIER	1960– 1964	1965– 1969
This Is Cinerama, 1952	How the West Was Won, 1962	
	Goldfinger, 1964	Thunderball, 1965
The Robe, 1953 Ten Commandments, 1957 Ben-Hur, 1959	Cleopatra, 1963	Doctor Zhivago, 1965
Bridge on River Kwai, 1958	The Longest Day, 1962	The Dirty Dozen, 1967
South Pacific, 1958	West Side Story, 1961 My Fair Lady, 1964 Mary Poppins, 1964	Sound of Music, 1965 Funny Girl, 1968
Around the World in 80 Days, 1956	Mad, Mad World, 1963 Tom Jones, 1963	The Odd Couple, 1968
		Valley of the Dolls, 1967 To Sir, with Love, 1967 Guess Who's Coming to Dinner, 1968
		Bonnie & Clyde, 1967 The Graduate, 1968 Butch Cassidy, 1969

Source: Adapted from *Variety*, January 6, 1971, pp. 12, 34, 36

To make my point it is not necessary to argue that every film produced in recent years is a freakish product. Some films gain their novelty in the flow of contemporaneous production precisely by their archaic quality. *The Odd Couple* is in some ways an old fashioned film not unlike the films made thirty-five years ago. Its very squareness separates *The Odd Couple* from other 1968 films that were its direct competition: *The Graduate, 2001,* and *Rosemary's Baby.*

Periodically, there are other successful releases for thoroughly old-fashioned films like *Love Story* and *Airport.* Despite the industry optimism that the bizarre cycle was coming to a close with these films, they were followed almost immediately by such increasingly grotesque films as *Straw Dogs, Dirty Harry, Clockwork Orange, The Godfather,* and, more recently, *The Exorcist.*

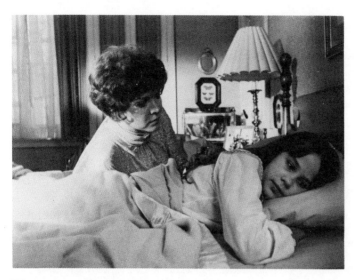

Ellen Burstyn and Linda Blair in *The Exorcist* (1973).

All of this has nothing to do with aesthetic evaluation but does have to do with artistic integrity. Good pictures and bad can be made with and without bizarre extravagances; yet, in contemporary film production, the benefit of the doubt is apparently given to the odd, the unusual, the titillating.

One is at hazard in making blanket condemnations; whether gore and skin are relevant to a particular film is an aesthetic matter. Would *The Last Picture Show* have been less valued without the female frontal nudity of the swimming pool sequence? It might even be argued that the honesty of the scene is called into question by the contrast between the bluntness of the female nudity and the delicacy of the male nudity. Artists, along with businessmen, seem to be affected by institutional influences on the shape of works of an era.

It is probably demonstrable that novelty and sensation cannot support an indifferent picture at the box office. The important point is that many successes do incorporate such elements. Each success influences subsequent production, exhibition, and ultimately, creative decisions. In the process, the production of increasingly sensational films is encouraged.

By their novelty, these films appear to preempt their subject matter. There is a sense of having created the definitive presentation of their characters and their milieu. The question that must be asked about the films is whether, in spite of first appearances, they have in fact exhausted their subject matter.

In the atmosphere created by present production and exhibition arrangements, I suspect that attempts to deal with, for instance, an alienated middle-class college graduate may be forgone on the logic of "it's been done before." Are adolescent fantasies of illicitly mating under the family roof, or with a girl friend's mother, really all there is to say on the subject?

To the extent that such restrictions exist, contemporary film-makers are only slightly more free than their Big Studio predecessors.

NOTES

1. Earlier antitrust proceedings were against corporations attempting industry control through licensing of equipment; equipment was not at issue in the 1921 case against Famous Players-Lasky Corporation and its affiliate, Paramount Pictures Corporation. Michael Conant, *Antitrust in the Motion Picture Industry* (Berkeley: University of California Press, 1960).
2. *Historical Statistics of the United States* (Washington: Bureau of the Census, 1958), p. 224. Home entertainment expenditures include expenditures for radios, television sets, records, musical instruments, and repairs to radios and television sets. A detailed table is available from the author.
3. *Statistical Abstracts, 1970* (Washington: Bureau of the Census, 1970), p. 204.
4. *Historical Statistics*, p. 22.
5. *Variety,* January 6, 1954, pp. 5, 59; January 5, 1955, p. 59.
6. Distributor's gross is the money forwarded by exhibitors to the distributor as rental on films. From the producer's viewpoint, these are the crucial figures.
7. These data probably underestimate the actual increase in phenomenal grossing films. Films released earlier have had a longer period to build up phenomenal grosses due to the practice of re-release. Thus, some films are counted as phenomenal grossers that might not have been if only the original grosses had been considered. This underestimate is leveled somewhat by using 1970 data as a base to allow for the sometime extended playoff times for films originally released toward the end of 1969.
8. *Film Daily Yearbook, 1956,* p. 97. A table detailing the flow of films is available from the author.
9. For the ten-year period 1932–1941 there were an average of 707 films per year in release from all sources, major studios, independent, U.S. produced and imports. The comparable figure for the ten years 1955–1964 is only about two-thirds of that average (465 films per year average). A substantial portion of the latter figure consists of imported films (which may or may not have been in English). Considering only the U.S. produced films for the later period, the decrease is even more severe. The number of U.S. produced films for the later period is only 39 percent of the comparable number for the earlier period. *Film Daily Yearbook,* 1965, p. 97. A detailed table is available from the author.
10. A complete list of the titles of all the high grossing films including those grossing more than the equivalent of ten million 1970 dollars is available from the author.

From the Outdoors to Outer Space:
The Motion Picture Industry in the 1970s

BRIAN ROSE

Moviegoers may not be entirely aware of it, but they're being treated differently in the 1970s. With only about half of Americans over the age of twelve even seeing one film a year,[1] Hollywood is doing everything in its power to understand and keep the audience that it still has left. The task is not easy, especially since the size and nature of the film-viewing public has changed dramatically in the last three decades. The boom years audiences of the mid-1940s, when 90 million people went to the movies weekly,[2] are now a cherished memory. The box-office patrons of the 1970s represent a far smaller percentage of the population (from about 75 percent in 1946 to 50 percent in 1976), and they are infrequent filmgoers at best.[3] According to recent figures released by the Motion Picture Association of America, they are also a much younger audience—in 1975, nine out of ten tickets were purchased by people under forty.[4]

Increasingly, Hollywood's attempt to reach its current public (and hopefully lure the hundred million or so who no longer go to movies) is taking the form of a renewed catering to the broadest of popular tastes. Producers and distributors, eager to minimize risks, search even more energetically for proven vehicles, time-tested formulas, and bankable stars. The industry, anxious to protect investments, looks to the techniques of marketing and product testing as valuable ways of not only selling movies, but also creating them. The results, predictably enough, are films characterized by their willingness either to comfort an audience with nostalgic truths or to shock it into senselessness.

In this effort to reach and attract the public of the 1970s, new approaches to distribution and exhibition have developed. The growth of "four-walling" is perhaps the most interesting phenomenon of the period. Though it started in the silent era, this procedure of renting out a theater for the run of an engagement assumed tremendous popularity in the product-starved 1960s and '70s. Exhibitors are only too glad to receive a flat fee in exchange for allowing the distributor to handle the promotion, the risk, and any box-office profits. If the film is successful, the theater owner reaps additional revenue from popcorn sales; if the film bombs, he still earns enough money to cover his expenses and put a little in the bank (something he can't be assured of with regularly exhibited products). For the distributor, the potential for profits is enormous.

Recognizing that fortunes could be made given the right handling, firms like Sun International Enterprises and Pacific National Enterprises introduced a new element into four-walling by systematically investigating every possibility. Using sophisticated demographic studies, they would rent dozens of theaters located within the viewing area of the nearest TV station; then they would saturate the airwaves with an aggressive and incessant ad campaign. Box-office response was usually so strong that it was not uncommon for a film like *The Vanishing Wilderness* (1974), which cost $300,000 to produce, to gross $1.5 million in one week's showing at 144 theaters.[5]

Of course, this kind of success also depended on a careful reading of moviegoing audiences. The activities of the oldest four-waller, American National, typify how that knowledge was obtained. In business since 1964, the Salt Lake City-based company started out by showing an animal documentary called *Alaskan Safari* to enthusiastic crowds at Kiwanis clubs and high-school auditoriums. Subsequent releases convinced them that there existed a great untapped public for family-oriented wilderness films, particularly in small towns and rural regions. In order to target their audience more closely, American National embarked on an ambitious program of marketing research. Movies were tested and evaluated to determine consumer need and appropriate advertising campaigns; theaters were rented according to detailed studies of population patterns and media playoff effectiveness. Every measure was taken to insure that each G-rated release had the chance to reach its intended market throughout the country.

The other companies engaged in regional four-walling, such as Ambassador Releasing and Phoenix International, all followed American National's lead. The key to success quickly became not only the product (seldom other than inexpensively produced wildlife documentaries and adventures) but also an effective television strategy. Since the audiences for these films were not frequent moviegoers, it was important to make each picture an event, something that could easily be achieved through a nonstop barrage of commercials. Specialists carefully planned every ad to maximize public motivation; and factors such as the weather, competing sports events, and even TV programs were considered in booking multiple theater locations.

Probably the biggest winners in the four-wall sweepstakes were Tom Laughlin and Delores Taylor. In the resolution of a suit against Warner Brothers in 1973 for improper handling of their 1971 movie *Billy Jack,* they agreed with the studio on a massive re-release plan, with the profits to be split fifty-fifty. Laughlin, who made and starred in the picture, and his wife, Taylor, who co-starred in it, obviously knew their audience well and realized the time was ripe for their cowboy-hippie fairy tale, with its unusual mixture of sweetness, mysticism, and kung-fu action. During the first week alone, $750,000 was spent on promotion and $1 million was allocated for renting out 389 theaters.[6] The entire campaign was organized like a military endeavor, with detailed charts mapping out the income levels, population density, and transportation facilities of each market. The film's engagingly innocent flavor was either highlighted or downplayed, depending on who the ads were trying to reach. From its original roots with underground, underage audiences, *Billy Jack* quickly became a phenomenon attracting all types and classes. It ended up grossing more than $30 million. Its sequel, *The Trial of Billy Jack* (1974), did almost as well at the box office, thanks to an equally shrewd marketing campaign. Theater owners were forced to pay $8,000 to $10,000 in front money just to have their houses four-walled, which gave Laughlin and Taylor $10 million before they even started. The movie opened simultaneously at one thousand theaters in 1974, and was supported by more than $3 million in advertising. Within seven days, it had earned almost $11 million.[7]

The success of Laughlin, Taylor, and Warner Brothers convinced other major production/distribution companies to try this new approach to exhibition. Films like *The Day of the Dolphin* (1973) and *Jeremiah Johnson* (1972), which had proved disappointing on their original releases, were remarketed in the hopes of attracting the broad, general audience that constituted the special province of four-walled vehicles. Distribution firms took their cue from *Billy Jack* and the wilderness pictures: they planned enormous advertising strategies emphasizing the family/adventure elements of their product. Saturation television spending became the name of the game, with the idea that 95 percent of the viewers in a given area would see more than four commercials promoting the movie. Producers and distributors increased their spending in local TV ads from $28.4 million in 1972 to $40.1 million in the first nine months of 1974 alone.[8] The encouraging results at the box office made this kind of investment seem worthwhile.

The popularity of four-walling grew so rapidly among the majors that eventually their own greediness defeated them. Recognizing the potential lucrativeness of a technique that guaranteed them 100 percent of the gross revenues, Warner Brothers and United Artists started to four-wall large attractions like *Fiddler on the Roof, Last Tango in Paris,* and *The Exorcist,* thereby depriving theater owners of any percentage of the profits. This was a clear violation of the 1948 consent decree, which required a breakup between production/distribution and exhibition. The U.S. Department of Justice finally stepped in: acting on a complaint filed by the National Association of Theater Owners, they issued an order in April, 1976, that prohibited Warner Brothers and other major producing firms for ten years from renting theaters, fixing admission prices, and demanding all money generated at the box office. Four-walling once again belonged to the independent firms who had pioneered the practice.

One of the direct outgrowths of the four-walling phenomenon was a new responsiveness on the part of major companies to test-market their films. Firms like Audience Studies Incorporated conducted elaborate consumer reaction surveys for new movies to determine public appeals and effective advertising pitches. In a typical project, a demographically selected group of 350 people were invited to watch an advance screening at a specially equipped theater. While they viewed the picture, their reactions were carefully monitored, second by second, through finger sensors and small, hand-held feedback units that permitted them to dial their interest levels, from very dull to very good. When the film was over, the group filled out detailed questionnaires about the characters and plot and participated in an intensive discussion session conducted by a staff researcher. A final evaluation was then made concerning the most appropriate age levels and income types the picture should aim for. Costs for the entire procedure usually ran from $3,300 to $4,100, depending upon the length of the movie.[9]

In addition to pretesting their product, some producers were also beginning to pay greater attention to the demands of unexpected audiences. The experiences of Cinerama Releasing Corporation with their 1973 film *Walking Tall* are a case in point. Though the movie opened slowly in spite of a violent ad campaign, reports soon started to circulate of people suddenly standing up and cheering at the conclusion. The film's true story of redneck retribution seemed to strike a forceful chord in rural viewers, and Cinerama quickly changed their advertising to stress this inspirational appeal. Theater owners who allowed the picture to gather steam were surprised by its remarkable staying power: cities like Little Rock and Chattanooga had runs of more than thirty weeks. Eventually, the movie grossed $17 million.[10]

The majority of the pictures mentioned so far were designed to attract the working-class audience, which had largely stopped going to films. According to a 1975 study by the Motion Picture Association of America, only 50 percent of those people with a high-school education and 25 percent of those without one attend movies regularly.[11] Films like *Walking Tall* and the wilderness documentaries were able to tap the huge market of infrequent moviegoers by offering a product and a promotion that stressed conservative, small-town values. But appealing as it might be to strike box-office gold in the hinterlands, Hollywood could not ignore the fact that its most consistent patrons came from an entirely different social and economic class. College-educated men and women in their twenties and thirties now saw more movies than anyone else,[12] and the movies of the 1970s became shaped by the industry's efforts to figure out exactly what they wanted to see.

Several different approaches were explored. As the decade began, it seemed as if the wave of the future would be dictated by the surprising success of the

1969 low-budget saga of rebellion, *Easy Rider*. Movie-makers felt they recognized a trend when they saw one; and, in their haste to capture the youth audience, dozens of misbegotten projects with long-haired radicals and druggy atmospheres were rushed into production. None really caught on. Even the stars who had created the most memorable bikers of the period were at a loss about what to do next. Peter Fonda and Dennis Hopper, buoyed by their sudden prominence, drifted off into separate ventures of self-indulgence and soon lost whatever bankability they might have possessed. Other efforts at specifically reaching the youth market, such as *The Strawberry Statement* (1970), *R.P.M.* (1970), and *B.S. I Love You* (1971), met similar fates. Clearly, the time was ripe for a renewal of creative direction in film-making.

Most of the major talents that would dominate in the 1970s scored their first successes in the opening years of the decade. They were, by and large, a young group of actors, directors, and producers who began their careers with apprenticeships in Hollywood's low-budget, exploitation studios. American International Pictures, which specialized in motorcycle and horror films, served as an enormously important training ground. Under its producer Rodger Corman, novice film-makers and performers were given the chance to develop their craft, as long as they completed their work quickly and cheaply. Corman demanded movies filled with fast action and violent thrills, but he also permitted a degree of creative freedom that was not generally available in other parts of the industry. The offbeat, eccentric films created for him by people like Francis Ford Coppola (*Dementia 13,* 1967), Martin Scorsese (*Boxcar Bertha,* 1972), and Peter Bogdanovich (*Targets,* 1968) testify to his ability to attract new talent and his willingness to support it.

When they finally left the low-budget system in the late 1960s and early 1970s, Corman's graduates found the fragmented movie audience made it almost impossible to predict what films might go over at the box office. Conventional rules and practices seemed to be changing overnight. Expensively mounted musicals and adventure epics, which the industry had always regarded with confidence, now ended up falling flat on their faces; cheaply made pictures with controversial themes, like *Easy Rider* and *Joe* (1970), surprised everyone, including their producers, by becoming big hits. In their confusion, the majors reluctantly found themselves becoming more open to new avenues of expression. If the moviegoing public was growing somewhat more catholic in taste and able to embrace unusual products, such as *M*A*S*H* (1970), *They Shoot Horses, Don't They* (1969), and *Z* (1969), perhaps the time was right to expand the creative range of film-making.

It was this kind of changing Hollywood climate that produced some of the most critically acclaimed and most popular films of the 1970s. The big studios were now willing to support and release movies which were often idiosyncratic in appeal and intensely personal in nature. Talents like Francis Ford Coppola, Robert Altman, Peter Bogdanovich, and Mike Nichols found themselves receiving financial backing for projects that would have been unthinkable ten years earlier. The *Last Picture Show* (1971) is an example of the industry's new production attitudes. With only one low-budget film to his credit, director Peter Bogdanovich created a movie which seemed to break all the rules. It was made in black and white, its cast was largely unknown, and its story of rural teenage sex was deliberately bleak. Nonetheless, the picture was a great success. Other films with unconventional approaches also did well at the box office in 1971. Mike Nichols' interesting but rather cartoonish sexual saga, *Carnal Knowledge,* grossed more than $12 million; Alan Pakula's intriguing story of a high-class call girl, *Klute,* made $8 million; and Robert Altman's hauntingly evocative *McCabe and Mrs. Miller,* while not a huge hit, still earned a respectable $4 million.

Though it was just as much a part of the 1970s atmosphere of artistic independence and experimentation, Francis Ford Coppola's *The Godfather* (1972) ushered in a new era of blockbuster film-making. The movie's astronomical success (it has currently grossed about $86 million) prompted Hollywood to embark once again on big-budget, broad-appeal productions. A frantic search began for no-risk properties, which guaranteed either presold audiences or large-scale thrills, or, hopefully, both. From their somewhat weakened position in the late 1960s, big-name stars reemerged as one of the most dependable ways to insure a hit. Four actors and one actress—Robert Redford, Paul Newman, Steve McQueen, Dustin Hoffman, and Barbara Streisand—brought people rushing to the box office, even if the stars' vehicles were wildly erratic in quality. When two male superstars teamed up, the profits seemed to double, which led to a series of male "buddy" films with every permutation imaginable: Redford and Newman in *The Sting* (1973), Hoffman and McQueen in *Papillon* (1973), McQueen and Newman in *The Towering Inferno* (1975), and Redford and Hoffman in *All the President's Men* (1976). Through the middle seventies, however, there was only one romantic pairing—Redford and Streisand in *The Way We Were* (1973).

In its pursuit of big hits, Hollywood became increasingly attached to the same kind of action/disaster formulas that the exploitation studios had always employed. The only difference, of course, was budget; and in this area, the majors went all out to give their products a first-class sheen. No expense was spared in making natural and unnatural catastrophes look completely convincing. Universal went a step further and developed a special theatrical sound system, called Sensurround, which encouraged audiences to go deaf as they watched the collapse of Los Angeles in *Earthquake* (1974), the triumph of the allied forces in *Midway* (1976), and the bumpy ride of *Rollercoaster* (1977).

New approaches to shaking up viewers were constantly being explored, ranging from a young girl vomiting on priests and masturbating with a crucifix in *The Exorcist* (1974), to a great white shark taking particular delight in eating friendly New Englanders in *Jaws* (1975). The fact that these two pictures rank as number four and number two, respectively, in *Variety*'s list of all-time film rental champs indicates the enormous popularity shock tactics enjoyed among the modern moviegoing public.

Nineteen seventy-four through 1978 were peak years for the film industry, largely because of the successes of superstar films like *The Sting, Papillon,* and *All the President's Men,* disaster pictures like *The Exorcist, The Towering Inferno,* and *Jaws,* and rock-music youth-movies like *Saturday Night Fever* and *Grease.* Probably more than anything else, the characteristic genre of the late 1970s has been the science fiction film, which rose to meteoric heights of popularity. In just the first nine months after its release, *Star Wars* grossed more money than any movie ever made ($207 million as of this writing)[13] and its future earning power overseas and at home with continued re-releases seems virtually unlimited. The film was shrewdly merchandised, proving once and for all that soundtrack albums and tie-in dolls, lunch pails, and jewelry can bring in even more revenue than box-office receipts. Another other-worldly movie, *Close Encounters of the Third Kind,* came out at the end of 1977 and in its first two months made $62 million. Audiences of the 1970s were clearly enthralled with the thrills that only outer-space or superhuman heroes (like 1978's major film bonanza *Superman*) could provide.

The box-office grosses of 1974 were the best since the end of World War II ($1.725 billion). The grosses for the next two years were even better, and the figures for 1977 were the best ever recorded ($2.325 billion).[15] The tremendous response to each year's big releases boosted the general level of the entire box office: eighteen pictures earned $10 million or more in rentals in 1974 — double the number of each of the previous two years. Hollywood was riding high, a condition some people felt would last as long as the economy stayed sluggish and the public searched for escape.

But there was an underside to these boom years. As the potential profits for films seemed to skyrocket, the studios developed a multi-million dollar mentality. Since only a few big films were needed each year, they concentrated their energies on just one or two large projects. With more to be gained, fewer risks were taken — the wave of innovation and experimentation that opened the decade was no longer as actively supported. Recycling became an appealing alternative, as hits from the past were either spun off into sequels (*Godfather Part II,* 1974; *The French Connection II,* 1975; *Walking Tall II,* 1976) or simply remade (*King Kong,* 1976; *A Star Is Born,* 1976).

The decline in production, from 400 films in 1955 to just 180 in 1975,[16]

Jessica Lange in *King Kong* (1976).

affected everyone. Independent talents were finding it harder to get their work financed or released as the number of major distributors decreased. Exhibitors, in the wake of a rapid expansion to multiple-screen complexes, were unable to locate enough product to fill their theaters year round and, because of higher rental demands, were forced to charge more for admission. That one-half of the population which went to movies at all now saw only one or two films a year.[17]

As a result of these factors, the motion picture industry faces an uncertain future. The trend towards the spectacular thriller and the preprocessed superstar package seems an ominous replay of Hollywood's desperate behavior during the 1950s, when any type of surface novelty was employed to draw people away from their television sets. Major studios may earn much more money now, but they are slowly strangling themselves by drastically reducing the range of products reaching the screen. The emphasis on bigger, but fewer, pictures makes it increasingly difficult for specialized, innovative films to attract an audience. Without a broad variety of movies featuring new elements and fresh approaches, the size of the filmgoing public has little chance of expanding. The motion picture industry may be content with its once- or twice-a-year patrons; but, unless it begins to reach out actively for different ideas and audiences, it may discover that America's already infrequent box-office habit could diminish even more.

NOTES

1. *New York Times*, January 27, 1977.
2. Tino Balio, *The American Film Industry* (Madison: University of Wisconsin Press, 1976), p. 225.
3. *New York Times*, January 27, 1977.
4. *Variety*, January 19, 1977.
5. *Variety*, February 26, 1974.
6. *Variety*, November 7, 1973.
7. *Variety*, November 20, 1974.
8. *Business Week*, March 3, 1975.
9. *Variety*, May 12, 1976.
10. *New York Times*, March 10, 1974.
11. *U.S. News and World Report*, March 17, 1975.
12. Ibid.
13. *Variety*, February 2, 1978.
14. Ibid.
15. *Variety*, January 11, 1978.
16. *Variety*, May 15, 1976.
17. *New York Times*, January 27, 1977.

All box-office rental figures are from *Variety*, January 5, 1977.

TWO/MOVIE STARS

CHARLIE CHAPLIN, MARY PICKFORD, Douglas Fairbanks, Rudolph Valentino, Gloria Swanson, James Cagney, Humphrey Bogart, Katherine Hepburn, Bette Davis, Marilyn Monroe, John Wayne, Sidney Poitier, Barbra Streisand, Robert Redford, Clint Eastwood, Jane Fonda—these are names with magic. Our movie stars have always been special people. Their real lives are like ours. Hundreds of stories in dozens of fan magazines tell us every week that stars have personal and family problems and that they desire happiness just as we do. But on-screen, their lives are glorious. And their bodies are transformed by the skill of the cinematographer and the size of the screen to the beauty and proportion of demigods. In movie stars we find our apotheosis, our elevation from the mundane to the celestial.

The stars provide a focal point for understanding the particular appeal of popular movies. Each star embodies special qualities which the audience reveres and therefore subscribes to as qualities to be emulated. We worship Greta Garbo for her cool reserve and Mae West for her earthy participation. Clark Gable is loved for his blue-collar simplicity, Cary Grant for his high-society sophistication. We are capable of an infinity of moods and feelings, and there are stars to personify and redeem all of them.

The essays in this chapter illustrate that stars also serve as touchstones for the particular eras in which they are most admired. James Damico describes how Ingrid Bergman's screen persona was carefully formed by David O. Selznick to embody a combination of the spiritual and the natural—a perfect combination for a decade that was sick of war and anxious to get back to family life and normalcy. In describing the public furor that followed Bergman's infamous Roman escapade, Damico also illustrates the deep seriousness with which we worship our stars. Being a divinity in America is a full-time job, both on- and off-screen: when a star's public and private lives are not consistent, the public reaction is likely to be immediate and cruel.

Julian Smith writes of his own strong personal link with a minor screen deity, Audie Murphy. For Smith, Murphy defines an aspect of the 1950s that would not find full expression until the 1960s and the American heart of darkness in Vietnam.

Gene D. Phillips describes another star who straddles decades. Paul Newman is by no means our only screen rebel. John Garfield, Marlon Brando, James Dean, and Steve McQueen, among others, all have shown disdain for American norms. None, however, for so long or with such consistent public approval as Newman.

Ingrid from Lorraine to Stromboli: Analyzing the Public's Perception of a Film Star

JAMES DAMICO

> Oh, sing me a saga of Joan
> Whose actions we cannot condone.
> From Boudoir to Altar
> Her steps never falter.
> She quips, "Get me God on the phone."
> Who is this pure maid of Lorraine?
> Whose voices she cannot explain?
> From a life so licentious
> She is turned so repentious,
> It's driven her simply insane. . . .[1]

Today when adultery and a panoply of what were once held to be sexual sins are not only publicly admitted by film stars, but often committed and filmed as part of their work, and when actresses openly form liaisons specifically to have children whom they intend to rear outside marriage, all without fear of adverse public reaction, it is intriguing to recall there was a recent time when one film star's adultery with and illegitimate child by a film director was headline news for more than a year, caused the entire motion picture industry a long moment of apprehension, prompted local, state, and national lawmaking bodies to indignant tirades and to the preparation of restrictive legislation, mobilized professional, religious, and civic groups to vociferous protest, and moved a legion of everyday moviegoers to towering outrage.

Exactly what caused the extensive and spontaneous national reaction that attended Ingrid Bergman's affair-cum-marriage with Roberto Rossellini is not easy to identify, but it is important to speculate on in the context of determining the function that films and film stars have in society and is especially informative in tracing the process by which the public arrives at a perception of a star's personality.

Ingrid Bergman was born in Sweden in 1915, married Dr. Peter Lindstrom in

1937, had a daughter in 1938, was brought to America in 1939 by David O. Selznick, and very soon thereafter became an important Hollywood star. Though not generally known, by at least 1946, her marriage had begun to sour; and it has been suggested that she had at a minimum a pair of extramarital affairs at this time (with Robert Capa, the photographer, and Victor Fleming, the director).[2] But, in critical contrast to her subsequent involvement with Rossellini, these were discreetly managed, and the public remained totally ignorant of them.

In 1948, struck by the power of *Open City* and *Paisan,* she wrote worshipfully to Rossellini, in effect pleading to work with him.[3] He responded enthusiastically; and, during the shooting of *Under Capricorn* in England, she and her husband (who also acted as her business manager) met with the Italian in Paris on numerous occasions to plan the production of what was finally called *Stromboli* (named after the film's locale specifically to capitalize on the international tide of notoriety that identified the volcanic island as the place where Ingrid and Roberto had carried on their romance). Subsequently, they all repaired to Hollywood, ostensibly to find a way to shoot their film there, but it seems Rossellini had the further intention, as he announced to a reporter, of putting "the horns on Mr. Bergman."[4] Soon though, finding that he couldn't work in Hollywood, he returned to Italy, where it was decided the film would be done.

What initially directed all the curiosity toward Bergman's arrival in Rome on March 20, 1949, was the much-ballyhooed meeting of two diametrically opposed cinematic worlds—the Hollywood glossy and the Italian neorealistic. But what inflated worldwide interest to extraordinary proportions and created the bedlam that never really afterwards subsided, was the openly conducted, apparently flaunted romance between the married actress and director begun in full view of the assembled international press from the moment she stepped off the plane. Front-page articles and photos documented the affair, Ingrid and Roberto strolled hand-in-hand across full pages in *Life,* and gossip column items became superfluous.

In the temper of the times, it was, to be sure, tactless, brazen, and almost calculated to create a scandal. But totally unexpected was the breadth of the attack on Bergman, which reached epic scale when the news broke that she was pregnant and when eventually she had Rossellini's child out of wedlock.

Ministerial groups, women's organizations, and private citizens bombarded Hollywood with resolutions and letters. Legislatures the country over spent hours discussing the scandal. A Sioux City Catholic bishop declared that it was about time Hollywood did something about "persons whose dirty, lousy, filthy conditions are ruining the industry."[5]

Editorials were written by newspapers of all sizes and persuasions, most condemning Bergman but some championing the artist's right to individual freedom. Her death scene from *Joan of Arc,* which had been included as part of an educational film, *History Brought to Life,* was hurriedly excised from final prints.[6] Louella Parsons, in announcing her pregnancy, compared what she called Bergman's "sacrifice for love" to those of Mary, Queen of Scots, and Lady Hamilton, and to the abdication of Edward VIII.[7]

Senator Edwin Johnson of Colorado, a leader in the Swedish-American community, felt particularly aggrieved, having previously held up Bergman as a perfect model of Nordic womanhood. For more than an hour on the floor of the U.S. Senate, he fulminated against the actress, calling her "a free-love cultist," "a powerful influence for evil," and "Hollywood's apostle of degradation;" and he urged passage of a resolution barring her forever from returning to the United States for "moral turpitude," predicting that "from the ashes of Ingrid Bergman a better Hollywood will rise."[8]

Attempts were made to get the then very active local and state censor boards to ban *Stromboli* as immoral, not because of any salacious content in the film, but by virtue of the extra-cinematic conduct of its principals. A Memphis censor tried unsuccessfully to ban all Bergman pictures, present and past, stating that "Miss Bergman's conduct is a disgrace, not only to her profession, but to all American women. I'm glad she's a foreigner." This was balanced by the police captain and head of Chicago's censor board, who said, "If we're going to delve into the past of every Hollywood actor, we'd be eliminating about two-thirds of all films."[9]

Not satisfied with oratory, Senator Johnson presented to the Senate a bill which would have made it mandatory for all entertainment industry members to be licensed before being permitted to work. This would have given those responsible complete control over all film artists simply by investing in them the power to revoke licenses for whatever they deemed reprehensible public behavior. It failed to gain acceptance.[10]

The extent of the furor this affair aroused, however, is evident; and it indicates the wide social implications of what amounted in reality to little more than a sexual peccadillo in an element of society well known for and indulged in its promiscuities. The question therefore arises: Why did this particular film star's affair generate such a momentous reaction when many another's hardly caused a ripple? And why was this adulterous act so condemned when, for instance, at approximately the same time, Robert Mitchum's apparent transgression of an even stronger societal taboo was revealed with his arrest for drug possession, and it, though widely reported, barely affected his career and raised nothing like the storm of disapproval that Bergman's actions did?

Essentially, the answer lies in the way in which the public perceives film stars and in the peculiarities of the Bergman image. The public images of a majority of stars are constructed out of a mixture of the off-screen characters of the actors, their on-screen personas, how publicity defines both of these, and how the general public interprets and fuses all the foregoing elements into assimilable phenomena which it then labels with, and thereafter identifies by, the stars' names. Although audiences and professional observers, such as critics and reviewers, are often perceptive in recognizing authentic artistic temperament, they are by no means infallible in correctly interpreting the nature of and defining that temperament. Arbitrarily, or out of their own psychological needs, or from suggestions made by publicity, they will often ascribe to film

Cary Grant and Ingrid Bergman in *Notorious* (1946).

personalities characteristics, attitudes, beliefs, virtues, and vices for which they think they see validation on the screen in the stars' behavior and expression. Such judgments, however, may in fact be essential misunderstandings of these indicators of authentic temperament and consequently of the personality components of which they are expressive (as has been the case, for example, in such popular and basic misconceptions as of Wallace Reid's "wholesomeness," Will Rogers' "lack of sophistication," Jayne Mansfield's "dumbness," etc.). It is this kind of critical misinterpretation that seems to have been made of Bergman's personality.

From her initial appearance in Swedish films, through her Hollywood years, which included many public and stage appearances, Bergman provoked reactions whose language verged on the monotonous. "Beautiful," "natural," "clean," "fresh," "glowing," and "spiritual" turned up again and again in articles and reviews. Her performance in *Intermezzo: A Love Story,* her first American film, brought from Frank S. Nugent, the not normally effusive critic of *The New York Times,* an analysis of the actress and her acting that might be thought of as cutting the pattern to be followed by most subsequent reviewers:

> She is beautiful, and not at all pretty. Her acting is surprisingly mature, yet singularly free from the stylistic traits—the mannerisms, postures, precise intonations—that become the stock in trade of the matured actress. Our impression of her Anita, who is pallid one moment, vivacious the next, yet always consistent, is that of a lamp whose wick burns bright or dull, but always burns. There is that incandescence about Miss Bergman, that spiritual spark which makes us believe that Selznick has found another great lady of the screen.[11]

Six months later, in appraising her first English-speaking stage performance in *Liliom,* Brooks Atkinson matched his colleague's enthusiasm:

> Ingrid Bergman acts with incomparable loveliness . . . is personally beautiful and endows Julie with an awakened, pulsing grace of spirit. One is timidly reluctant to praise an actress too highly on her first appearance, but the time will come when it will be hard to praise Miss Bergman enough. There is something wonderfully enkindling about the way she illuminates Julie's character.[12]

These are, of course, exceptional notices from different observers of her work in entirely different media, and they testify to a common recognition of authentic and essential qualities in the Bergman acting persona.

It was precisely these qualities that Selznick had seen in the original Swedish *Intermezzo* and that he took great care to ensure Bergman projected in his remake. In a memo to Gregory Ratoff, the director of the American *Intermezzo,* the producer issued methodical instructions about photographing her:

> The [Gregg] Toland tests of Miss Bergman prove indubitably . . . the difference between a great photographic beauty and an ordinary girl with Miss Bergman lies in proper photography of her—and that this in turn depends not simply on avoiding the bad side of her face; keeping her head down as much as possible; giving her the proper hairdress, giving her the proper mouth make-up, avoiding long shots so as not to make her look too big [she was nearly 5'10"], and, even more importantly, but for the same reason, avoiding low cameras on her, as well as being careful to

build people who work with her . . . but most important of all, on shading her face and in invariably going for effect lighting on her.[13]

Selznick's painstaking attention to the actress' physical appearance extended not only to her make-up, but made a rather large issue out of her eyebrows — as it turned out, a matter of some significance.

Thanks to clubbing everybody on the head about avoiding make-up on Miss Bergman, it looks as though we have a new star in her, with the public and the press all commenting widely on the fact that her eyebrows look natural, and that she isn't smeared with Hollywood make-up.[14]

Ann Rutherford [a young film actress] told me . . . that all the girls she knows are letting their eyebrows grow in as a result of Bergman's unplucked eyebrows. . . . So apparently our decision about Miss Bergman's eyebrows, based upon this studio's feeling that the public was sick and tired of the monstrosities that had been inflicted on the public by most of Hollywood's glamour girls, is going to have a national reaction.[15]

The studio's internecine battles over seeming inconsequentialities, such as the retention of the actress's eyebrows, her unmade-up look, and her name (which raged hotly for a time), were all settled in favor of her "naturalness" and had the desired effect not only upon audiences, but also on critics, as Graham Greene's review of *Intermezzo* testifies:

The film is most worth seeing for the new star, Miss Ingrid Bergman, who is as natural as her name . . . a performance that doesn't give the effect of acting at all, but of living — without make-up.[16]

But beyond being methodically built, the image of the actress was just as precisely disseminated. Long before her first picture was released, the producer assiduously labored at shaping the public's concept of his star-to-be:

I think Miss Bergman's interview in the [*Los Angeles*] *Examiner* was awfully bad publicity . . . our being quoted as thinking she is sexy . . . is not the way we should publicize her. . . . Please don't have her interviewed unless somebody you can rely on . . . can be present.[17]

In a subsequent memo to his publicity department, he set out the correct "angle" on the actress. It involved stressing for public consumption her conscientiousness as an artist, her devotion to her work, her thrift and her unaffectedness (manifested, for example, in her acceptance of less than a star's dressing room and her desire not to have a stand-in).

All of this is completely unaffected and completely unique and I should think would make a grand angle of approach to her publicity, spreading these stories all around, and adding to them as they occur, so that her natural sweetness and consideration and conscientiousness become something of a legend. Certainly there could be nothing more popular, and nothing could win for her the affection of fans more than this. . . . It is completely in keeping with the character she plays in the picture and completely in keeping with the fresh and pure personality and appearance which caused me to sign her. . . .[18]

Through his campaign, Selznick was in effect offering filmgoers a ready-made lexicon with which to label all the startling qualities of the Bergman personality, in the expectation that the provided labels would be synthesized into a sympathetic interpretation of both the actress's personal character and her screen performances. The process, of course, was a Hollywood tradition, and had been tried before with great and, more often, utterly no success. Its obvious risk was that the public would not agree that the lexicon provided for it was appropriate to what it saw on the screen. But a more essential risk underlay the first: even if the public did accept them, the proffered labels and consequent directed interpretation of the star's qualities might eventually turn out to be misleading and false, and that, out of a sense of having been duped, the general audience might turn on and reject the star.

Almost unanimously, however, the public did accept Selznick's campaign on Bergman. Not only did descriptions and judgments of the actress in reviews match the producer's scenario, but countless interviews and articles reemphasized the same points. The *Richmond* (Va.) *News-Leader,* for example, said she looked like an American college girl and made other stars look phoney because she "buys her own groceries and even wears her own eyelashes."[19] The *Milwaukee Journal* praised her for having her family "form the background of her life away from the studio," and for never posing for cheesecake art.[20] But this *Baltimore Sun* summation of August 20, 1944, can serve as the essence of the public conception of Bergman:

A big star who is satisfied with her roles, her salary, and her life in general. . . . There isn't a superlative left which hasn't been used about her person and her acting. She is probably the only woman here [Hollywood] who hasn't an enemy. She has never in the five years she's lived here been mentioned unfavorably in a gossip column. . . . There is nothing star-ish about her, except her personality, smile, and charm . . . she doesn't dear and darling everybody. She never wears make-up, except a little lipstick occasionally, and she lives quietly with her

husband . . . and daughter. . . . She has no conceit, except about her
ability as an actress. . . .

These quotations make evident how much the supposed stability of her
family life had entered into the publicity picture, when, in reality, her domestic
situation at the time was rapidly deteriorating.

Equally a part of the Bergman "legend" from its beginnings was her identification with Joan of Arc. She had had a fixation on the French saint from
girlhood and got Selznick to announce, as her second American film, a dramatization of Joan's life. The film was not made, because the approaching war
rendered it inappropriate to portray the British burning France's woman saint.
But a publicity barrage at the time implanted the historical figure in the public's
consciousness as a kind of alter-ego for the actress. The alter-ego was finally
given palpable form shortly before the Rossellini affair when Bergman appeared on Broadway as *Joan of Lorraine* in Maxwell Anderson's play. Not
only did she triumph, but she was also "immortalized" in the role for the
nation at large on the cover of *Life*. This was immediately followed by the
culmination of her personal and career aspirations with the filming of *Joan of
Arc,* which, though a financial and artistic failure, was critical in solidifying the
connection between the actress and the saint.

Ingrid Bergman in *Stromboli* (1950).

But entirely hidden from the public during this time, besides her romantic involvements, were what has been called "the Bergman temper,"[21] her obstinancy, her chronic restlessness, her compulsive eating,[22] and the fact that as a girl her next most cherished personage after Saint Joan was Isolde, because she "was a symbol of earthly love."[23] There appeared no public hint of the woman Robert Capa described as:

> all tied up in a million knots . . . so naive it hurts . . . afraid to let go . . . a damn sight more woman than actress. And people should stop treating her like an adolescent schoolgirl—or like a saint.[24]

Or of the person that a Hollywood producer saw as "a very selfish, self-centered woman . . . only interested in herself."[25] Or of what Bergman said of herself to her press agent:

> We Swedes are not supposed to show our emotions in front of strangers. That's the way we're brought up. On the set, when I'm working, they think I'm so placid, and the fan magazines keep saying I'm so normal and simple. But you know me better.

> I wish I could rage and throw things, but if I did I'd feel foolish and wonder how I looked. So when I get angry I think to myself, will I lose my dignity? And I hold it inside and wait until I'm alone in my bedroom, then I throw myself on the bed and scream and cry.[26]

And after Rossellini:

> I was regarded as the wholesome, well-mannered girl, the actress without make-up, the Hollywood exception. People didn't expect me to have emotions like other women.[27]

Selznick has also testified to the importance of his publicity campaign and the image of the actress it attempted to present to the public:

> I'm afraid I'm responsible for the public's image of her as Saint Ingrid. I hired a press agent who was an expert at shielding stars from the press, and we released only stories that emphasized her sterling character. We deliberately built her up as the normal, healthy, unneurotic career woman, devoid of scandal and with an idyllic home life. I guess that backfired later.[28]

One thing the promulgated image of Bergman did do was to cause the general public to ignore or rationalize away the specifically sexual character of the largest proportion of her roles and, even more essentially, the almost totally sexual nature of her screen persona.

In her twelve American films prior to *Joan of Arc,* Bergman is a whore or promiscuous in four *(Dr. Jeykll and Mr. Hyde, Saratoga Trunk, Notorious, Arch of Triumph),* is having or has had an affair in four *Intermezzo, Casablanca, For Whom the Bell Tolls* [in which she has also been gang-raped], *Spellbound),* and is a virtual slave of sexual dependency in one *(Gaslight).* Of the three remaining films, she is accused of infidelity in *Rage in Heaven,* self-sacrificingly admits to someone else's infidelity in *Adam Had Four Sons,* and even in *The Bells of St. Mary,* as James Agee observed, uses,

> . . . sex appeal . . . to play a Mother Superior . . . and in general, I grieve to say, justifies a recent piece of radio promotion which rather startlingly describes a nun: "Ingrid Bergman has never been lovelier, hubba hubba hubba."[29]

Most critics, however, ambivalently sought to reconcile the Bergman "legend" with those of her roles containing sexual specifics too obvious to ignore by simply accepting the validity of her acting while denying the character it portrayed. Of her Clio Dulane in *Saratoga Trunk,* for example, Bosley Crowther said:

> Miss Bergman gives ample surface evidence of a coquettish, impulsive miss and looks quite fetching with dark hair and eyebrows, but there is no genuine spirit in her act. It is hard to accept this proper lady as the willful courtesan she's supposed to be.[30]

And of her "unemployed courtesan" and "tramp" in *Arch of Triumph:*

> . . . we watch love as it is made by two of the movies' most able craftsmen [Bergman and Charles Boyer, but] she with her cleancut, graceful style [is] quite hard to reconcile with her characterization.[31]

Even her co-workers saw this "able craftsman's" love-playing as spiritual. As her press agent put it after *The Bells of St. Mary* was released:

> Forgotten were the "bad girls" she had previously played, which had never fooled anyone anyway. Through all the painted women of her former films had shone the artless, virginal look, which her adherents now insisted was the true Bergman.[32]

The difficulty in reconciling the actress's publicity image with her screen persona lay in the fact that the two were not identical but complementary. In contradiction of the "legend," the constituents of Bergman's film persona arise from a central motivating concept of an "earthly love" that is total, orgasmic, all-consuming and the only essential experience in life. It is a love desperately to be hoped for, anxiously anticipated, struggled with, but then surrendered to entirely—mind, heart, soul, and body: a surrender in its complementary concept of "unearthly" love no less applicable to the Maid Joan than to Isolde.

Surrender, as Selznick realized in recognizing "how superbly" Bergman played "scenes of surrender,"[33] is possibly the prime element of her screen personality. It is the action to which *Casablanca* builds and which is capped by her line, "You'll have to do the thinking for both of us." It is the emotional impetus behind the celebrated kissing scene in *Notorious* that makes it more than just a technical exercise—the sense of her natural giving in contrast to Cary Grant's rather removed acceptance of her.

Of the many physical manifestations of the passionate intensity of her portrayals (misunderstood not only by audiences but by old Hollywood hands as well, who are as susceptible to the processes of legend-making as the general public), one was singled out by Sam Wood, director of both *For Whom the Bell Tolls* and *Saratoga Trunk*. He attempted to explain it, however, in terms of the Bergman publicity image.

> Bergman's loveliness is more than external. It comes from in here (he patted his abdomen). When she plays a love scene, she blushes—real blushes. And when her cheeks get pink, you can see it on the screen because there's no make-up to hide it. It's a beautiful sight to see.[34]

The distinction between blush and flush is more than alphabetical. Bergman's coloring in such circumstances is less an indication of her virginal tendencies than an expression of the restraint she is exercising before the overwhelming character of her understanding of love—her tremulous anxiety at the prospect of a surrender that will mark the commitment to an all-encompassing passion.

It was a characteristic of the actress that another director, Anatole Litvak, recognized and defined:

> Her great quality is that, the moment she understands a part, her intellect gives way to emotion. When her emotion takes over, it comes out all right.[35]

Ben Hecht recounts that Bergman did not want to do *Spellbound* because, as she said:

I don't believe the love story. The heroine is an intellectual woman, and an intellectual woman simply can't fall in love so deeply.[36]

The author wryly remarks that she played the part convincingly. What he doesn't note is that she played it as she did all her successful roles—with an underlying emotional rationale—and that the woman in the film consequently came out far more emotional than intellectual. According to the producer, Walter Wanger, this approach extended beyond the confines of the part. "She always imagined herself in love with the leading man or director in every picture she did."[37] In other words, the entire filmmaking process was an extension of the total and emotional nature of the love experience at the center of her films.

The close relationship that an all-encompassing and finally transcendental romantic sexual love bears to a spiritual love of an equal intensity is critical to the misapprehension of Bergman's film persona, for those physical and emotional attributes that constitute her screen personality could just as easily be read as expressive of the spiritual torment of a soul reaching for communion with and salvation from God. Her nearly metaphysical agony at the prospect of a total personal surrender could as well delineate the agony of a surrender to the will of a heavenly power, and her fear and trembling before the commitment to an overwhelming romantic love might as well express a deep anxiety at the possibility of loss of one's identity in the acceptance of God.

It would appear, therefore, that filmgoers accepted the ready-made interpretation provided by the actress's publicity image of those qualities comprising the phenomenon they knew as Ingrid Bergman and which they recognized as authentically artistic, because they assumed that the judgments already devised for them were accurate and that the view which saw Bergman as essentially representative of spiritual concerns had been validated by the persona itself as it appeared and performed on the screen.

As it turned out, however, those judgments were neither accurate nor complete, and in their errors of omission and commission, they provided, at least partially, the basis for the broad social disappointment, anger, and resentment that attended Bergman's affair with Rossellini, for it is possible to speculate that, in accepting the publicity image of the actress, a segment of the moviegoing public came to regard her as a totem figure (as it often seems to do other celebrities, out of other needs and to fulfill other functions) because her apparent film persona could conveniently serve as a focus, reflector, and symbolic rehearser of the audience's indefinite spiritual longings and aspirations. But when it was dramatically shown that the central passion of the Bergman personality was not exclusively spiritual, but also quite specifically sexual, when the totem had in effect despoiled itself, the now wrathful public rose up in an effort to pull down what it saw as a self-proclaimed false idol.

Such a speculation, at any rate, offers a partial explanation of how a film star's inconsequential act of adultery could be aggrandized into an international incident and become a matter of legislative, professional, and deep personal concern. It also provides a further sounding of the profound depths of the public's psychic investment in films and film stars.

NOTES

1. Doggerel by Lewis Milestone, David Lewis, Charles Boyer, Russell Metty, and Norman Lloyd, sent to Bergman during the first week of October, 1946, on the occasion of the start of rehearsals for *Joan of Lorraine;* quoted in Joseph Steele, *Ingrid Bergman: An Intimate Portrait* (New York: David McKay Company, Inc., (1959), pp. 111–12. The "life so licentious" is that portrayed by the actress in *Arch of Triumph,* which she had just completed filming in collaboration with the writers of the verse, and in which she played another Joan (Madou), a prostitute. The sudden change from this Joan to Joan of Arc is what has "driven her simply insane."
2. Steele, pp. 63–66, 91–92, 138–39.
3. The letter may be found in Bill Davidson, "Anatomy of a Scandal," in *The Real and the Unreal* (New York: Harper & Brothers, Publishers, 1961), p. 161.
4. Steele, p. 168.
5. *New York Herald Tribune,* February 7, 1950.
6. *Variety,* February 15, 1950.
7. Steele, p. 261.
8. Ibid., p. 142.
9. *Variety,* February 8, 1950.
10. Jack Vizzard, *Speak No Evil* (New York: Simon and Schuster, Inc., 1970), p. 148.
11. October 6, 1939.
12. *New York Times,* March 31, 1940.
13. David O. Selznick, *Memo From David O. Selznick,* ed. Rudy Behlmer (New York: Viking Press, 1972), p. 130.
14. Ibid, p. 280.
15. Ibid, pp. 133–34.
16. *Spectator,* 26 January, 1940.
17. Selznick, p. 130.
18. Ibid., pp. 131–32.
19. February 15, 1940.
20. October 26, 1943.
21. Steele, p. 52.
22. Davidson, p. 144.
23. Steele, p. 17.
24. Ibid., p. 92.
25. Davidson, p. 148.
26. Steele, p. 75.

27. Davidson, pp. 157–58.
28. Ibid.
29. *Nation,* January 5, 1946.
30. *New York Times,* November 22, 1945.
31. Ibid., April 21, 1948.
32. Steele, p. 76.
33. Selznick, pp. 338–39.
34. Steele, p. 39.
35. Davidson, pp. 149–50.
36. *A Child of the Century* (New York: New American Library, 1954), p. 449.
37. Davidson, p. 145.

Innocence Preserved or Audie Murphy Died for Your Sins, America

JULIAN SMITH

November 11, 1955. With two or three other officers, I am marching at the head of a battalion of fine young Americans. It is Armistice Day (I've never liked the new name, Veterans' Day).

I am wearing the basic uniform of the U.S. Army since World War Two: the short Ike Jacket and matching olive drab trousers. Beyond that, from top to bottom, all is changed, magical. On top, a chrome plated helmet, carefully stored in tissue paper except when taken out for ceremonial occasions; below, spit-shined paratrooper boots.

In between, a gleaming Sam Browne belt, huge brass buckle, silver-plated scabbard, stainless steel cavalry saber, insignia of rank and regimental badge (two of each), shoulder patches, service stripes, the crossed rifles of the infantry on each lapel, white silk scarf, rope-like fourragères (one blue, one red, one white, one yellow) with brilliant brass pips, medals (just gobs of them), marksmanship badges, and (closest to my heart) four rows of ribbons (red, white, blue, yellow, green, orange, purple, brown, and combinations thereof) absolutely spotted and clotted with stars, bars, and oak leaf clusters.

The truly marvelous thing about all this is that I'm only seventeen years old, a cadet major in the Junior ROTC battalion at West Phoenix High School, and I am marching down the main drag of Phoenix, a captive city. This parade means a lot to me and to almost everyone else in Phoenix, a city that takes pride in the military competence of its children.

No one scoffs at the ROTC in Phoenix. Is it not democracy in action? Is not the battalion commander at Camelback an Afro-American (or, as they said in those days, a fine, upstanding colored boy)? At Phoenix Union, he's a Polish-American. And look at my own West Phoenix, the city champion in last spring's military competition and the most ethnic conglomerate of all: I'm just a WASP from the South, pure American, but one of the company commanders, my good friend Danny DeLeon, is a Mexican-American, another company commander is a compact little Japanese-American, and the cadet colonel, Herbie Dreiseszum, is a fine Hebrew-American, just like the owner of Goldwater's department store downtown who is both a United States Senator and a brigadier general in the Arizona National Guard.

I'm in the National Guard too, and so are Danny and a lot of the other cadet officers; but, as we're only privates and corporals in the guard, bare of brass and real campaign ribbons, we prefer to march with our Rotcy units all decked out in full glory.

The parade reaches its end. We've marched four or five miles, and Army trucks are waiting to take us back to our local assembly areas. With another cadet major, I decide not to ride back to West Phoenix. Instead, we walk back past Goldwater's to the central downtown area, clanking under the weight of our medals and paraphernalia, through the admiring crowds of post-parade shoppers and sightseers. We're going to a movie, to see Audie Murphy in his own life story (if you can credit a life ending with the hero only a few years our senior). For three years, my friend and I have tried to outdo each other in winning medals and badges and fourragères. Audie, the most decorated soldier of World War Two, is our hero.

November 11, 1969. My son Joshua is being baptized in the Sage Chapel at Cornell University. The priest is Dan Berrigan, and the infant, a symbol of innocence, is the focus of an act both religious and political. Dan prays that the child will grow into a man of peace, that the old significance of Armistice Day will not be lost. It's a long way from Phoenix.

November, 1972. It is not to brag that I have played back the home movie of me at seventeen, at half-life, for the image I summon up embarrasses me and would puzzle those who know me as a shaggy gray beard whose gaudiness runs to turtlenecks and bell bottoms. So far have I moved beyond rank and insignia that I won't even wear love beads, peace symbols, or smile buttons like the counter-culture shock-troops around me.

No, I want you to know I am speaking as one who once admired what Audie Murphy stood for (and who may yet, in a strange way), as one who has traveled a long road from the days when he stood at the top of his class at N.C.O. school at Fort Hood, Texas (the general shook his hand)—as one who still can't bear to throw away his awards from the American Legion, the Sons of the American Revolution, and the National Rifle Association, but hides them away with his old stamp collection, another relic of a happy middle-American childhood and adolescence.

I want you to understand that this investigation into the ironies of Audie is, for me, a journey back into time, a journey in which I see, not with old eyes but a new vision, what I saw in movies and magazines half a life and more ago.

Finally, I want you to understand that Audie Murphy's death [in 1971] struck me as a reminder of both personal and national mortality. I had forgotten him, had seen none of his films since 1958, had left him as an all-American boy-faced hero. And there he was splashed on the front page of a local paper, middle-aged, jowly, heavy-eyed, wearing the face of an outwardly successful auto dealer who might, any day now, be indicted for fraud.

Audie. The image he makes. Our very own Dorian Gray. In death, the jowls drop away, the fat melts, the movie runs backward, and suddenly we see the timeless youth once more, an image frozen in the mold set by this twenty-year-old *Saturday Evening Post* head:

HE DOESN'T WANT TO BE A STAR

He ran away to war at 17, won 23 decorations and the Medal of Honor by personally killing 240 Germans. A semidisabled veteran at 21, Audie Murphy reluctantly became a big-money Hollywood star, but he's still just a sharecropper's kid—lonely and sometimes afraid of his own dreams.

Afraid of his own dreams . . . the real world was safe, but the world of dreams full of snares and delusions. "I had nightmares about the war—men running and shooting and hollering, and then my gun would fall apart when I tried to pull the trigger." So at first he slept with a loaded pistol under his pillow, with a gun that wouldn't fall apart—if he couldn't pull the trigger in the dream world, at least he could in the real. One night, awaking to find a luminous switch glaring at him in the dark, he blasted away, startling out of her own dreams the starlet sleeping at his side.

THE GREAT AUDIE MURPHY DREAM AND TIME MACHINE
PART ONE: CEREMONIES AND CELEBRATIONS

When the lieutenant general pinned the Medal of Honor and the Legion of Merit on Audie, nine United States senators on a jaunt to Berchtesgaden stood in line to shake his hand.

He came back from the war, stood on a reviewing stand on Fifth Avenue next to another general. "Where do you plan on going, Murphy, now that the war is over?" the general is supposed to have asked under his breath. "Home, General. Is there any other place to go, sir?"

Home, of course, was Farmersville, Texas, and we know he went back, for *Life* went with him, and the *Saturday Evening Post* proclaimed the homecoming too. He didn't stay long. Whether Farmersville had changed or Audie had changed makes no difference. Everything seemed changed, even the old battle fields when he went back to France in 1948 as the guest of M. le President Auriol: "He traveled 1,500 miles visiting battlefields where he fought but even after they were pointed out to him by former members of the Maquis he had difficulty in recognizing the localities." General de Lattre de Tassigny, the chief of staff, pinned the Legion of Honor and the Croix de Guerre on Audie, and home he came, to Hollywood.

Whatever happened to Farmersville?

When a girl wanted his autograph in Dallas in 1948, Audie signed himself a "fugitive from the law of averages." He meant that he had escaped death when so many had not. But one law of averages he was never able to escape: that, by winning more medals than anyone else, he marked himself for life. Few writers, no matter how brief the space provided nor the reason for writing, were able to avoid some version of the magic formula: "The Most Decorated American Soldier of World War Two."

To his dying day, Audie carried not one but a whole flock of albatrosses, and the biggest hung around his neck on a star-spangled blue ribbon.

He tried to give them away in 1950. The Medal of Honor went to his eight-year-old nephew back in Farmersville, the Distinguished Service Cross, to a girl in Tennessee as a high-school graduation present. But there was no escaping the medals, the awards dead men couldn't collect ("I feel," he once said, "as if they handed their medals to me and said: 'Here, Murph, hold these.' "—Murph, the patsy), for the Army quickly replaced them, gratis.

He was like a man who had broken the law of averages in a crazy crap game played for symbols; and, though the symbols could be exchanged for money (and were—as *Life* put it in commercial metaphors, "He got the big one for a *day's work* near Holtswihr. . . . His medals got Murphy a *contract* in Hollywood"), they carried with them a doom.

THE GREAT AUDIE MURPHY DREAM AND TIME MACHINE
PART TWO: REAL LIFE

My country. America! That is it. We have been so intent on death that we have forgotten life. And now suddenly life faces us. I swear to myself that I will measure up to it. I may be branded by war, but I will not be defeated by it.

Gradually it becomes clear. I will go back. I will find the kind of girl of whom I once dreamed. I will learn to look at life through uncynical eyes, to have faith, to know love. I will learn to work in peace as in war. And finally—finally, like countless others, I will learn to live again.

As the last words of his autobiography suggest, Audie Murphy was the kind of childlike man who knew too much about death before he knew about life. Trouble was, *Life* knew about *him*. As Citizen Kane is seen through the Lucean newsreel, so with Audie through *Life,* the picture magazine.

He burst forth upon America on the cover of *Life* for 16 July, 1945. There he is, in all our libraries today, smiling down at the camera as though at a younger brother. (Perhaps I'm that younger brother, for I first saw him there myself.) Strong, even white teeth, hundreds of freckles, and for caption the inevitable formula: "MOST DECORATED SOLDIER." There he was, full blown, the all-American boy that press agents would blather about for another generation. James Cagney saw his picture, called his brother, a producer, and, the story goes, a star was born. Well, almost.

The four-page spread inside ended with a picture of Audie, back home in Farmersville, getting his tie straightened by his "special girl," nineteen-year-old Mary Lee: "Audie hopes she is his own girl, but he isn't quite sure yet, because he usually blushes when he gets within ten feet of any girl."

Life just couldn't leave him alone. As long as he kept his boyish looks, he was good for yet another four-page spread. So, two years later, he is seen showing his medals to yet another nineteen-year-old girl friend, Wanda Hendrix, an aspiring (as they used to say) starlet he had first seen on the cover of another magazine: "At present, Wanda and Audie consider each other more important than any career. They are reportedly engaged, and the love affair, unlike so many others in moviedom, is said to be the real thing. . . . Audie has simply given Wanda his medals—'just for safekeeping.' "

Life was right: it was the real thing, though they didn't do a spread on the end of the affair two years later when Wanda was granted a divorce on uncontested grounds of mental cruelty (that shootout with the lightswitch didn't help things).

The bloom was off the Texas rose, but *Life* was still game for yet another four-page spread when Audie starred in his own life story based on his own autobiography. The combination of art and life was just too much, so there, in the 1955 Fourth of July issue, was Audie manning the machine gun on a burning tank under the head "A War Hero Turned Actor Acts Himself as Hero."

Sixteen years passed before Audie returned to *Life*. It took his death to do it. No more the four-page spread, but half a page by his old colleague-in-arms and fellow actor, Bill Mauldin, who rendered the immortal last testimonial: "Long before his plane flew into a mountain, he was nibbled to death by ducks."

No more the front cover, but now the "Parting Shots." *Life* had given Audie fame twenty-six years before, and Audie had blown it. The final irony, surely unconscious, was that the last of the Parting Shots for that issue was the full-page photograph of a baby-faced South Vietnamese general, absolutely dripping with medals, ribbons, fourragères, badges, and gew-gaw, receiving his thirty-first decoration. The caption reads, "It has been a very long war in Vietnam."

It's been many years since I've read *Life* with any regularity. I'm a *New York Times* man, nowadays, and the only time I get to see *Life* is in my dentist's waiting room. Thus I associate *Life* with decay. *Life* also brings back my green youth. I feel ambivalent about *Life*—and don't we all?

So, researching this essay has been a trip back to my own personal Farmersville, that metaphorical Farmersville of the mind in which we knew the streets and landmarks, and the heroes wore the friendly faces of neighbors.

THE GREAT AUDIE MURPHY DREAM AND TIME MACHINE
PART THREE: THE MOVIE BEGINS

To examine Audie Murphy's life as a work of art is like reading a novel by a deranged disciple of Kurt Vonnegut. Audie was (is?) just as much the unwilling traveler as that other victim of wartime excess, Billy Pilgrim. Where Billy came unstuck in time, Audie came unglued in reality. Actors, you say, don't really live their parts—but Audie was no actor and made no pretensions along that line, as when he told a director he had a "hell of a handicap: no talent."

The people who first put Audie Murphy in front of a camera were interested in what he was, not in what he could pretend to be. He was, simply, a war hero on a scale as spectacularly wholesome as anything Hollywood could dream of.

His movies, then, are not so much roles, as alternative life styles. Quick, let's examine that life before you suspend disbelief. His first bit part was a simple extension of the life he had begun to dream of while in the Army: he had wanted to go to West Point after the war, but a battle injury kept him out— yet he wound up there as a cadet in *Beyond Glory* (1948), a film about the problems of a veteran (played by Alan Ladd) still recovering from the effects of combat.

Then Audie began reliving the possibilities of his old life before the war: in *Bad Boy* (1949), his first top billing, the orphan from Texas played another Texas orphan, a teenager afoul of the law (but basically a good kid, the kind a stint in the Army or Marines would soon straighten out). The story continues in his very next movie, *The Kid from Texas* (1950); but, instead of joining the Army and becoming the Audie Murphy we know, the bad boy from Texas gets kicked back in time and becomes Billy the Kid, the Billy of myth, not history—a misunderstood boy who kills a score of men to revenge the murder of a friend and benefactor.

Traveling back in time, see. First a contemporary boy, then a youth of the 1870s, then all the way back to the Civil War in 1951, a vintage year for Audie, the year in which he played a nameless Union soldier in *The Red Badge of Courage,* then acquired a name (Jesse James) and joined Quantrill's *Kansas Raiders* to take revenge on the Yankees. A pretty good trick for a boy who began the Civil War in the Union camp.

Once he came unstuck in reality, it was hard for him to get back to his starting point—so the peak of his acting career was when he attempted the impossible for a boy without talent: to be himself, to play Lieutenant Audie Murphy in an adaptation of the book by Audie Murphy about Audie Murphy (he was the first actor to star in his own life story on the screen; Arlo Guthrie was the second, and therein lies one difference between two generations).

"I didn't think I was the type myself," he told a *New York Times* interviewer. Maybe he wasn't: when he delivered in the reel world lines he had first spoken in the real, it was with the embarrassed self-consciousness of the little boy repeating for Mommy the cute thing he once said spontaneously and had now lost.

Loss. When Audie acted himself, he left something behind on the screen, as if fulfilling that fear anthropologists have found among some primitive peoples: the camera can steal the soul.

"War is like a giant pack rat," Audie said at the time of the autobiographical *To Hell and Back.* "It takes something from you, and it leaves something behind in its stead." Movies too. "We changed the part where Brandon died in my arms. That was the way it had really happened, but it looked too corny, they said. I guess it did."

Audie seems to have been programed for loss, like the hero of Hemingway's

"Soldier's Home," a cruel little story about a boy who comes home from the war to find that he can't talk honestly about his experiences: "All of the times that had been able to make him feel cool and clear inside himself when he thought of them; the times so long back when he had done the one thing, the only thing for a man to do, easily and naturally, when he might have done something else, now lost their cool, valuable quality and were lost themselves. . . . Krebs acquired the nausea in regard to experience that is the result of untruth or exaggeration. . . . In this way he lost everything."

Not that Audie lied or exaggerated, God forbid. But, like Hemingway, he lived for decades on the dividends of a small amount of experience, he transmuted a brief portion of his life into art, he cashed in his medals.

No, not that he lied, though one suspects that much of what he said to interviewers or published under his own by-line in the popular press had been combed and cared by press agents. Thus, with the piece he wrote for *Colliers* on the strange position of "a man who has fought an honest war, then come back and played himself doing it": "Twelve years stood between this powder-puff battle and the real war, between the lucky and the dead. And time, I'd learned, can be a good thing. It stretches quietly between the present and the

Audie Murphy in *The Red Badge of Courage* (1951).

past, like a membrane. But I was beginning to discover that the membrane can be broken, and suddenly you are back at the beginning, in the real war. The charges going off in the make-believe battle are blanks, but the shrapnel goes off in your mind.''

The automatic reaction of the sophisticate is that Audie Murphy couldn't have written this—but then, are Hollywood press agents any more given to existential paradox and irony than simple Texas farmboys caught up in the ''strange jerking back and forth between make-believe and reality, between fighting for your life and the discovery that it's only a game and you have to do a retake because a tourist's dog ran across the field in the middle of the battle''?

THE GREAT AUDIE MURPHY DREAM AND TIME MACHINE PART FOUR: PREVIEWS OF COMING ATTRACTIONS

In 1957, when Audie, taking advantage of contract clauses that gave him story approval, began asking for vehicles such as *Peer Gynt* and Dostoevsky's *The Idiot,* his producer sued him for a million dollars, claiming Audie was trying to break his contract by proposing unsuitable parts. But think! What if there was no trick? What if Audie *was* beginning to see himself as Prince Myshkin? It's not impossible, after all—get your mind straight, clean out your prejudices, and you too can see that Audie might have made a native American Myshkin, an innocent, trusting, childlike, and misunderstood figure too good for the world around him.

In fact, that's just the role he played in his very next film, *The Quiet American.* From the opening montage of happy, smiling Vietnamese faces (and how long has it been since you've seen a smiling Vietnamese?) to the closing dedication to the People of the Republic of Vietnam and Their Chosen President (i.e., the late lamented Ngo Dinh Diem), the film evokes a lost innocence and springs back upon us a holy idiocy in which Audie plays a Yankee Myshkin, an idealistic young entrepeneur who wants to bring democracy and plastics to Southeast Asia. Ah, but wicked men doubt his motives and have him betrayed and murdered.

As it is fit and proper for our heroes to set examples for the young, it is worth noting that Audie was one of the first Americans to die in Vietnam, if only on the screen. Note also that the whole damn war may well have started with the production company that shot *The Quiet American* on location in Vietnam—*vide* the *New York Times* account: ''When Rocky Cline and George Schlicker, experienced Hollywood special effects men, detonated explosives to recreate Saigon during the Indochinese war, the city's population became noticeably jumpy, Saigon's Mayor was even summoned to President Diem's office to explain what all the shooting was about. The country, after all, has been at complete peace for only a little more than a year, and nerves are still a trifle frayed.''

AND NOW, A WORD FROM OUR SPONSOR

Audie's involvement in the Cold War did not end with *The Quiet American*. In his very next film, *The Gunrunners* (also 1958), he was a fishing boat captain forced to smuggle arms to Cuban revolutionaries. He killed the smugglers and did his part to prevent the Communist overthrow of a dependable ally in the bastion of freedom. The producers of the film were trying to exploit popular interest in Castro and to refine Audie's image by having him repeat the role of Hemingway's Harry Morgan as played by Bogart in *To Have and Have Not* and John Garfield in *The Breaking Point*. And in *Trunk to Cairo* (1966), he was an American agent in conflict with a former Nazi scientist helping the Egyptians plot the ruin of Israel.

In retrospect, the casting of Audie Murphy in certain specific roles—as the democratic spokesman in Vietnam, as the defender of Israel, as the boy learning to bite the bullet in four or five different wars—becomes a political act. Go back over his career, and you'll find he was an unwitting salesman for grass roots militarism in the days when the movies were a perpetual public service announcement. In his very first minor role, he played a West Point cadet in a film about a villainous (and, of course, unjust) attack on the principles of the United States Military Academy. The film ended with General Eisenhower delivering a graduation speech about the traditions of the Academy—with fine boys like Audie preparing to be career officers, how could anyone doubt the essential rectitude of the Academy, the Army, and the Pentagon for which it stands?

THE GREAT AUDIE MURPHY DREAM AND TIME MACHINE PART FIVE:
APOTHEOSIS

Ask the man in the street about heroes, and, if he isn't demonstrating, he'll probably respond along these lines: the greatest American hero of World War I was Sergeant Alvin York, a quiet, humble boy from the South who killed and captured more enemy soldiers singlehanded than just about anyone else (Hollywood turned him into Gary Cooper, and all was well); the greatest American hero of World War II was another quiet, humble boy from the South who won more medals and killed more enemy than anyone else (and Hollywood turned him into Audie Murphy).

And then came Vietnam and a time when some said The Greatest was an unquiet, unhumble, and unwhite boy (though you better not call him *boy* to his face) from the South—and he wasn't even in the Army and hadn't even killed any one, though he did make a mess of Sonny Liston.

The times were confused, the landscape unclear, so when a genu-wine old-fashioned quiet humble boy from the South saw his opportunity and took it, suddenly the magic didn't work anymore.

But lo, the very season that Lieutenant Calley was convicted rather than rewarded for doing what he thought the movies and the history books had all told him to do, George C. Scott (though unquiet and unhumble and definitely no boy) got the Academy Award for *Patton.* Hollywood protects its own.

And Lieutenant Murphy (Retired) traveled about speaking in behalf of Lieutenant Calley ("I'm not so sure that in those days, having been indoctrinated to a fever pitch, I might not have committed the same error—and I prefer to call it an error—that Lieutenant Calley did"), but he lost his bearings and found, like the title of his last movie, *A Time for Dying.* Searchers found his body on Memorial Day, but the younger generation was protesting too loudly to take much heed.

General Westmoreland came to the funeral, and President Nixon sent his aide across the tumid Potomac to represent him at Arlington. The President released a statement:

> As America's most decorated hero of World War II,
> Audie Murphy not only won the admiration of millions
>   for his own brave exploits,
> He also came to epitomize the gallantry in action
>   of America's fighting men.
> The nation stands in his debt
> And mourns at his death.

Paul Newman: Anti-Hero
of the Alienated Generation

GENE D. PHILLIPS

A photograph in Laurence J. Quirk's *Films of Paul Newman* shows the young actor in the custody of two policemen. They are hustling him into a station house to book him on the charge of leaving the scene of an accident. He wears an arrogant half-smile on his face, and his hands are jammed insolently into his pockets. This picture is not a still photo from an early Newman film but a record of a real-life arrest in 1956, when Newman was just on the brink of stardom. The photograph serves, however, as an example of the screen personality that Newman was developing at the time, which he has maintained, with certain refinements, ever since.

Paul Newman came to young manhood in the optimistic postwar period, when high expectations for progress and advancement were aroused in the younger generation in what was assumed to be a new era of peace and prosperity. But these expectations were not realized for those numberless young Americans who went off to fight and to die in Korea and Vietnam for causes that seemed no clearer to the politicians who sent them than to the youths themselves. Furthermore, even those young people who enjoyed the fruits of their parents' affluence resented parental indulgence as a kind of uncaring neglect, and to some extent they were right. As Steven Roberts wrote of the younger generation of this period, "These youngsters were so coddled that they never developed a sense of responsibility; but they were so ignored that they never developed a sense of values."[1]

A cumulative disillusionment set in which was to be echoed in fiction, drama, and film. Indeed, youthful disappointment turned to frustration, cynicism, and anger, as young America came to view its elders as comprising an impersonal "Establishment" that ignored their needs and aspirations; these tensions exploded into the youthful rebellion of the sixties. Paul Newman came along as a major screen actor at just this time. No movie actor could project these tensions to the mass audience quite as convincingly as he.

Newman's anti-heroes were, of course, embraced especially by young audiences, because the characters symbolized the general alienation and rebellion that the fifties passed on to the sixties. Newman began his career in the tradition established by James Dean and Marlon Brando in the early fifties by playing confused, inarticulate rebels who strike out at the world without knowing why. He later turned to playing rebels who were older, more articulate, and therefore more in personal control of themselves and their destinies. They became loners because that was the only way they could survive. Summing up Newman's lasting appeal as a superstar, Michael Kerbel wrote in his book on the actor, "He ascended to prominence because he was able to embody best the rebellion and dissatisfactions of his era, while possessing a classic handsomeness that his contemporaries lacked. He was at once the perfect modern anti-hero and the link with a glamorous Hollywood that was rapidly fading into memory."[2]

In other words, the source of Newman's charisma as a superstar was, and continues to be, his ability to project to audiences of various age groups an ideal image of their own unfulfilled dreams and desires. To the young, he came to represent the outsider who could confront society with more resourcefulness than they could; to their elders, he came to be the handsome screen idol who could meet the disappointments and hardships of life with more equanimity than they. Both groups recognized his sex appeal and looked up to him as someone who might be felled in the battle of life, but who would nevertheless win our admiration for going down swinging. In short, moviegoers have always needed someone to root for, whether it was a swashbuckling Errol Flynn or a more vulnerable Brando or Dean. Paul Newman filled this prescription for a variety of filmgoers, enabling them to identify with those aspects of his screen personality which particularly appealed to them.

Newman's most characteristic roles at the beginning of his career projected the loneliness and alienation of a young man who was bitter because the older generation (usually personified in a father or father-figure) had let him down. As he grew older, Newman went on to play immature young adults who were still grappling with the unresolved emotional conflicts of adolescence. And even the roles which he has enacted in middle life often reflect the mentality of an overaged adolescent dropout who has yet to come to terms with the problems of youth. Though Newman's screen personality has mellowed with the years, it is still in essence the same as that of the young man who was snapped by a newspaper photographer on his way to jail in 1956: the defiant outsider rejected by a society that does not care to try to understand or accept him.

Newman's quintessential screen image becomes clear in analyzing how it surfaces in the key performances of his career—in such films as *The Hustler, Hud,* and *Harper,* as well as in his two Tennessee Williams movies, in *Cool Hand Luke,* and in his two films with Robert Redford.

His first important role was that of Rocky Graziano in *Somebody Up There Likes Me* (1956), Robert Wise's screen biography of the famous fighter. Newman delineated Rocky's personality as that of a mixed-up adolescent who learned in the ring to work off the frustrations of his unhappy and underprivileged home life. In so doing, Newman created the definitive screen character which he was to play with variations in his best pictures for years to come: the aggressive but sensitive and basically likable young man who could be totally disarmed by unexpected acceptance.

Young people found it easy to identify with Newman's screen image, because the inner tensions he exuded made him, like Dean and Brando before him, one of them. Alexander Walker noted in *Stardom* that actors like these three gave expression to the unformulated need of growing numbers of mixed-up young people to see their own growing pains reproduced in films, especially their inability to find meaningful affection in their starved family groups.[3]

Brick Pollitt in Tennessee Williams's *Cat on a Hot Tin Roof* (1958) clearly still suffers from the lack of affection which he experienced as a youngster, even though he is a married man when the story opens. Brick is typical of the very vulnerable Newman protagonist who has withdrawn into his own private world because of the psychic wounds he has sustained from life, a bitter and isolated figure with whom we can easily sympathize.

The reason for Brick's morose withdrawal into sulking and drinking is the fear that his close relationship with Skipper, a college pal and later teammate in pro football, had been basically homosexual. Because homosexuality was a taboo topic for films in the fifties, however, writer-director Richard Brooks had to find a substitute motivation with which to explain Brick's anxiety and despair. Brooks' solution was to emphasize Brick's fundamental immaturity, his refusal to grow up and face the responsibilities of adult life. Brick's alliance with Skipper, who was even more immature, represented their mutual effort to remain boyish athletic heroes well beyond their allotted time. This strain of immaturity was present in Brick's personality as Williams conceived it for the stage; but Brooks brought it much more into relief in the movie and, in so doing, brought Brick's character into much closer alinement with Newman's typical screen persona.

In a confrontation scene with Big Daddy (Burl Ives), Brick forces his father to admit that part of the reason he has remained frozen emotionally in adolescence for so long is that his cold and domineering father denied him the paternal affection he needed to grow to manhood. This sequence takes place in the basement of Big Daddy's mansion, where all of Brick's athletic trophies are gathering dust. As Brooks described it recently, "The basement sequence is one in which the father and son finally confront one another on a gut level. At its conclusion, they mount the stairway out of the cellar, out of the lower depths into which they have descended, out of the past with its cobwebbed trophies." They help each other up the steps, signifying the mutual support which they have now founded on their newly discovered trust and understanding.

That Newman received the first of his four Academy Award nominations for his performance as Brick demonstrated that no young actor around could better portray the problems of the alienated younger generation than Newman. Brooks was also to write and direct the screen adaptation of Williams' *Sweet Bird of Youth* (1962) with Newman once again in the lead. But this time Newman was re-creating for the screen a Williams role that he had already done on the stage. In 1959, Newman had returned to Broadway, where he had gotten his start in the early '50s, to stake out a Williams character that would be his alone. When he came to play Chance Wayne in the film of *Sweet Bird,* therefore, he had already "rehearsed" his performance 336 times on the stage.

Williams seems almost to have conceived Chance Wayne, the aging adolescent with romantic illusions of becoming a movie star, with Newman's screen persona in mind. Chance leaves his small home town to become a star in

Paul Newman and Burl Ives in *Cat on a Hot Tin Roof* (1958).

pictures but returns as the paid escort of a faded movie queen, Alexandra del Lago (Geraldine Page). Nevertheless, he hopes to reclaim his boyhood sweetheart, Heavenly Finley, daughter of the town demagogue, Boss Finley. Once again, Newman shows us a pathetic young man who is all swagger and charm on the outside, all insecurity and weakness within. He is the young man on-the-make who is not going to make it, but who will not admit it—even to himself.

Once again, Brooks had to alter Williams' plot to suit censorship specifications. In the somewhat "sanitized" movie version of the play, Chance has gotten Heavenly pregnant, and her father forces her to have an abortion. At the film's end, Boss Finley has Chance's face scarred, but Chance and Heavenly are reunited. Nonetheless, the sobering elements of Williams' play are still present in the film's softened finale. Chance had cynically depended on his youth and beauty as his meal ticket and his entrée into Hollywood. As the film concludes, however, Boss Finley's henchmen deprive him of his beauty. That Chance was already losing his youth is made painfully apparent by flashbacks showing him in the full vigor of young manhood. One of these flashbacks represents the finest visual symbol in the film: we see a slow-motion shot of Chance in a swan dive; his beautiful body floats across the screen for a few seconds and then slowly glides downward into the water. Here is the perfect image of the elusive, ephemeral, sweet bird of youth as embodied in Chance, soaring for a moment into the incandescent blue sky and then disappearing, never to be recaptured.

With Chance deprived finally of both youth and beauty, his immature and unrealistic aspirations for easy success are likewise shattered once and for all; he is ready to salvage his relationship with Heavenly, after Alexandra has abandoned him and gone back to Hollywood. Chance's change of attitude is suggested by the shift from the lush colors in which most of the film is photographed, which depict the phoney dream world of instant success and glamorous romance in which Chance has sought to take refuge, to the darker, more somber hues of the last scenes, which betoken Chance's more sober approach to the harsh realities that he must ultimately face.

Paul Newman and Jackie Gleason in *The Hustler* (1961).

Williams' theme of the inevitable loss of youth and the futility of trying to prolong it comes through just as much in Newman's portrayal of Chance in this film as it did in his acting of Brick in *Cat*. [4] In both films, Newman's anti-hero has time to rebuild his life on his new, dearly bought self-knowledge. This self-knowledge comes too late, however, for Fast Eddie Felsen in *The Hustler* (1961).

Fast Eddie is another young man on-the-make who is willing to sacrifice anything or anyone to become a first-class professional pool player and ultimately to beat the acknowledged champion, Minnesota Fats (Jackie Gleason). He accomplishes these goals; but the suicide of Sarah (Piper Laurie), his fragile, sensitive lover, makes him realize that he has sacrificed too much for too little.

Newman garnered his second Oscar nomination for his interpretation of Fast Eddie, who radiates tenderness for Sarah until he becomes convinced that the crippled girl will stand in the way of fulfilling his obsessive ambitions. At the film's moving finale, Newman wrings every ounce of pathos out of Eddie's rejection of the money which he has won for finally beating Minnesota Fats. He refuses the fruits of his victory because, as he explains, ''I loved her, and I traded her in on a pool game.'' The money he refuses, in essence, is his down payment on the price of expiating Sarah's death.

No such regrets or moral scruples are discernible in Hud Bannon, the role for which Newman deserves to be best remembered. Newman received his third Oscar nomination for *Hud* (1963), in which he played the title role of a cattle rancher who is gradually deserted by the people around him when each of them in turn sees through his superficial charm and clever façade. Hud manages to ruin the only meaningful relationships in his life: that with his father, Homer (Melvyn Douglas), his housekeeper, Alma (Patricia Neal), and his nephew, Lon (Brandon de Wilde).

Hud is despised by his father for the crass opportunism with which he wants to run the ranch; and he loses Alma after trying to rape her, just when she was growing to love him on her own initiative. Searching his face one last time for some sign of genuine feeling and finding none, she wearily boards a waiting Greyhound bus for nowhere in particular. At the end of the movie, Hud cannot even bring himself to tell his disillusioned nephew Lon how much he would value his friendship now that everyone else has turned away from him. With his customary bravado, Hud shouts after Lon, from one side of the vast wide screen to the other, that this world is so corrupt, a man is going to be tainted by it sooner or later whether he wants to or not. Then Hud swaggers into the kitchen of his now-empty ranch house, opens a can of beer, and slams down the shade of the screen door against the late afternoon sun: he is a deservedly deserted loner.

Although Hud is a grown man, the generation gap again appears to explain, at least in part, how the anti-hero came to be the cruel, cold man that he is. Hud truly loves his father and makes intermittent efforts to win his regard, only to be rejected anew. At one point, Homer suggests that his son is simply unloveable, and Hud retorts, while still smarting from the biting remark, "My mama loved me—but she died." One infers that the genuine affection which Hud cherishes for Lon (as well as for Alma) might have served to rejuvenate the better side of his nature. But this does not happen, and Hud remains the isolated outcast to the end.

Brandon De Wilde and Paul Newman in *Hud* (1962).

Cinematographer James Wong Howe, who won an Oscar for photographing *Hud,* sought to underscore visually the gap between Hud and his nephew Lon by photographing their night scenes together with light falling more directly on the boy's face so that he would look clean and young; but Howe lighted Hud's face more indirectly so that he seemed a darker, more shadowy figure and thus appeared lonely and older. In daytime scenes, Howe emphasized Hud's grim loneliness by making him stand out against the arid landscape of West Texas. "I wanted to create the isolated atmosphere of a small town on the plains," the late Mr. Howe once recalled, "and so I took along wind machines on location in Texas and had handfuls of dust thrown in front of the camera. Later, the mournful sound of the wind was mixed in on the sound track, and that increased the sense of desolation in which Hud lived." Howe also used filters to wash out any clouds that happened to be in the sky so they were not visible in the scene as photographed. The stark, bright stillness of the cloudless, burntout landscape made Hud's lonely figure stand out all the more in relief, and provided the perfect context for what I consider Newman's finest and most nuanced performance.

Newman was surprised to find that some young people admired Hud as a man who could get along on his own, an attitude indicated in John Schlesinger's film *Midnight Cowboy* (1969), in which Joe Buck (Jon Voight) leaves family and friends in Texas to seek his fortune in New York City. His guiding inspiration is Hud, as evidenced by an enormous poster of Newman in the film, which Joe proudly hangs on his dingy hotel room wall. The point the admirers of Hud missed, said Newman, is that Hud really did need others but was just too stubborn to admit it.

A Newman character more worthy of admiration is Lew Harper, whom Newman played in *Harper* (British title: *The Moving Target,* 1966). Harper is a private investigator who sleeps in his underwear and socks on a cot in his grubby office and starts the day by making his breakfast coffee from yesterday's grounds. He clearly has no illusions left about the fabled glamor of a private eye's life. A rich socialite (Lauren Bacall) hires Harper to search for her missing husband. As his investigation continues, he becomes increasingly aware that the man is not worth finding and the woman who hired him is not worth helping. But he continues his sordid investigation because of his determination to be a success. "The bottom is full of nice people," he cynically quips at one point. "Only cream and bastards rise." He implies that, since he does not have what it takes to be the former, he will just have to settle for the latter as the only way for him to get ahead in a tough world. But he really has too much decency for that; and so he will always be a good-natured loser, regardless of his remarks to the contrary.

When his old and trusted friend, lawyer Albert Graves (Arthur Hill), asks Harper if he is disappointed that being a private detective so often involves him in tawdry activities like "popping flashbulbs in dirty hotel rooms," Harper replies that about every four months or so he gets a case that makes him feel that he is helping someone who needs him; and that makes it all seem worthwhile.

In the end, Harper must arrest Graves, one of the few people involved in the case who seemed to have some integrity, as the culprit. Harper intentionally turns his back on Graves to allow his old friend to shoot at him and escape. After Graves fails to fire, the final shot of the film freezes on the disconsolate look on Harper's face just after he murmurs, "Oh hell," indicating that he will do his duty, as he always has, and turn Graves in. Harper, as one critic put it, will continue, almost in spite of himself, to sympathize with the lonely and the flawed. Neither cream nor bastard, he will never rise.

Newman's depiction of Harper is the most underrated performance of his entire career. Judith Crist was one of the few reviewers who appreciated it when the film appeared, noting how Harper as Newman plays him is truly a human rather than a superhuman detective: "Harper hurts when he is hit; he needs time to catch his breath. Harper tries not to kill; he is sickened when he is forced to. He has compassion, and he has righteous wrath. . . . He knows that the job began as a matter of 'a bitch sending him to find scum,' but, even though he'd rather have been sent after Cinderella by Prince Charming, he hasn't lost his awareness of what is right and what is wrong. He happens to love his estranged wife (Janet Leigh), and he knows that nothing, not even right and wrong, is quite that simple."[5]

Janet Leigh and Paul Newman in *Harper* (1966).

Harper engages the audience's emotions in the way that Newman's gallery of loners often do. The same can be said for the title role of *Cool Hand Luke* (1967), one of the most appealing characters Newman has ever played. Luke belongs to the same band of outsiders as Fast Eddie, Hud, and Harper, and proved to be the perfect rebel hero for the young people of the sixties.

Having left the army as he entered it, a private, and having failed in marriage, Luke finds himself interned in a Southern penal camp for drunkenly lopping off the tops of parking meters—pointlessly irresponsible behavior. Yet, once in the camp, he assumes some responsibility: he tries to put a little excitement and even some meaning into the lives of his degraded fellow prisoners, often despite the personal cost to himself. He is soundly but heroically beaten in a boxing match by the biggest of the inmates; he bets that he can down fifty hard-boiled eggs in an hour and painfully succeeds; finally, he gives the prisoners a vicarious taste of freedom by escaping three times. Before he is inevitably shot down, in a church, he shouts to his pursuers, "What we have here is a failure to communicate," ironically repeating an earlier comment by the sadistic prison warden.

On the thematic level, that is precisely what we have. Although the viewer easily and obviously identifies with Luke, one is not entirely certain in just what light we are intended to see him. Luke may simply be a likable nonconformist whose unwillingness to live by society's rules would bring him into conflict with any circumstance in which he found himself.

On another level, *Luke* seems to be stretching for Gospel status, due to the Christian symbolism throughout the film. Luke more than once assumes a cruciformed posture; and, in general, he seems to be sacrificing himself for his fellow prisoners. In death, the lingering image of the smile on Luke's face implies he is fully aware his memory will live on among the men he has left behind, as an encouragement and possibly an inspiration. So he does seem a Christ figure of sorts.

Even though Luke's temples are now tinged with grey, he is still touched by the generation gap as so many Newman anti-heroes are. In this case, it is reflected in the visit to the camp of his wretched invalid mother (Jo Van Fleet), who comes propped up in the back of a truck to see Luke. In a single scene, she sketches for us the miserable background against which Luke must have grown up. "Sometimes I wish folks was like dogs," she tells Luke, "because dogs let go of their pups without love or pain." And the supreme insight Luke offers us, despite some of the cloudy symbolism in the movie, is that people are not dogs, even when they are treated like them. Perhaps this last reflection is the ultimate message of the Gospel according to Luke.

For *Cool Hand Luke,* Newman won his fourth Oscar nomination and once again was denied the ultimate honor. But, like one of his own screen incarnations, he shrugged off his disappointment. "It's nice to be nominated, but I don't think my life will be incomplete if I never win an Oscar."

In seeming recompense for his being deprived of the recognition of the Hollywood community which he so richly deserves, Newman went on to make two enormously successful films in which he co-starred with Robert Redford under George Roy Hill's direction. The first was *Butch Cassidy and the Sundance Kid* (1969). Newman's Butch is like Luke, a greying adolescent. He and Sundance rob banks and trains with the carefree cameraderie of a couple of kids playing cops and robbers. Inevitably, the game turns serious, and they are finally gunned down by a host of soldiers.

Earlier, their girl friend, Etta Place (Katherine Ross) had told them that she would go anywhere with them and do anything for them—except watch them die. "If you don't mind, I think I'll miss that scene," she says. Hill spares the audience that scene, too, for as Butch and Sundance are about to face a hail of bullets, the frame freezes and the film ends, so that we, like Etta, can remember these two overgrown boys as they were in life.

In *Butch Cassidy,* the Newman character is a rebel outsider who has mellowed, if not matured, with age. Newman used the same approach to the role of Henry Gondorff, a down-at-the-heels gambler in *The Sting* (1973), his other co-starrer with Redford. The pair this time are boyish pranksters intent on perpetrating an elaborate con job on Doyle Lonnegan (Robert Shaw), a rich gangster against whom both nurture a grudge. Newman is once more an anti-establishment anti-hero; but this time out, the Establishment is principally organized crime, as represented by Lonnegan.

With the glee of a couple of mischievous youngsters, Gondorff and his sidekick Hooker (Redford) pull off the big con as they put the sting not only on Lonnegan, but on the audience as well, with a spectacular surprise ending. There is no difficulty in siding and sympathizing with Gondorff and Hooker, since opportunists like Lonnegan deserve what they get.

The Sting won seven Academy Awards, including Best Picture of the Year, and, along with *Butch Cassidy,* is one of the most popular Newman films to date. One is prompted to ask if Newman's popularity will abide now that he has passed fifty and the roles of even overaged adolescents are pretty much behind him. Newman's own response to this question is, "I just want to get through life with some kind of grace and style, both as an actor and a human being."

One can only speculate, but it would seem, even as he graduates into more mature roles such as the architect hero of *The Towering Inferno* (1975) and character parts such as the title role in Robert Altman's *Buffalo Bill and the Indians* (1976), he will remain a handsome superstar who also happens to be a fine and accomplished actor. In *Inferno,* he played the resourceful architect who joins forces with the fire chief in a race against time to save a group of guests trapped in a new office-residential tower by a fire on a lower floor. Newman not only succeeded in saving most of the guests, but managed to more than hold his own on the same screen with an impressive array of Hollywood denizens, including Steve McQueen, William Holden, Faye Dunaway, Fred Astaire, Richard Chamberlain, and Jennifer Jones: he was frequently singled out by reviewers as one of this blockbuster movie's chief assets.

Newman's triumphs of the past return on TV to revive our cherished memories of his best work. For that reason, concludes Kerbel, the very mention of his name still evokes an aura of moody rebelliousness, cool detachment, and sex appeal. Fast Eddie Felsen, Brick Pollitt, Chance Wayne, Hud, Harper, and Cool Hand Luke, to mention only his best roles, have earned Paul Newman a lasting place in the most prestigious Hollywood Hall of Fame: the fond memories of the filmgoers who continue to admire the work of his long and significant career.

NOTES

1. Steven V. Roberts, "What Really Happened to the Class of '65?" *New York Times Book Review,* October 3, 1976, p. 8.
2. Michael Kerbel, *Paul Newman* (New York: Pyramid Books, 1974), p. 18.
3. Alexander Walker, *Stardom* (New York: Stein and Day, 1970), pp. 338–39.
4. For a more detailed treatment of *Cat on a Hot Tin Roof* and *Sweet Bird of Youth,* see Gene D. Phillips, *Tennessee Williams and the Movies* (New York: Barnes, 1977).
5. Judith Crist, "Return to the Pre-Bond Man," *New York Herald Tribune,* April 3, 1966.

THREE/MOVIE GENRES

C̲ERTAINLY THE MOST PROLIFIC AND perhaps the most significant form of cultural film criticism, genre studies have greatly enriched our understanding of popular movies. Popular films can generally be grouped according to certain emphases: theme, approach to subject matter, characterization, etc. Certain "types" or genres of popular movies—such as Westerns or musicals—become successful because they consistently fulfill certain identifiable needs and interests of the movie audiences which support them. In short, they creatively and effectively represent the collective dreams and nightmares of their audiences.

The articles in this chapter are attempts to understand the cultural significance of five successful movie genres. Michael Marsden deals with the essentially religious appeal of the Western. Timothy Scheurer builds a basis for the evaluation of movie musicals on an understanding of the key elements popular audiences consciously and unconsciously use in distinguishing movie musicals. Walter Evans provides us with an explanation for the tremendous appeal monster movies hold for a specialized audience—adolescents. Stuart Kaminsky turns his attention to the significance of the Kung Fu films, which he sees as providing a unique type of moviegoing ritual for urban youth. Finally, Joe Slade gives us a useful guide to contemporary trends in the porn film genre, an area of film which, largely because of its notorious content, has received scant serious critical attention.

Genre criticism helps us gain a firmer grasp of the cultural significance of film forms which, because of their consistent and frequent repetition, seem to fulfill our continuing cultural needs and desires. We can better understand ourselves and our society by better understanding the significance of the movies we consistently enjoy over an extended period of time.

Western Films: America's Secularized Religion

MICHAEL T. MARSDEN

Just as Americans struggled to uncover a truly American culture in the late nineteenth century, so they celebrated an Americanized religion in the Western film in the twentieth century. The most popular filmic form of the new entertainment industry in the early part of the twentieth century was the Western film, and no more common plot evolved in this genre than the triumph of the essentially priest-like hero representing the forces of goodness and civilization over the forces of the wilderness, or evil, often represented by the wilderness itself, the American Indian, or man corrupted in the wilderness.

While the Western film has been the object of considerable critical attention in recent years,[1] the latent religious implications of the genre have received scant attention.[2] While some films make these religious parallels obvious, as in the case of *Shane* (1953), *El Topo* (1971), and *High Plains Drifter* (1973), most other Westerns carry the religious parallels just below the surface, visible to the trained observer on the conscious level, but powerfully effective for the common filmgoer on the unconscious level.

Clint Eastwood in *High Plains Drifter* (1973).

The Western formula in both fictional and filmic forms is at its very basis religious in its implications. Westerns are essentially romances, depicting the West not as it was but, to paraphrase John Ford, as it should have been. Westerns depict a moment in our national American past when the American choice was made and when we as a people decided who we were and where we were headed. That moment, of course, never actually existed. But we believe it did; and, as John Cawelti has so aptly pointed out in his *Six-Gun Mystique,* every Western is a type of Fourth of July celebration where we relive our American choice.[3] The icons of the gun, the horse, and the landscape, associated with the Western ritual, provide it with depth and meaning and take on religious significance themselves because of their close association with the religious ritual. The gun, the horse, and the landscape become the sacred tools of the hero-priest-messiah who stands between the forces of wilderness and civilization and provides the necessary advantage so Progress and the American Way can survive and thrive.

It is a commonly held American belief that American culture is distinct from European culture, and in some ways superior to it, because of its organic relationship to the American Experience itself. This point of view found its most effective spokesperson in Frederick Jackson Turner at the end of the nineteenth century as the frontier was officially declared closed. His "frontier thesis" has become part of standard American mythology. It is the Western formula itself, however, that makes the Turner thesis most visible and vital every time it is dramatized on movie screens in this country and abroad.[4]

Because of the essentially evolutionary nature of American culture in the popular imagination, it would seem reasonable to posit that a popular entertainment form such as the Western film would reflect that same belief. Thus, given the essentially religious nature of the Western drama, it would follow that the Western formula would alter the Christian mythology to reflect its contact with the Western landscape. More specifically, the European savior-messiah would have to be transformed into a hero-priest appropriate to the Western landscape, a man who could serve the various cultural needs of a large mass audience.

For the transplanted European frontiersman, the wilderness existed as a force to be reckoned with, to be tamed, to be dominated. When confronted with the essentially different ecological perspective of the American Indian, the frontiersman was unable to deal with it. For example, the Indian asked permission of a tree's spirit before chopping it down; the Army Corps of Engineers simply felled it in the name of progress. The wilderness was seen not as beautiful but as fearful, since it defined all that was not civilization.

The Western hero had to evolve from the captivity narrative through the dime-novel tradition and into the Western film and novel of the twentieth century, where he took a more permanent form that fused the instincts of the frontiersman with those of the American Indian, or man of nature. The Western hero represents a synthesis of the best qualities of both worlds, advocating Progress on the one hand, while, at the same time, keenly aware of the influence of the natural environment on the other. The wilderness and the natural environment in general were not mere abstractions for him; they profoundly influenced man's relationship to fellow man and to nature.

The Western hero also had to evolve religiously. Beginning as a messiah out of the New Testament, he had to adopt the trappings of the Old Testament Yahweh.[4] It was Gary Cooper who, in a documentary film entitled *The Real West* (1961), put the issue most succinctly. He said that in the Western hero's Colt .45, the five bullets in the cylinder were law and order, and the one in the chamber was justice. As the Western formula evolved in the popular imagination, it clearly indicated the savior figure of the New Testament was inappropriate for this new, savage land, for, west of the Mississippi, the landscape was ambiguous. It could harbor gods as well as demons. This view of the landscape was essentially different from the one held by the frontiersmen who pushed the outward circle of civilization westward. It was a hybrid view of nature born of frontier mythology and tempered with the wisdom of the mountain man and the American Indian. The West needed a messiah who could survive the Great American Desert, help found a civilization, and dispense justice to those who would attempt to stand in the way of Progress. This messiah also had to have an affinity with nature, because it is from nature that the Western hero draws his moral and spiritual strength: after he has established order, he cannot remain with the townspeople but must, like Shane, return to the wilderness from whence he came. The American West needed a hero-priest who could ride in from nowhere when needed, dispense justice with a finality that would make the angels envious and a skill that John Cawelti likens to that of a surgeon,[5] and ride out as mysteriously as he rode in. His perspective was not that of the easterner pushing westward; to the contrary, it was the perspective of the mountain man who, having tasted of the Western landscape, refused to return to civilization.

The transformation of the American Western hero of popular nineteenth-century romances into the twentieth-century hero of Westerns required a two-pronged development; one prong involved his attitudes towards his environment, and the other concerned his modified Christianity which combined the New Testament Messiah with the qualities of the wrathful God of the Old Testament. As the loving and forgiving and merciful Christ of the New Testament, the Western hero could not survive West of the Mississippi. The essential lawlessness of the West required a hero with a strong sense of divine justice at times untempered with mercy. The coming of the Western hero is a kind of second coming of Christ, but this time, he wears a gun instead of carrying a cross, and he wears the garb of a gunfighter, not of a carpenter.

The Western film, which has been one of our most consistently popular art forms, has, from its very beginnings at the turn of the century, synthesized a number of important cultural myths into a popular Western mythology. The Western hero retains his viability in the culture generation after generation because he serves in the central role of a secularized religious drama for a people whose needs and desires may change but whose needs for ritual continue to be fulfilled by the Western, among other popular entertainment forms.

The importance of secularized religious ritual in American popular arts is evident in the popular theatrical traditions of the late nineteenth century and early twentieth century, especially vaudeville. Albert McLean, in his significant study of the religious implications of vaudeville, *American Vaudeville as Ritual,* focuses on the redemptive vision of urban life that was projected by this most popular entertainment form.[6] According to McLean, vaudeville served three key religious functions: to inculcate the audience with a sense of their common humanity; to provide the audience with a feeling for community that transcends boundaries caused by ethnicity, occupation, etc.; and to point a way towards a type of neoprimitive ecumenicalism.[7] McLean sees vaudeville as a central cultural ritual in the lives of its patrons. It would seem logical to argue for the extension of that cultural centrality to the movies, which replaced vaudeville as the common ritual for American society in the early years of the twentieth century.

Movies, more than any other medium up to that time, provided their huge audiences with common experiences as they worshipped the gods and goddesses on their local silver screens. And Westerns were the most staple offering of movie theaters across the country from the earliest days of the industry until the end of the Second World War. It has been conservatively estimated that Westerns comprised between 25 and 30 percent of all American-made features before 1950.[8] A sampling of a few key and essentially representative Westerns may help to establish the central religiosity of this filmic form.

In 1916, William S. Hart directed and starred in an allegorical Western, *Hell's Hinges.* Rarely has the screen witnessed such wrongness righted, or such innocence preserved, as in this film. Hart, as Blaze Tracy, represents, as one title in the film tells us, a two-gun "embodiment of the best and the worst in the early West." A young preacher is sent to this den of iniquity to begin his ministry. He soon learns, however, that God does not have a home in Hell's Hinges, a truth that is most painful for the young preacher and his innocent sister-companion, Faith. When Blaze gazes into the eyes of Faith, he realizes that he has met goodness; from that moment on, his mockery of religion and his general unruliness decline, until he begins to act in defense of formal religion. His conversion begins with this statement on a title: "I reckon God ain't wantin' me much ma'am, but when I look at you, I feel I've been ridin' the wrong trail."

The townspeople proceed to have a local barmaid seduce the young minister, disgrace him, and drive him mad. He is forced to put the torch to his own church in a final act of humiliation. It is Blaze Tracy who then serves up vengeance and justice in proper measure. His actions are not born of the New Testament (for, as the preacher and Faith's experience evidence, that fails to work in the uncivilized Hell's Hinges) but of the Old Testament, and they are as effective as they are final. Blaze proceeds to prove the appropriateness of his name as he shoots down the evil saloon owner and puts the match to the entire town in just revenge for the monumental blasphemy.

In the 1931 film *Cimarron,* Yancey Cravat (Richard Dix) is an incurable wanderer who finds himself in Oklahoma as a result of the land rush into the Indian territory opened for settlement. He becomes in turn poet, gunfighter, lawyer, and editor in this raw, new land, and, in order to bring some type of religion into this environment, he himself preaches a sermon. As he pulls a Bible out from his back pocket and draws it around front, it crosses the butt of his holstered but obviously readied gun as a warning to all who would attempt to interrupt his sermon. The saloon becomes his church; and, instead of the traditional crucifix in the background, there is the appropriate saloon nude. Christ visits this frontier town in an unexpected garb, but comes with a vengeance for having been kept out too long.

George Stevens' masterful *Shane* depicts a clearly savior-like hero who rides down from the Grand Tetons to the West at the beginning of the film and into the valley where an epic struggle between the farmers and the ranchers is in progress. Shane is the new Christ, the true frontier messiah, coming to aid the forces of civilization (farmers, fences, families) against the forces of the pioneering ranchers who hold out for the open range, unorganized society, and the rule of the gun. Shane, who at the film's end entrusts his sacred mission to young Joey Starrett, brings with him all the trappings of a wrathful Old Testament God, tempered by the knowledge of the strengths of the New Testament. Despite the fact that Shane, in New Testament fashion, adopts the farmer's garb and gentle manners, his past will not be denied and the challenges he was born to face prevail upon him once again.

That George Stevens intended for us to perceive Shane as a Christ-like figure is fairly obvious (Shane is even wounded in the left side), but what is not as obvious is that the film's essential religious drama goes well beyond the simplistic battle between the forces of good and evil. The ranchers, led by Reichert, do not represent evil as such, for that is personified in the gunfighter Jack Wilson; rather, they represent the stubborn past which refuses to give way before the demanding present of churches, schools, and families. This Western religion demands we worship at the altar of Progress.

A more recent film, *El Topo,* directed by and starring Alejandro Jodorow-

Alan Ladd and Brandon De Wilde in *Shane* (1953).

sky, pivots around the Old Testament/New Testament tension. The first part of this complex film details the desert exploits of El Topo as he seeks adventures and encounters all varieties of mankind. After he has been left for dead by a female companion, he is rescued by a tribe of cave-dwelling mutants who are kept in underground confinement by the tyrannical townspeople. While he recovers from his physical and spiritual wounds, he finds himself becoming the leader of these people, a kind of messiah who leads them from the caves of darkness into the land of light. But when these freed mutants encounter the townspeople, they are promptly and summarily slaughtered. Having witnessed the slaughter, El Topo grabs a rifle, and declaring in turn that he is Justice and God, he becomes the personification of revenge, consecrates the bullets with his words, and guns down the evil populace, seemingly invulnerable to bullets himself. The film ends in a holocaust, as El Topo sets fire not to the town, in the tradition of *Hell's Hinges,* but to himself, in the tradition of the radical Buddhist monks of the late 1960s. Justice through violence is the unmistakable message of this remarkable film.

The Western film genre has remained a viable secularized religious ritual for

Americans through generations of changing mythology and consciousness.[9] It tells a morality tale for a people who have confronted the American wilderness and survived and wish to celebrate their dominance over nature and all manner of evil. Every Western is a ritualistic driving out of the devils who lurk in the savage wilderness, ready at the slightest sign of human weakness to reestablish the law of the wilderness where once proud Progress stood.

During the last seventy-five years of American film history, the Western film formula has changed and continues to change in the never-ending challenge to meet the needs and interests of the people who view Westerns.[10] Recently, film-makers have been doing a considerable amount of experimentation with

Katharine Hepburn and John Wayne in *Rooster Cogburn and the Lady* (1975).

the Western formula—casting John Wayne as a peppery gent who spends his time righting wrongs with one hand and wooing a quaintly cute and disarming Katharine Hepburn with the other in *Rooster Cogburn* (1975), giving Marlon Brando and Jack Nicholson the opportunity to try to upstage each other in the untraditional *Missouri Breaks* (1976), and encouraging Robert Altman to film his version of an American institution in *Buffalo Bill and the Indians* (1976).

Yet, despite the experimentation with the Western formula, one of the few Westerns in recent years to make a respectable showing at the box office is Clint Eastwood's *The Outlaw Josey Wales* (1976), a most conventional Western. If popular movies take any of their direction from television, they would certainly note the success of James Arness' return in a traditional made-for-television movie, *The Winning of the West* (1977). Conventional Western movies continue to account for a considerable amount of television programing across the country in any given scheduling period.

While the evidence is limited and the pattern far from closely defined, it is tempting to suggest that the future direction of the insecure Western film genre is in an innovative return to the basics of the formula itself. The lesson may well reside in the saga of professional football, another secularized American religion.[11] Football has changed many of the accidentals of its Sunday liturgy, but not the essentials; the rules are varied slightly every now and then, and the media coverage becomes more sophisticated, but the basic formulaic structure of the game, its essential liturgy, remains the same.

Should such a march backward into the verities of our cultural past and present become the route for Western films to follow, it is certain that the formula's central core, its secularized religious ritual so clearly present in Western classics such as *Hell's Hinges* and *Shane* and visible to the trained observer in most traditional Westerns, will remain the magnet which attracts audiences to an experience they are familiar with, a ceremony they know and appreciate, but a ceremony whose ministers have had such interesting liturgical variations for the particular occasion.

NOTES

1. The list is certainly a long one. For a most useful bibliography, see *Focus on the Western,* edited by Jack Nachbar (Englewood Cliffs, N.J.: Prentice-Hall, 1974), pp. 138–146.
2. Peter Homans' article, "Puritanism Revisited: An Analysis of the Contemporary Screen Image Western," in *Studies in Public Communication,* No. 3 (Summer, 1961), pp. 73–84, is an excellent analysis of the Western as a puritan morality tale.
3. Bowling Green, Ohio: Popular Press, 1971, p. 57.
4. Nachbar discusses this point in some depth in his Introduction to his *Focus on the Western.*

5. I have developed this concept much more fully in an article entitled "Savior in the Saddle: The Sagebrush Testament," *Illinois Quarterly,* Vol. 36, No. 2 (December, 1973), pp. 5– 15. The article was reprinted in *Focus on the Western,* pp. 93– 100.
6. Cawelti, p. 59.
7. Albert F. McLean, Jr. (Lexington, Ky.: University of Kentucky Press, 1965), p. 41.
8. McLean, p. 217.
9. Nachbar, "Introduction," p. 2.
10. Jack Nachbar's, "Seventy Years on the Trail: A Selected Chronology of the Western Movie," in his *Focus on the Western,* pp. 129– 37, originally published in the *Journal of Popular Film,* Vol. 2, No. 1 (Winter, 1973), pp. 75– 83, provides at a glance a perspective of the amazing viability of the genre during the last almost three-quarters of a century.
11. Michael R. Real develops this idea successfully in his article "Super Bowl: Mythic Spectacle," *Journal of Communication,* Vol. 25, No. 1 (Winter, 1975), pp. 31– 43.

The Aesthetics of Form and Convention in the Movie Musical

TIMOTHY E. SCHEURER

What do you go for—Go see a show for?
Tell the truth, you go to see those beautiful *Dames*
— Al Dubin and Harry Warren

In the scene from Ray Enright and Busby Berkeley's *Dames* (1934) from which the above lyric is taken, the energetic young producer (Dick Powell) and his "backers" involved in "putting-on-the-show" are discussing what makes a show popular with an audience; oddly enough, after forty years, the question is still being discussed among *aficionados* of the Film Musical and popular film in general. In spite of the facts that critical response to the Film Musical has been traditionally less than edifying and that film scholars have only touched on it tangentially, large crowds have flocked to see musicals since movies first learned to talk. Unfortunately, most of the criticism of the Film Musical has run along one track, an essentially historical one, and its primary thesis has been similar to one offered by Roy Paul Madsen, who echoes an ostensible consensus opinion by opting for the "escapist" argument:

> Although escapism can be used to justify anything, the thin stories and minuscule messages of the average musical make it clear that the only reason it thrives during days of ordeal is that it offers the national audience collective pleasure, relaxation and escapism. Film and television musicals really find their social value, if they need one, in giving the viewer something to sing about and in providing a respite from continual confrontation with The Problems.[1]

It's a familiar argument—one at least as old as Dubin and Warren's lyrics for *Dames:* the Film Musical offers entertainment for entertainment's sake and in this way it serves some cryptic utilitarian purpose.

The "escapist" theory is ultimately too confining, even though it seems to have the popular culture in mind. Neither should it be assumed that Madsen's argument is invalid—one need only look at the great proliferation of musicals during the Depression, World War II, and the Korean conflict to understand that—but it really only treats one side of the popular response to the Film Musical. For in examining the socio-historico-cultural tableau shrouding a popular art form, we tend to dismiss the question of what sort of inherent aesthetic appeal a film genre as genre may have. Perhaps, then, it would be useful to suspend the prevailing critical tide and examine the forms and conventions of the Film Musical and how they function, discussing briefly its aims on a broad structural plane, and then (reversing yet another prevalent critical trend)[2] moving into a discussion of the major components intrinsic to the genre and its form: music, dance, and libretto, and how they function and distinguish the Film Musical as a whole.

The whole idea of the Film Musical is predicated on the concept that music and, in the majority of cases, dance are used in part to tell a story. There are a few instances where a story is rendered entirely through the medium of music, as in Jacques Demy's *The Umbrellas of Cherbourg* (1964), but for the most part the musical is distinguished by its finely balanced interplay and synthesis of non-musical and musical sequences. In the context of the musical as a whole, music is the most important governing principle in the style, structural unity and movement of the film. The use of music in drama as such first of all forces us to reexamine, on a large contextual basis, the mode of reality presented by the Film Musical.

Louis D. Giannetti has noted that "realistic film theorists either ignore the musical, or make an exception of it;"[3] the reason for this is that the musical is a highly stylized representation of life where the reality is not revealed through the actions we normally associate with everyday living, but where a different mode of reality, the inner reality of feelings, emotions, and instincts are given metaphoric and symbolic expression through the means of music and dance. The musical is not so much a reflection of life as it is an *interpretation* of life; it dispenses with normal dialogue or soliloquy in favor of the more metaphoric medium of music where elements like harmony, melody, and rhythm coupled with a lyric phrase become manifestations of the inner feelings and motivational impulses of the characters, and which, consequently, control the action and impel it forward.

To understand the Film Musical demands that we understand the roles stylization and expression play in the song and the dance sequences which in large part determine the structural movement of the film as a whole; as Rouben Mamoulian notes, "Stylization, integrally and properly carried out, conveys a deeper reality to the audience than everyday kitchen naturalism can."[4] Thus it is essential that the audience not only understand—or better, perhaps, accept— the mode of reality presented in a musical, but that the director and other artists involved in the musical create a world where it is natural to sing and dance about something when the feeling arises or is demanded. If an audience is to become involved in or derive any sort of aesthetic experience from a Film Musical their sensibilities must be engaged on this level and the elements of music, dance, and libretto must be directed toward this end.

How well a Film Musical works as a whole, how well it creates a specific mode of reality, is heavily incumbent upon how well musical numbers are varied, coordinated, and integrated. Music is capable of expressing many emotions or underscoring any variety of moods and actions;[5] a song with a tendency toward repetition of notes has, depending to a certain extent of course on rhythm, an aggressive quality;[6] while a song written, let us say, stepwise and at a slower or moderate tempo often flows and is capable of vacillating between poles of elevation and calm. Both types of song, and the variants of these two types, serve as important structural components in the musical. *On the Town* (1949), for example, is a tremendous success because it begins on a note of aggressive intensity with the song "New York, New York" which the three sailors (Gene Kelly, Frank Sinatra, and Jules Munshin) sing as they begin their quest for love and laughs during their leave in New York. The film maintains that same intensity through Ann Miller's song and dance in the museum ("Prehistoric Man") to the number performed atop the Empire State Building by the sailors and their girls ("On the Town") and into the dream ballet, "A Day in New York," (a modification of the Jerome Robbins and Leonard Bernstein ballet *Fancy Free*) which both rhythmically, melodically, and thematically underpins Gaby's (Gene Kelly) problems in trying to establish a permanent romantic relationship with Ivy (Vera-Ellen). The Ballet is particularly effective in light of an earlier sequence, a charm song, "Main Street," performed by Kelly and Vera-Ellen which sheers off some of Ivy's stolid and pretentious veneer to reveal her real self and her affection for the love-struck Gaby.

Another film, *It's Always Fair Weather* (1955), begins, like *On the Town,* with a rather aggressive song and dance number performed by three servicemen (Kelly, Dan Dailey, and Michael Kidd) just returned from the war, but it does not sustain this feeling throughout. The most obvious omission in the film, however, in terms of thematic and musical structure is the absence of a good romantic love ballad and accompanying love dance which should be performed by Kelly and Cyd Charisse, his romantic interest; throughout the film Kelly has been struggling with his inability to commit himself to anything, but by the film's end he is firmly committed to Charisse. A dance performed by the two would have established a solid medium of expression for their somewhat ambiguous feelings, reinforcing the theme of the film and at the same time answering the conventional exigencies of the genre. In the latter film a lack of varied songs is clearly a weakness because it has not, through song, offered the viewer the opportunity to experience and understand the multifaceted natures of the different characters and their relationship to one another. It is exactly this implementation of a balanced and yet varied score which makes the Astaire-Rogers musicals so successful. In *Top Hat* (1935), for instance, there are two rhythm numbers ("No Strings" and "Top Hat, White Tie and Tails") which help delineate Jerry's (Fred Astaire) character; there is a "charm song" ("Isn't This a Lovely Day") which sustains an optimistic mood at a crucial point; there is a "love ballad" ("Cheek to Cheek") which, with its unusual 64 bar chorus, offers Jerry a perfect opportunity to woo and win Dale (Ginger Rogers); and, finally, there is a musical scene number ("The Piccolino"). A well rounded musical score is essential in a good Musical for more than just entertainment's sake: it is our direct encounter with the characters' ways of looking at the world and life.

In creating effective musical numbers for a Musical the film medium commands a special power because it can complement and explore the melodic, rhythmic, and lyrical possibilities of the music through a variety of cinematic techniques. This, of course, is more evident in dance sequences, but it is also important in filming the simple rendering of a song by a character. During the singing of a love ballad, for instance, the camera not only can register the feelings of the singer through close-ups, but also, with, perhaps, the smallest most fluid movement, can record the reaction of the partner as a particularly melodious or lyrically meaningful phrase is sung. Or through inventive editing it can capture the joyful rhythm of one man's statement about himself and life as in Norman Jewison's filming of "If I Were a Rich Man" in *Fiddler on the Roof* (1971). In any case, what the director must do is complement in filmic terms what is being sung and said in musical terms; he must capture that element which all good songs have in common: the neat fusion of the general (or familiar) and the particular.[7]

For a song to function effectively in a Musical, it must not only capture and communicate the total mood of the dramatic situation, but also be familiar enough to the audience, both musically and lyrically, to engage their attention. A song of any type written in a twelve tone row will probably detract more

Topol in *Fiddler on the Roof* (1971).

from the situation than further it, no matter how relevant the lyric may be to the situation or to the people's lives in the audience. Popular music lends itself well to the Film Musical as, generally, the dramatic situations depicted are meant to communicate something not only within the film but to the audience, who can apprehend more readily the basic song structures of popular music as well as the native language idioms characteristic of the musical's song lyrics. In a song situation, then, the melodic, harmonic, and rhythmic elements of the music do the most in establishing a "general" feeling for the situation; music should serve as a metaphor in a song situation: it should match and develop the meaning, mood, and rhythm of the dramatic situation through appropriate musical structure. The film-maker must, in turn, complement this general feeling established by the song in filmic terms. While keeping his eye on the general structure and movement of a scene, the film-maker must also be aware of the degree of particularization presented in the lyrics of the song; the lyrics of a song serve as the bridge between various sequences by helping us keep a finger on the spoken story line. The lyric is also the verbalization of a particular feeling or idea (underlined by the music) that a particular character is attempting to express. Lehman Engel states: "One element all best lyrics have in common is directness and precision of idea and image."[8] The film-maker must complement the lyric with a similar eye toward precision of idea and image. A good example occurs in *Cover Girl* (1944) when Rita Hayworth sings the Ira Gershwin–Jerome Kern ballad "Long Ago and Far Away" to Gene Kelly in the night club. The director, Charles Vidor, begins with a medium shot of Hayworth reassuringly singing to Kelly of her love for him; the next shot is a close-up of Kelly with a troubled look on his face but at the same time resolutely set in rejecting her plea; back to a close-up of Hayworth, now more saddened, singing rather ironically, "The dream I dreamed was not denied me." Vidor then opens the scene to take in both the principals while Hayworth sings: "Just one look and then I knew/That all I longed for, long ago, was you." At this point Kelly changes mood (a two shot inserted here) and as he goes to her the camera pulls back and the dance begins. In this scene, Vidor not only has captured the evocative longing sort of quality in Kern's melody but also has reinforced the specific message of the lyrics through specific film techniques. It is this sort of treatment of songs that enables the Film Musical to transcend what is normally done on the Broadway stage, and, consequently, makes it a special form of art.

The lyrics of a song clearly help identify and particularize character in a song situation, but it is the dance which strives further to bring to the surface the complexity of emotions residing within a character. Just as the appropriate lyric phrase must be welded to the given musical phrase, so the dance must also work closely with the music but in a much more sophisticated fashion. Dance, in the majority of cases, evolves out of a song situation; it extends and amplifies through bodily and, essentially, non-verbal movement what was stated in the lyric, and, at the same time, it attempts to move the degree of expression and interpretation onto a more elevated or, at least, more metaphoric plane. Peter Hogue, in an article on *The Band Wagon* (1953), illustrates this principle in his discussion of Fred Astaire's "By Myself" number from the film: "Though piqued by neglect, his vigor and sense of purpose are quickly renewed as his walk from the station inevitably (because of the genre) yet spontaneously (because of Astaire) elicits a song and dance. The song tells us of Hunter's determination to live in "a world of my own," and the dance reveals his inner resources for self sustenance. In the early scenes in particular, dance is more than entertainment and more than art; it is both a catalyst for, and an expression of, the quintessential vitality which is itself the meaning of Hunter's life."[9] The dance situations in a Film Musical, then, should, in the context of the film as a whole, bring us to a closer understanding of the characters as individuals and how they stand in relationship to one another and their environment.

Within this broader context, the dance serves more specific functions. Bob Fosse says in John Kobal's *Gotta Sing Gotta Dance: A Pictorial History of Film Musicals*[10] that the dance can "set the environment or atmosphere or character behavior of a particular locale or particular set of characters. . . ." This type or function of dance enables the audience to get a general feeling for a place in the musical and it also serves to reinforce the basic texture and mood of the musical as a whole; a dance of this sort is also instrumental in establishing basic conflicts among and motivational patterns in different characters. The opening sequence of *West Side Story* (1961), for instance, serves both ends. The high aerial shot moving into a more specific view of the Jets on the

Rita Moreno in *West Side Story* (1961).

playground and the unfolding dance illustrates and delineates not only the dismal surrounding of New York's west side but also, through Jerome Robbins' marvelous jazz ballet choreography and Robert Wise's crisp camera work, the intensity of the basic conflict between the gangs.

Another end that dance should attempt to achieve is to "Move the story and character along. Further the action. . . ." This, of course, is the most obvious of all criterion for effective dance numbers; in essence the dance should be of such a nature that it seems all of a piece with the action preceding and following the number. A good example of a song and dance which fulfills this end is "Goin' Courtin' " in *Seven Brides for Seven Brothers* (1954) where Jane Powell gently initiates the bumbling brothers to the "glories" of wooing and dancing to a point where they are joyously involved in their new found ability to dance and are ready to go to the forthcoming barn raising. Still another fine example of this type of dance is the "Dancing in the Dark" sequence from *The Band Wagon*. In the film, prior to the dance sequence, Astaire and Cyd Charisse believe they cannot work together, but as they are walking together late one evening, the sounds of Arthur Schwartz's melody drift in, and they find themselves dancing to the music and subsequently with one another; tensions are resolved.

Fosse states that dance can also be employed to "Express a particular emotion. This does not necessarily move the story along but does elaborate on a particular feeling of the moment. Dances of 'love' would fall into this group. Also dances of elation. . . ." In this type of number, the dynamic fusion of music, dance, and cinematography are of the utmost importance, because so much of what is to be expressed is reliant upon the type of melody used in conjunction with the combined rhythms of song, dance, and camera work. The most notable examples of this type or function of dance are the ballad or love dances in the Astaire-Rogers films ("Night and Day" from *The Gay Divorcee,* 1934; "Cheek to Cheek" from *Top Hat,* and "Let's Face the Music and Dance" from *Follow the Fleet,* 1936, to name but three). Another real classic of this type is Gene Kelly's "alter ego" dance in *Cover Girl* in which Kelly dances with his own image by means of double exposure photography. In deference to Fosse, most dances should, and oftentimes do, advance the story. Because emotions are so important in character motivation, dances of this nature enable us to understand better why a character acts as he does and where his emotions will eventually lead him or her in the total movement of the story.

"The last group that comes to mind," Fosse states, "are really what could be called just 'entertainment'. . . ." Here Fosse cites his own "Steam Heat" number from *Pajama Game* (1957). The most obvious dances of this type, however, are Busby Berkeley's playlets ("42nd Street" from *42nd Street,* 1933; "By a Waterfall" from *Footlight Parade,* 1933; "I Only Have Eyes for

You'' from *Dames*, etc.) and the large production numbers from revue Musicals (*Ziegfeld Follies*, 1946, etc.) and those in musical biographies ('*Till the Clouds Roll By*, 1946; *Three Little Words*, 1950; *Night and Day*, 1946; etc.). In entertainment numbers, the dance is filmed almost exclusively for effect with the camera eye directing all its attention on the form. By the same token, however, entertainment numbers can be neatly integrated into a film's structure. For instance, in backstage musicals like *42nd Street*, the entertainment numbers are designed to show us how well the show (which has been a "blood and guts" effort to put together) is going; we should, in a sense, get a feeling of being "wowed" much like the fictional audience supposedly watching the number in the theater is.

An effective dance number in a Film Musical should attempt to achieve all the above ends, and, in fact, most good numbers do so without seeming pretentious or too caught up in their own art. Dance, by its nature, is a stylized reflection and interpretation of reality; thus as the audience views a dance they should be aware of the element of communication being expressed by the characters either internally or between one another. The film-maker's and choreographer's task is to engage their audience's interest and involvement in this abstract mode of reality being presented in the dance, and to do this they have a multitude of cinematic techniques at their disposal. The principal concern, however, in filming dance sequences is choreographing the camera to suit the individual dance routine. As Walter Sorell points out: "Filmed dance must . . . be a compromise. The movement of the camera must serve the movement of the dance, and the dance must be choreographed with an eye to the camera."[11] In essence, what this "compromise" means is that the director not only turns an eye inward toward the form and movement of the dance itself, but that he also turns his eye outward toward how the audience will and should perceive the action. By choreographing the camera as such the film-maker and choreographer give it the stature of a participant in the dance.[12] Through movement, or compression and expansion of the visual image, or editing, the film-maker is able to anticipate and embellish movement and, ultimately, control the message being communicated in the dance. Any dance can become a failure the minute the film-maker allows his camera to take off on its own flights of fancy or the minute he allows the camera to "assert its own personality."[13] As in ballet, where the male figure often is most important as the support for a ballerina in a *pas-de-deux*, the film-maker serves his most important function in supporting the total sweep and message of the movement going on before him. Walter Terry, in discussing Gene Kelly, states: "Not content with simply photographing dances, he used the camera's inherent mobility and almost magical perceptiveness to seek out dance details or, through absolutely appropriate fantasy, make the dancer a part of the wind, the rain, the sky, just as a dancer really is in his own dreams."[14] The Film Musical has broken past the proscenium arch in recording dance; the camera's flexibility makes it an explorer: it can delineate character more sharply with a multiplicity of shots and movements, it can create "real" alter egos, it can move from reality into fantasy with no jarring of sensibilities, and it can translate the rhythms of a person's imagination and feelings into the rhythms of life.

The third essential element of the Film Musical is the libretto or, as it is oftentimes called, the "book." The book in the total structure of a Film Musical is the basic subject matter or idea for the plot—minus the song and dance numbers as totally conceived segments of the plot—which determines what direction the musical will take in terms of conflict and theme. In the case of filmed musicals, the book would be a basic scenario. The fusion of music, dance, and book ideally evolve a unity so balanced and integrated that the three elements appear as one.[15] There is a tendency, when a musical does not achieve this fusion, to concentrate most of the criticism on the book, forgetting in the process the formal distinguishing factor implied by the genre: the communication of the story through the use of music.

Music and dance, in the main, are implemented in the context of a Film Musical to explore and bring to the surface the intricacies of the underlying structure of the book. An effective Film Musical will take statements of importance, i.e., pieces of the dramatic action where the conflicts, motivational patterns, and ideas concerned with the theme of the film are of heightened importance, and express them in musical and/or choreographic terms; this is a demand—a demand of convention—implied in the genre of the Film Musical. In *Silk Stockings* (1957), for instance, the starchy Ninotchka's (Cyd Charisse) first "flowering of feeling" is structurally important and is done by means of the song "All of You" sung by Fred Astaire and a dance number between the two which beautifully illustrates her hidden (up to this point) potential for feeling and expressiveness. Nothing of the movement of the film as a whole is destroyed by an obtrusive number here, because fidelity, not only to the story but also to the conventions of the genre, has been maintained. This fidelity to convention is essential to the formal qualities of the Film Musical, and convention also plays an important role in the popularity of the genre.

The Film Musical, like other popular art forms, is highly formulaic; it has always relied upon a solid core of conventions especially in its books to engage the audience's interest, but it has also been an evolutionary art form in terms of the artistic inventiveness executed within the formulaic structures. Up to the mid-1950s most musicals could be located within one of the following formulas[16]: (1) the revue, one of the earliest forms, generally presents a variety of acts ranging from dramatic scenes to musical production numbers; sometimes, but oftentimes not, there is a thematic idea which unites the acts; *Hollywood*

Revue of 1929 and *Ziegfeld Follies* are good examples of this formula; (2) the screen operetta is most often a love story set in some exotic locale[17]; the music is highly melody-oriented and does not often draw on typical American jazz rhythms so often implemented in the "musical comedy," and, for the most part, the lyrics for the songs aspire to quasi-poetry and do not draw on common speech idioms of the present culture; *The Desert Song* (1929), *Maytime* (1937), and *The Student Prince* (1954) are good examples; (3) the backstage musical is concerned with getting the big show ready for its Broadway debut and all the problems accompanying this process; *42nd Street* and Busby Berkeley's "Gold-diggers" series fall into this category, as well as later films like *Summer Stock* (1950) and *The Band Wagon*. A variant of the formula is *Singin' in the Rain* (1952), which basically uses the same conventions but deals with the motion picture industry; (4) the Cinderella or "rags-to-riches" formula generally chronicles the rise in the world of a star or some semi-waif like Deanna Durbin or Shirley Temple; (5) the love/hate, mistaken notion, or mistaken identity formula is often seen in the Astaire-Rogers musicals, and a whole complex of mistaken notions keep *Easter Parade* (1948) (with Astaire and Judy Garland) predictable yet lively; essentially in this formula hate at some point turns into love, and then to further complicate the plot one principal or the other generally accepts some idea (false, of course) about the other which must be overcome if love is to triumph; (6) the musical biography traces the life or career of some individual whose life is intimately associated with music or the performance of music. *The Jolson Story* (1946) and *Rhapsody in Blue* (1945) (a biopic of George Gershwin) are two of the most popular. The majority of these formulas had their inception on the early Broadway stage where producers and artists became aware of their consistent popular appeal and continued to implement them. The Film Musical essentially adopted the formulas but, like the stage musical, continued to refine them through a process of evolving inventiveness in the use of music and dance.

A common critical complaint directed against the musical is that the creators are relying on the same old conventions in their books. There is a good reason for drawing upon formula: a formulaic book or storyline can prove to be a necessary adjunct to the aesthetic form of the Film Musical. By providing the audience with a storyline that is basically familiar, and, in fact, almost archetypal[18] the artists involved in the musical are able to first, present the audience with "familiar shared images and meanings [which] assert an ongoing continuity of values,"[19] and, second, they are able to exercise a greater degree of artistic freedom in those areas which define and distinguish the art: music and dance. By the same token they are able, through their artistic inventiveness, to present and confront the audience with, as John Cawelti states in his essay on "The Concept of Formula in the Study of Popular Literature," "a

Fred Astaire and Ginger Rogers in *Shall We Dance* (1937).

new perception or meaning which we have not realized before.''[20] In drawing upon some fairly well-established formulas, the artists in Film Musicals are able to infuse new life into characters and situations about which the audience has a reasonable amount of prior knowledge. We all know that Gene Kelly is out to woo and win Leslie Caron in *An American in Paris* (1951), but when will the crucial first romantic encounter come? How will Kelly's character go about winning her? In keeping with the conventions of the genre, he sings "Love Is Here to Stay," and the ensuing dance of give-and-take solidifies the love relationship; yet it is very different from other scenes of its kind. This is not to say that the book for a musical must be idiotically simple so that artists can be more artistic; on the contrary, a musical book may be totally imaginative, unlike anything written before, but it still must be able to assimilate the more abstract art forms of music and dance and use them to their full advantage in the whole of the film. Formula enables the audience to draw easily discernible relationships between the "conventional" story set in the everyday world and the stylized representation and interpretation of the inner mode of the reality of feelings, emotions, passion, etc., brought to the surface by means of music and dance; what then becomes important to recognize is that the burden of not only the genre's popularity but also its artistic content falls into the realm of *how* effectively the Film Musical presents its subject matter.

The Film Musical is a highly conventional film genre, as opposed to the strict "art" film where convention becomes subordinate to inventive themes or ideas. In the musical, the elements of music and dance woven into the libretto not only serve the end of reinforcing a formulaic type of film but also serve in creating and distinguishing a distinctive film genre. Moreover, if a new idea (a novel and progressive artistic concept) is expressed, it is, most often, found in the song and dance sequences. It is not surprising, then, in light of this to understand the popularity of the Film Musical: on the one hand we have a genre with a solid core of conventions which can be counted on to strike a responsive chord in the viewer, and on the other we have the audience's obvious appreciation of the talents of artists like Fred Astaire and Gene Kelly, or composers like the Gershwins, Jerome Kern, Cole Porter, Irving Berlin, Harold Arlen, and Jule Styne.[21] The Film Musical presents us with a popular phenomenon in terms of the directors, composers, and choreographers who have consistently taken the conventional fabric of the musical and progressively and imaginatively shaped it into a form which can present us with freshness of perception and variety of experience hitherto unseen, emphasizing in the process *how* both common and new ideas are presented rather than *what* the implications of these ideas are. Instead of always searching immediately outside a film genre to find some reason for its popularity, we should begin by accepting the art form within its own sphere—recognizing first the parameters and dimensions of that sphere. Hopefully, this introductory analysis of the Film Musical's form will help balance our perspective at least in terms of this genre.[22]

NOTES

1. *The Impact of Film: How Ideas Are Communicated Through Cinema and Television* (New York: Macmillan Publishing Company, 1973), p. 308.
2. See Pauline Kael's review of *Funny Girl* in *Going Steady* (Boston: Little, Brown and Company, 1968, 1969, 1970), pp. 133–37; in the review she does not even mention the composer of the score, Jule Styne.
3. *Understanding Movies* (Englewood Cliffs, N.J.: Prentice-Hall Inc., 1972), p. 115.
4. "Rouben Mamoulien: 'Style Is the Man,' " in *Discussion* (The American Film Institute), No. 2 (1971), p. 9.
5. Lehman Engel, in his *American Musical Theater: A Consideration* (New York: Macmillan Company; a CBS Legacy Collection Book, 1967), lists a variety of song types most often used in stage musicals; I believe the same list is applicable to the Film Musical:

1. *Song* . . . The verse is free in form, usually establishes or sets up a subject, and is melodically secondary to the chorus—which introduces and develops the main theme. In musical theater and popular song practice, the 32-bar chorus (or variants) [AABA is the usual melodic structure] is the commonest form. . . .

2. *Ballad.* Most often a love song, but it can also be a narrative, soliloquy, or character song. . . . 3. *Rhythm song.* One primarily carried along on, or propelled by, a musical beat which is most usually a regular one [oftentimes up-tempo]. . . . 4. *Comedy song.* Divided into two main and quite opposite forms— each of which has many variants . . . might be generally classified as the "short joke" and the "long joke". . . . 5. *Charm song.* One usually combining music and lyrics in equal importance. The subject matter . . . is light, and . . . no attempt to make a comedy point. The musical setting is generally delicate, optimistic, and rhythmic and may have, more than the music of comedy songs, a life independent of its lyrics. . . . 6. *Musical Scene.* A theatrical sequence . . . set to music, for one or any number of characters. It may include a song and may be held together formally by its literary structure, guided by . . . musical balance. It may include speech, recitative, song, and incidental music (underscoring) [pp. 118–20].

6. Alec Wilder, *American Popular Song: The Great Innovators, 1900–1950* (New York: Oxford University Press, 1972), states in his discussion of George Gershwin, "The constant, and characteristic, repeated note found throughout Gershwin's songs is a basic attestation of this aggressiveness" (p. 122).

7. The word "particularization" is taken from Lehman Engel's discussion of music in *Words with Music* (New York: Macmillan Company, 1972), pp. 92–112.

8. Engel, *Words with Music,* p. 108.

9. "The Band Wagon," in *The Velvet Light Trap,* No. 11 (Winter, 1974), p. 33.

10. John Kobal, *Gotta Sing Gotta Dance: A Pictorial History of Film Musicals* (London: Hamlyn Publishing Group Limited, 1971), pp. 299–300; all the subsequent quotations are from these pages.

11. *The Dance Through the Ages* (New York: Grosset and Dunlap, 1967), p. 261.

12. Gene Kelly substantiates this concept of choreographing the camera and having it act as a participant in the dance when he states: "You learn to use the camera as part of the choreography." From Tony Thomas' *The Films of Gene Kelly: Song and Dance Man* (Secaucus, N.J.: Citadel Press, 1974), p. 27.

13. Sorell, *Dance Through the Ages,* p. 291.

14. *The Dance in America* (New York: Harper and Row, 1971; revised edition), pp. 228–29.

15. A good example of this is in Lehman Engel's *Words with Music,* pp. 115–16, where he relates that when someone asked him after seeing *Fiddler on the Roof* what he thought of the score he "could only reply that [he] had been totally unaware of it" because he was "completely absorbed in the total experience."

16. The following formulas are also mentioned and illustrated a little more fully in the following books: John Kobal, *Gotta Sing Gotta Dance* (Mr. Kobal mentions the formulas but does not often define them; he does provide many examples); John Russell Taylor and Arthur Jackson, *The Hollywood Musical* (New York: McGraw-Hill, 1971) (the authors here only mention formula tangentially); Arlene Croce, *The Fred Astaire and Ginger Rogers Book* (New York: Outerbridge and Lazard, Inc., 1972). Ms. Croce discusses the formulas used in the Astaire-Rogers films quite extensively.

17. Leonard Bernstein in his chapter on "American Musical Comedy" in *The Joy of Music* (New York: Simon and Schuster, 1959), p. 167, cites the outstanding characteristic of the operetta as its use of exotic locale.

18. Because so many of the "books" in Film Musicals are comedies I believe Northrop
    Frye's comments about archetypal structure in comedy is particularly relevant at
    this point; I will parenthetically cite *The Pirate* by way of illustration:

    What normally happens [in a comedy] is that a young man wants a young woman
    [Serafin woos Manuela in *The Pirate*], that his desire is resisted by some opposi-
    tion, usually paternal, and that near the end of the play some twist in the plot
    enables the hero to have his will . . . the movement of comedy is usually a
    movement from one kind of society to another. At the beginning of the play the
    obstructing characters are in charge of the play's society [like Don Pedro], and
    the audience recognizes that they are the usurpers. At the end of the play the
    device in the plot that brings the hero and heroine together causes a new society
    to crystallize around the hero [in *The Pirate,* Serafin (Gene Kelly) puts on a small
    show and uses his hypnotist act to draw the truth out about Don Pedro], and the
    moment when this crystallization occurs is the point of resolution in the action,
    the comic discovery, *anagnorisis* or *cognito.*

    The appearance of this new society is frequently signalized by some kind of
    party or festive ritual, which either appears at the end of the play or is assumed to
    take place immediately afterward [in most musicals it is the promise of marriage
    often symbolized in the reprise of a love ballad or another song; in *The Pirate*
    Kelly and Garland (Serafin and Manuela) perform Cole Porter's "Be a Clown,"
    symbolic of their union to one another and to a life on the stage]. The preceding
    is from *Anatomy of Criticism: Four Essays* (New York: Atheneum, 1957),
    p. 163.

19. John G. Cawelti, "The Concept of Formula in the Study of Popular Literature," in
    Journal of Popular Culture, Volume 3; No. 3 (Winter, 1969), p. 385.
20. Ibid.
21. Once again I refer the reader to the books on dance cited above where the names of
    Astaire and Kelly are most often mentioned in regards to achievement in filmed
    dance, and also to Alec Wilder's *American Popular Song* cited above for discus-
    sion of American composers and their compositions.
22. The author wishes to express his gratitude to Mr. Gary Don Luckert, whose interest
    in and knowledge of the musical spurred my own interest and to Mr. Jack Nachbar
    for his helpful suggestions in focusing and framing my subject matter.

Monster Movies: A Sexual Theory

WALTER EVANS

As has ever been the case, Dracula, Frankenstein, the Wolfman, King Kong, and their peers remain shrouded in mystery. Why do they continue to live? Why do American adolescents keep Dracula and his companion monsters of the 1930s and early 1940s alive yet largely ignore much better formula movies of the same period, Westerns *(Stagecoach)*, gangster movies *(Little Caesar, Public Enemy)* and others?[1] What is the monster formula's "secret of life"? Is this yet another of the things which "man was not meant to know"?

The formula has inspired a plethora of imaginative theories, including several which attempt to explain the enduring popularity of these movies in terms of: contemporary social prosperity and order[2]; political decay[3]; the classic American compulsion "to translate and revalue the inherited burden of European culture"[4]; the public's need for "an acceptance of the natural order of things and an affirmation of man's ability to cope with and even prevail over the evil of life which he can never understand"[5]; the "ambiguities of repulsion and curiosity" regarding "what happens to flesh, . . . the fate of being a body"[6]; our "fear of the nonhuman"[7]; the social consequences of "deviance from the norm," particularly physical deviance[8]; and "mankind's hereditary fear of the dark."[9]

Dracula, Frankenstein's monster, King Kong, and others have been fruitfully approached as cultural symbols, but their power and appeal are finally much more fundamental than class or political consciousness,[10] more basic than abstractions of revolt against societal restrictions, yet more specifically concerned with certain fundamental and identifiable features of human experience than such terms as "darkness" and "evil" seem to suggest. Their power, and that of the other movie monsters is, it seems to me, finally and essentially related to that dark fountainhead which psychically moves those masses in the American film and TV audiences who desperately struggle with the most universal, and in many ways the most horrible of personal trials: the sexual traumas of adolescence. Sex has a central role in many popular formulas,[11] but sexuality in horror movies is uniquely tailored to the psyches of troubled adolescents, whatever their age.

The adolescent finds himself trapped in an unwilled change from a comparatively comprehensible and secure childhood to some mysterious new state which he does not understand, cannot control, and has some reason to fear.

Mysterious feelings and urges begin to develop, and he finds himself strangely fascinated with disturbing new physical characteristics—emerging hair, budding breasts, and others—which, given the forbidding texture of the X-rated American mentality, he associates with mystery, darkness, secrecy, and evil. Similarly stirred from a childishly perfect state of nature, King Kong is forced into danger by his desire for a beautiful young woman, a dark desire which, like the ape himself, must finally be destroyed by a hostile civilization. And so, stirred from innocence and purity (see the wolfman poem which appears below) by the full moon which has variously symbolized chastity, change, and romance for millennia, the Wolfman guiltily wakes to the mystery of horrible alterations in his body, his mind, and his physical desires—alterations which are completely at odds with the formal strictures of his society. The mysterious, horrible, physical and psychological change is equally a feature of Frankenstein, of Dracula's victims, the Mummy and his bride, and countless other standard monster movie characters.

The key to monster movies and the adolescents which understandably dote upon them is the theme of horrible and mysterious psychological and physical change; the most important of these is the monstrous transformation which is directly associated with secondary sexual characteristics and with the onset of aggressive erotic behavior. The Wolfman, for example, sprouts a heavy coat of hair, can hardly be contained within his clothing, and when wholly a wolf is, of course, wholly naked. Comparatively innocent and asexual females become, after contact with a vampire (his kiss redly marked on their necks) or werewolf (as in *Cry of the Werewolf*), quite sexy, aggressive, seductive—literally female "vamps" and "wolves."[12]

As adolescence is defined as "developing from childhood to maturity,"[13] so the transformation is cinematically defined as movement from a state of innocence and purity associated with whiteness and clarity to darkness and obscurity associated with evil and threatening physical aggression. In the words of *The Wolfman's* gypsy:

> Even a man who is pure at heart
> And says his prayers by night
> May become a wolf when the wolfbane blooms
> And the moon is full and bright.

The monsters are generally sympathetic, in large part because, as remarked earlier, they themselves suffer the change as unwilling victims, all peace destroyed by the horrible physical and psychological alterations thrust upon them. Even Dracula, in a rare moment of self-revelation, is driven to comment: "To die, to be really dead. That must be glorious. . . . There are far worse things awaiting man than death.'' Much suffering arises from the monster's over-whelming sense of alienation; totally an outcast, he painfully embodies the adolescent's nightmare of being hated and hunted by the society which he so desperately wishes to join.

Various aspects of the monster's attack are clearly sexual. The monster invariably prefers to attack individuals of the opposite sex, to attack them at night, and to attack them in their beds. The attack itself is specifically physical; Dracula, for instance, must be in immediate bodily contact with his victim to effect his perverted kiss; Frankenstein, the Wolfman, the Mummy, King Kong, have no weapons but their bodies. The aspect of the attack most disturbing to the monster, and perhaps most clearly sexual, is the choice of victim: "The werewolf instinctively seeks to kill the thing it loves best" (Dr. Yogami in *The Werewolf of London*). *Dracula's* Mina Seward must attack her fiance, John. The Mummy must physically possess the body of the woman in whom his spiritual bride has been reincarnated. Even more disturbing are the random threats to children scattered throughout the formula, more disturbing largely because the attacks are so perversely sexual and addressed to beings themselves soon destined for adolescence.

The effects of the attack may be directly related to adolescent sexual experi-mentation. The aggressor is riddled with shame, guilt, and anguish; the victim, once initiated, is generally transformed into another aggressor.[14] Regaining innocence before death seems, in the best films, almost as inconceivable as retrieving virginity.

Many formulaic elements of the monster movies have affinities with two central features of adolescent sexuality, masturbation and menstruation. From time immemorial underground lore has asserted that masturbation leads to feeblemindedness or mental derangement: the monster's transformation is gen-erally associated with madness; scientists are generally secretive recluses whose private experiments on the human body have driven them mad. Masturbation is also widely (and, of course, fallaciously) associated with "weakness of the spine,"[15] a fact which helps explain not only Fritz of *Frankenstein* but the army of feebleminded hunchbacks which pervades the formula. The Wolfmen, and sometimes Dracula, are identifiable (as, according to underground lore, masturbating boys may be identified) by hairy palms.

Ernest Jones explains the vampire myth largely in terms of a mysterious physical and psychological development which startles many adolescents, noc-turnal emissions: "A nightly visit from a beautiful or frightful being, who first exhausts the sleeper with passionate embraces and then withdraws from him a vital fluid: all this can point only to a natural and common process, namely to nocturnal emissions accompanied with dreams of a more or less erotic nature. In the unconscious mind, blood is commonly an equivalent for semen"[11] (p. 59).

The vampire's bloodletting of women who suddenly enter into full sexuality, the werewolf's bloody attacks—which occur regularly every month—are certainly related to the menstrual cycle which suddenly and mysteriously commands the body of every adolescent girl.

Monster movies characteristically involve another highly significant feature which may initially seem irrelevant to the theme of sexual change: the faintly philosophical struggle between reason and the darker emotional truths. Gypsies, superstitious peasants, and others associated with the imagination eternally triumph over smugly conventional rationalists who ignorantly deny the possible existence of walking mummies, stalking vampires, and bloodthirsty werewolves. The audience clearly sympathizes with those who realize the limits of reason, of convention, of security, for the adolescent's experiences with irrational desires, fears, urges which are incomprehensible yet clearly stronger than the barriers erected by reason or by society, are deeper and more painful than adults are likely to realize. Stubborn reason vainly struggles to deny adolescents' most private experiences, mysterious and dynamic conflicts between normal and abnormal, good and evil, known and unknown.

Two of the most important features normally associated with monster movies are the closely related searches for the "secret of life" and "that which man was not meant to know." Monster movies unconsciously exploit the fact that most adolescents already know the "secret of life" which is, indeed, the "forbidden knowledge" of sex. The driving need to master the "forbidden knowledge" of "the secret of life," a need which seems to increase in importance as the wedding day approaches, is closely related to a major theme of monster movies: marriage.

For the adolescent audience, the marriage which looms just beyond the last reel of the finer monster movies is much more than a mindless cliché wrap-up. As the monster's death necessarily precedes marriage and a happy ending, so the adolescent realizes that a kind of peace is to be obtained only with a second transformation. Only marriage can free Henry Frankenstein from his perverted compulsion for private experimentation on the human body; only marriage can save Mina Harker after her dalliance with the Count. Only upon the death of adolescence, the mysterious madness which has possessed them, can they enter into a mature state where sexuality is tamed and sanctified by marriage.[16] The marriage theme, and the complex interrelationship of various other formulaic elements, may perhaps be best approached through a close analysis of two seminal classics, *Frankenstein* and *Dracula*.

Two events dominate the movie *Frankenstein* (1931): creation of the monster and celebration of the marriage of Henry Frankenstein and his fiancée, Elizabeth. The fact that the first endangers the second provides for most of the conflict throughout the movie, conflict much richer and more powerful, perhaps even profound, when the key thematic relationship between the two is made clear: creation of life. As Frankenstein's perverse nightly experiments on the monstrous body hidden beneath the sheets are centered on the creation of life, so is the marriage, as the old Baron twice makes clear in a toast (once immediately after the monster struggles out of the old mill and begins wandering toward an incredible meeting with Henry's fiancée Elizabeth; again, after the monster is destroyed, in the last speech of the film): "Here's to a son to the House of Frankenstein!"[17]

Frankenstein's fatuous father, whose naive declarations are frequently frighteningly prescient (he predicts the dancing peasants will soon be fighting; on seeing a torch in the old mill, he asks if Henry is trying to burn it down), declares, when hearing of the extent to which his son's experiments are taking precedence over his fiancée: "I understand perfectly well. Must be another woman. Pretty sort of experiments they must be." Later, after receiving the burgomaster's beaming report on the village's preparations for celebration of the marriage, he again associates his son's experiments with forbidden sexuality: "There is another woman. And I'm going to find her."

There is, of course, no other woman. The movie's horror is fundamentally based on the fact that the monster's life has come without benefit of a mother's womb. At one point Frankenstein madly and pointedly gloats over his solitary, specifically manual achievement: "The brain of a dead man, ready to live again in a body I made with my own hands, my own hands!"

Significantly, a troubled search for the "secret of life" is what keeps Henry Frankenstein separated from his fiancée; it literally proves impossible for Henry to provide for "a son to the House of Frankenstein" before he has discovered the "secret of life." Having discovered the "secret of life," he ironically discovers that its embodiment is a frightening monster horrible enough to threaten "normal" relations between himself and Elizabeth. Henry's attempts to lock the monster deep in the mill's nether regions are finally thwarted, and, in a wholly irrational and dramatically inexplicable (yet psychologically apt and profound) scene, the monster—a grotesque embodiment of Frankenstein's newly discovered sexuality—begins to move threateningly toward the innocent bride who is bedecked in the purest of white, then quite as irrationally, it withdraws. On his return, Henry promises his wildly distracted fiancée that there will be no wedding "while this horrible creation of mine is still alive."

The monster is, of course, finally, pitilessly destroyed,[18] and Henry is only ready for marriage when his own body is horribly battered and weakened, when he is transformed from the vigorous, courageous, inspired hero he represented early in the film to an enervated figure approaching the impotent fatuity of his father and grandfather (there is plenty of fine wine for the wedding feast; Frankenstein's grandmother would never allow grandfather to drink any), prepared to renounce abnormal life as potent as the monster in favor of creating a more normal "son to the House of Frankenstein."

The message is clear. In order to lead a normal, healthy life, Henry Frankenstein must—and can—give up dangerous private experiments on the human body in dark rooms hidden away from family and friends. He must learn to deal safely and normally with the "secret of life," however revolting, however evil, however it might seem to frighten and actually threaten pure, virgin womanhood; only then, in the enervated bosom of normality, is it possible to marry and to produce an acceptable "son to the House of Frankenstein."

Dracula's much more mature approach to womankind is clearly aimed at psyches which have overcome Henry Frankenstein's debilitating problem. *Dracula* (1931), obviously enough, is a seduction fantasy vitally concerned with the conditions and consequences of premarital indulgence in forbidden physical relations with attractive members of the opposite sex.

Of all the movie monsters, Dracula seems to be the most attractive to women; and his appeal is not difficult to understand, for he embodies the chief characteristics of the standard Gothic hero: tall, dark, handsome, titled, wealthy, cultured, attentive, mannered, with an air of command, an aura of sin and secret suffering; perhaps most important of all, he is invariably impeccably dressed. With such a seductive and eligible male around, it is certainly no wonder that somewhere in the translation from fiction to film Dr. Seward has become Mina's father and thus leaves Lucy, who also lost the two other suitors Bram Stoker allowed her, free to accept the Count's attentions. Certainly any woman can sympathize with Lucy's swift infatuation ("Laugh all you like; I think he's fascinating.") and Mina's easy acceptance of Dracula as her friend's suitor ("Countess, I'll leave you to your count, and your ruined abbey.").

Having left three wives behind in Transylvania, Dracula is obviously not one to be sated with his second English conquest (the first was an innocent flower girl, ravaged immediately before he meets Lucy and Mina), and he proceeds to seduce Mina, working a change in her which does not go unnoticed, or unappreciated, by her innocent fiancé: "Mina, you're so—like a changed girl. So wonderful—" Mina agrees that indeed she is changed, and, on the romantic terrace, alone with her fiancé beneath the moon and stars, begins, one is certain, the first physical aggression of their courtship. John is suitably impressed. "I'm so glad to see you like this!" Discovered and exposed by Professor Van Helsing, Mina can only admit that (having had relations with Dracula and thus become a Vamp) she has, indeed, suffered the proverbial fate worse than death, and shamefully alert her innocent, naive fiancé: "John, you must go away from me."

Only when John and his older, respected helpmate foil the horrible mock elopement—Dracula and Mina are rushing to the abbey, preparing to "sleep," he even carries her limp body across the abbey's threshold—only when the castrating stake destroys the seducer and with him the maid's dishonor is Mina free to return to the honest, innocent suitor who will accept her past, marry her in the public light of day, and make an honest woman of her.

Lucy, who has no selfless suitor to forgive her, marry her, and make an honest woman of her, is much less successful. When last seen, she has become a child molester, a woman of the night who exchanges chocolate for horrible initiations.

The thematic importance of such innocent victims turned monster as Lucy and Mina, Dr. Frankenstein's creation, King Kong, the Wolfman, and others points directly to one of the most commonly observed and perhaps least understood phenomena of monster movies, one which has been repeatedly noted in this paper: in those classics which are best loved and closest to true art, the audience clearly identifies with the monster. Child, adult, or adolescent, in disembodied sympathetic fascination, we all watch the first Karloff Frankenstein who stumbles with adolescent clumsiness, who suffers the savage misunderstanding and rejection of both society and the creator whose name he bears, and whose fumbling and innocent attempts at love with the little girl by the lakeside turn to terrible, bitter, and mysterious tragedy.

Clearly the monster offers the sexually confused adolescent a sympathetic, and at best a tragic, imitation of his life, by representing a mysterious and irreversible change which forever isolates him from what he identifies as normality, security, and goodness, a change thrusting him into a world he does not understand, torturing him with desires he cannot satisfy or even admit, a world in which dark psychological and strange physical changes seem to conspire with society to destroy him.

NOTES

1. Though many critics focus on adult themes in monster movies, I believe that adolescents provide the bulk of the audience for such films, particularly the classic films shown on late night television all across America. Adolescents, of course, may be of any age.

2. Curtis Harrington asserts that such movies are more popular in periods of depression and disorder. See "Ghoulies and Ghosties" in Roy Huss and T. J. Ross, eds. *Focus on the Horror Film* (Englewood Cliffs, N.J.: Prentice Hall, 1972), pp. 17–18. I should mention one of the finer essays in this fine collection, X. J. Kennedy's "Who Killed King Kong" (pp. 106–9).

3. Lawrence Alloway, "Monster Films," in *Focus on the Horror Film*, p. 123.

4. Frank McConnell, "Rough Beasts Slouching," in *Focus on the Horror Film*, p. 26.

5. R. H. W. Dillard, "The Pageantry of Death," in *Focus on the Horror Film*, p. 37.

6. Lawrence Alloway, p. 124. He is speaking specifically of the effects of death and decay.
7. John Thomas, "Gobble, Gobble . . . One of Us!" in *Focus on the Horror Film,* p. 135.
8. John D. Donne, "Society and the Monster," in *Focus on the Horror Film,* p. 125.
9. Drake Douglas, *Horror!,* Collier Books (New York: Macmillan, 1966), p. 11.
10. I feel this is clearly true in spite of the more superficial importance of, for instance, the Nazi allusions in such a film as *Return of the Vampire* (1944). The classic monster movies deemphasize such non-essential material.
11. According to Andrew Sarris, "There are no non-erotic genres any more." The statement was made on "Frame of Reference" following the "Film Odyssey" showing of *The Blue Angel.*
12. The transformation is less obvious, and perhaps for this reason more powerful, in *King Kong* (1933). Kong himself is safe while hidden deep in the prehistoric depths of Skull Island, but an unappeasable sexual desire (made explicit in the cuts restored in the film's most recent release) turns him into an enemy of civilization until, trapped on the world's hugest phallic symbol, he is destroyed. The psychological transformation of Ann Darrow (Fay Wray) is much more subtle. While alone immediately after exchanging vows of love with a tough sailor, she closes her eyes and, as in a dream vision, above her appears the hideously savage face of a black native who takes possession of her in preparation for the riotous wedding to the great hairy ape. Significantly, only when civilization destroys the fearful, grossly physical beast is she finally able to marry the newly tuxedoed sailor.
13. *Webster's New World Dictionary of the American Language,* 2nd College Edition (Englewood Cliffs, N.J.: Prentice-Hall, 1970). Interesting, in view of the fiery death of Frankenstein's monster and others, is one of the earlier meanings of the root word: "be kindled, burn."
14. It is interesting, and perhaps significant, that the taint of vampirism and lycanthropy have an aura of sin and shame not unlike that of VD. The good doctor who traces the taint, communicable only through direct physical contact, back to the original carrier is not unlike a physician fighting VD.
15. See Ernest Jones, "On the Nightmare of Bloodsucking," in *Focus on the Horror Film,* p. 59.
16. In "The Child and the Book," *Only Connect,* ed. by Sheila Egoff, G. T. Stubbs, and L. F. Ashley (New York: Oxford University Press, 1969) noted psychiatrist Anthony Storr has discussed a precursor of monster movies, fairy tales, in a similar context:

Why is it that the stories which children enjoy are so often full of horrors? We know that from the very beginning of life the child possesses an inner world of fantasy and the fantasies of the child mind are by no means the pretty stories with which the prolific Miss Blyton regales us. They are both richer and more primitive, and the driving forces behind them are those of sexuality and the aggressive urge to power: the forces which ultimately determine the emergence of the individual as a separate entity. For, in the long process of development, the child has two main tasks to perform if he is to reach maturity. He has to prove his strength, and he has to win a mate; and in order to do this he has to overcome the obstacles of his infantile dependency upon, and his infantile erotic attachment to, his parents. . . . The typical fairy story ends with the winning of the princess just as the typical Victorian novel ends with the marriage. It is only at this point that adult sexuality begins. . . . It is not surprising that fairy stories should be both erotic and violent, or that they should appeal so powerfully to children, for the archetypal themes with which they deal mirror the contents of the childish psyche; and the same unconscious source gives origin to both the fairy tale and the fantasy life of the child (pp. 93–94).

17. The dialogue is followed by a close-up of a painfully embarrassed Henry Frankenstein.
18. Significantly, the monster himself is pitifully sympathetic, suffering as adolescents believe only they can suffer, from unattractive physical appearance, bodies they don't understand, repulsed attempts at love, general misunderstanding. Though endowed by his single antagonistic parent with a "criminal brain," the monster is clearly guilty of little but ugliness and ignorance and is by any terms less culpable than the normal human beings surrounding him. He does not so much murder Fritz as attempt to defend himself against completely unwarranted torchings and beatings; he kills Dr. Valdeman only after that worthy believes he has "painlessly destroyed" the monster (a euphemism for murder) and as the doctor is preparing to dissect him; the homicide which propels his destruction, the drowning of the little girl, is certainly the result of clumsiness and ignorance. She had taught him to sail flowers on the lake and, flowers failing, in a visual metaphor worthy of an Elizabethan courtier, the monster in his ignorant joy had certainly meant only for the girl, the only being who had ever shown him not only love, but even affection, to sail on the lake as had the flowers. His joyful lurch toward her after having sailed his flower is, beyond all doubt, the most pathetic and poignant lurch in the history of film.

Kung Fu Film as Ghetto Myth

STUART M. KAMINSKY

The Kung Fu films are not to be confused with the ABC television series, *Kung Fu*, with David Carradine. The television series is not structured on violence.

The television battles take no more than three or four minutes of each show and are not particularly graceful. Thematically, the television series is like most television, reinforcement of middle-class attitudes: if you are kind to others and reserve your strength and ability, you will be rewarded and good will prevail because the orderly way is always right.

This is the direct opposite of the Chinese Kung Fu or Martial Arts films in which strength and ability must be displayed. There is no reward in Kung Fu films except the satisfaction of revenge and the opportunity to earn the respect of others who witness the performance of superhuman agility.

An understanding of the Kung Fu films depends on our acceptance of them as both violent myths and also as almost musical displays.

The essence of the Kung Fu film is performance.

Bruce Lee was the Fred Astaire of Kung Fu films.

To make such a statement implies a way of understanding the Kung Fu films. Such films can be viewed in two distinct, yet related, manners. On one hand, they are films of performance, very much like Astaire or Gene Kelly musicals. Many of the films even have a separate choreographer for the battle scenes.

In the Kung Fu film, as in the dance musical, we see the solo number, the ingenue number, chorus numbers, and dancing duos. Also, as in such musicals, the narrative of the film, while important, is a formalized manner of getting to and leading into the numbers.

That this is not idle fancy can be seen in (a) the way in which the battles are staged and (b) in the reactions of audiences to them. The battles are often prepared for by an establishing shot, a long shot showing the stage or "arena" in which the performance will take place. The obstacles and items to be used are also shown. Audiences accept these battles as performance by responding to the agility and grace of the performer. There is also the equivalent of the bow at the end of a number in the form of a medium shot or close up of the protagonist waiting for applause, which he almost always gets from audiences of children.

The performer even has props, like Fred Astaire's cane and hat. The prop can be a rough staff *(Fists of Fury, Duel of the Iron Fists, Deadly China Doll)* or a rather strange double club connected with chains *(The Chinese Connection, Enter the Dragon, Sacred Knives of Vengeance)*. When the Kung Fu protagonist uses these devices, they become part of a skilled performance similar to the way Astaire or Kelly might twirl his cane or flip his hat. The call is, clearly, for identification, and the identification depends on the myth of skill. For the American audience toward whom the dance musicals were directed, the skill was based upon dexterity, agility, and charm. The skilled performer was ambitious, got his chance, made it to the top. Fred Astaire was, thus, a middle-class identification figure, a self-made, socially accepted success. Bruce Lee is more clearly a ghetto figure whose skill and agility are devoted not to social success but to the execution of his skills to earn audience respect and destruction of his enemies.

The strength of Kung Fu films for black urban audiences is clear in the choice of theaters in which such films are shown. *Variety* reports for show dates in 1973 indicate that Kung Fu films are consistently strong box office in the overwhelmingly black downtown audience theaters in Chicago (the Oriental, the Woods), Detroit (Adams, Grand Circus), and Washington. (See *Variety,* Wednesday, November 14, 1973, or December 26, 1973.)

It doesn't matter that, in practice, to attain the Kung Fu hero's skill would require endless patience and practice, if it even were achievable. Certainly, no amount of practice would teach a young viewer to fly as the Kung Fu hero often does (in a film like *Fearless Fighters* or *The Chinese Professionals,* in fact almost all the skills are superhuman). However, identification is so strong that the myth persists often into the private life of the viewer. The number of

Bruce Lee in *The Chinese Connection* (1973).

black youths who practice pseudo-Kung Fu is strikingly evident on urban street corners. By the same token, the young man of the 1930s could not simply rise and start dancing in his room or on the deck of a ship as did Fred Astaire.

Another similarity between Kung Fu and dance films, especially those of Fred Astaire, includes the way battle sequences are shot. Generally, the protagonist is shown in full body. The more skillful the performer, and Lee appears to be the most skillful, the more of the total performance we see without cutting away to other angles or close-ups. In a Bazinian sense, our acceptance of the myth is to a great degree based on our belief that the performer is actually doing these things.

There are even particular movements like dance steps in Kung Fu films. These steps involve kicks, turns, elbow throws. One might at this point argue a qualitative difference between the dance and the Kung Fu performance. Such a broad distinction is based on taste and tradition rather than on an attempt to understand Kung Fu films by indeed accepting them as acrobatic or ballroom entertainment as were the performances of Astaire to a great degree.

A primary difficulty reviewers, critics, and some adults have in dealing with the Kung Fu films is that their performance is based upon violence, destruction, and death, not musical expression. Somehow, it is assumed that concentration on these aspects of human fear is too serious to handle in a mythic form, or, at least, too serious to be handled with any reference to the skill and grace of the person performing the killing regardless of his motivation within the films. This never seems to be raised as an issue when discussing the conclusions of *Richard the Third, Macbeth,* or *Hamlet,* however. It is the context of popular entertainment as somehow being an unfit arena for dealing with such concerns that turns the protective critic against such films.

If we wish to examine the Kung Fu films as potential expression of some mythic relationship to the ghetto viewer, the imposition of a moral posture gets in the way of our understanding of the genre. Such a posture also negates the possibility that valid creation can take place within it.

An analogy to Kung Fu films in terms of performance can be seen in the Samurai and Judo films of Japan which are somewhat more directly related to violence as expression than the musical. Certainly, few films can claim as bloody a battlefield as that which exists at the end of Kurosawa's *Yojimbo* or *The Seven Samurai.*

In those films, and the mass of Samurai films, our admiration is directed toward the individual performer who can destroy hundreds with his sword. However, the samurai is a middle-class figure in attitude, costume, and action. His deeds are motivated by an interest in the greater common good. The same is true of the judo expert. In films like Kurosawa's *Judo Saga,* the emphasis is on controlling one's skill, using it defensively for social good and never for individual revenge or attainment.

The Kung Fu hero, however, is invariably a lower-class working figure who has no extended interest in society. His motives are all personal, familial, and the tools available to him are never guns and seldom swords, which are a class above him, but his own body and, perhaps, a club, shaft, or crude blunt weapon.

The Samurai's and Judo expert's grace depend upon their interaction with their foes, who are performing part of a total ritual which both sides accept. The Kung Fu hero has his own ritual for which there are few rules and which allow for no mutual respect between adversaries. This dichotomy is most evi-

Bruce Lee in *Fists of Fury* (1973).

dent in *The Chinese Connection* and *The Screaming Tiger,* which deal directly with the conflict between the Kung Fu hero and the Japanese Judo and Samurai representatives, who are presented as arrogant, vain, and easily destroyed by the Kung Fu hero.

In one sense, Kung Fu as manifested in the films is simply graceful, dirty fighting. This is another distinction in kind and ethic from more traditional combat. It is radically different, for example, from the polite ritual of a Samurai film or from American genre films until the 1960s. In American genre films, one confronts his enemy face to face and obeys certain rules such as no hitting below the belt. But these are traditional American middle-class rules which the ghetto viewer has probably had difficulty accepting as valid. Survival, according to rhetoric of the recent past, is a matter of dirty fighting and staying alive no matter what you must do. The Kung Fu hero carries this principle to an "art." It becomes graceful to engage in dirty fighting. Not only is it graceful, there is a ritual pattern to it. Dirty fighting can be the means of righting mythic wrongs. It can be a respectable and admirable form of reaction to social ills and environment. The Kung Fu hero is not simply kicking his opponent in the face, he is doing it with grace and skill. It is ballet of violence.

Another important aspect of Kung Fu violence is that it allows dignity to the small protagonist. One need not be Clint Eastwood or Jim Brown, and few ghetto kids are. Bruce Lee, and others, by their size and nationality, are metaphors for the downtrodden. The Hong Kong Chinese laborer is certainly a disdained member of society from Japan to Europe and has never been considered hero material before.

Elements of the possibility of such grace through violence in the persona of the small, agile man can be seen in Edward G. Robinson or James Cagney in the early 1930s. Such films and stars were popular with children of an Irish/ Jewish urban lower class as are the Kung Fu films with black children.

Bruce Lee in *Fists of Fury* (1973).

There is at least one specific reference to presentation of graceful performance as violence in American film which might be mentioned here. In Vincente Minnelli's *Designing Woman* (1957), an issue raised by Kung Fu films is handled in an American context. Gregory Peck is a tough sports reporter surrounded by huge boxers. He is in love with Lauren Bacall, a designer, who is friendly with a number of "artsy" people including a small, effete male ballet dancer. At one point in the film, Peck is attacked by a gang of "mugs" and, surprisingly, is rescued by the little ballet dancer who performs with leaps, kicks, and studied grace. It is, indeed, a Kung Fu performance in an American film by a ballet dancer, the unity of Bruce Lee and Gene Kelly directed by Minnelli. However, there is a major difference. The ballet dancer has affirmed upper-class art and ballet as a functional motif. Peck's respect for him after the display of his essentially dirty but graceful style is a rapport with conventional art. In the recent Kung Fu films, however, the respect is a result of lower, not upper, class affirmation.

The plots of the Kung Fu films are also important. Invariably, the stories deal with a lower-class figure who contains his Kung Fu skill at first, makes the attempt to be a respectable working-class ghetto resident. He allows others, or witnesses others around him, usually his relatives, to fight the initial battles, because he wants to get along, has vowed to follow the acceptable route of behavior.

His resolve disappears when his family is attacked and destroyed and he sees that being a good worker and loyal citizen has ruined him. His family is almost always destroyed by the man who employs the Kung Fu hero. If the man does not employ him, the man is at least powerful enough to control the city or town where the action takes place. The destruction of the family releases the Kung Fu hero. All that the ghetto figure has is his body, his job, and his family. He rips off his shirt *(Fists of Fury, The Big Boss, Duel of the Iron Fists)*, tastes his own blood *(Enter the Dragon)*, displays great anguish, and proceeds to use his skill to get through the masses of underlings, who, like the creatures who confronted Theseus in the maze, have different skills and require a different display of grace and skill by the protagonist.

The minor villains always include one large or extremely powerful individual such as the Russian in *The Chinese Connection,* a large group of skilled Kung Fu fighters as in *Fists of Fury* or *The Queen Boxer,* an individual who can handle a particular weapon which the protagonist always takes from him and uses or discards as in *The Chinese Connection* or *Duel of the Iron Fists.* The final villain himself is always an older man, a father figure as clearly out of mythological consideration as Cronus or Seth, and the Kung Fu hero is as clearly a mythical extension of Zeus or Horus. Such mythical patterns also reflect psychological conflicts which are universal—the conflict of generations, the Oedipal situation. The father figure is always rich—a worthwhile symbolic adversary for a ghetto hero, lecherous—he is a dirty old man—and quite skillful. There is some implication, indeed, that he may be a self-made ghetto figure who has profited by betrayal of his origins, a terrible father who, like Cronus, has gobbled up his children and must be destroyed by the last of those children.

An important convention of the Kung Fu film is the handling of the final confrontation with the fatherlike villain. The fight is long and the combatants equal. It is invariably settled in slow motion. Both parties leap high into the air toward each other and meet. When they come to earth, the protagonist is torn and bloody, but alive. The father-figure is defeated and dead.

When viewed in this sense, the films are remarkably moral and unrevolutionary. They are films of revenge taken for destruction of one's family. The terrible villain is always destroyed for his conventional evils, which range from lechery and drinking to oppression of the lower classes. The films also frequently end with the protagonist about to be led off by the law to face his punishment for having violated the law.

The law itself, as in American gangster films of the 1930s, is almost non-existent in Kung Fu films. These are not films of law, but of myth; we are dealing with basic issues of life, meaning, and family. The fantasy resolution for a ghetto kid in mythology is not through the law. The fantasy is one of being able to right the wrongs of one's personal frustration through one's own limited ability. It is not surprising that films which deal with the skillful handling of wrongs done to one's immediate family should be popular among black American youths, particularly. This does not, however, mean that the myths and their execution do not have a broader appeal to all those who feel the same restrictions and helplessness and admire the performances.

Kung Fu films are remarkably intense. The percentage of time taken in battle

Bruce Lee in *The Chinese Connection* (1973).

and combat does parallel the time taken in actual dance and song in a Fred Astaire musical; however, the time taken in battle in a Kung Fu film is much greater than in so-called violent films from gangster pictures to Italian Westerns, although the latter come the closest. Only by realizing that the scenes of violence are at the core of the meaning and appreciation of these films can they be appreciated in terms of potential skill in presentation and performance and possible meaning to an audience. In *Duel of the Iron Fists,* for example, there is not even a resolution. The film ends in the midst of yet another battle with the hero still proving his skill. *The Chinese Connection* ends with Bruce Lee frozen in a leap toward a line of men with rifles. To dismiss these films as "junk," as the Italian Westerns were blanketly dismissed several years ago, is to fail to deal with their potential merit. That merit may, indeed, vary. All Kung Fu films are not alike in quality, as all Westerns are not; but to even begin to come to an understanding of which are which requires a willingness to understand the genre.

The Porn Market and Porn Formulas: The Feature Film of the Seventies*

JOSEPH W. SLADE

After nine years of exposure in theaters across America, the hard-core feature film is losing its appeal, or so say the pundits and some of the pornographers. Canny porn entrepreneurs are now taking out full page ads in *Variety,* touting "new" techniques like 3-D, and sending popular performers like Leslie Bovee, Linda Wong, and C. J. Laing on promotion tours with their movies. Some theater owners are cutting prices to draw crowds. Still, according to Phil Paresi, one of the original distributors of *Deep Throat,* demand has fallen so drastically that the average production will earn no more than $300,000 in rentals,[1] not a handsome return if expenses are high and the difference must be divided among several investors. To counter such pessimism, David Friedman, chairman of the Adult Film Association (yes, they are organized, like the

---

*This article was based upon research conducted in 1976–77.

conservative groups that oppose them), claims that the over one hundred porn features made in 1976 garnered sixteen per cent of the weekly U.S. film audience.[2] Probably both are correct: with more porn features than ever in release, the take from each is declining. Curiously, the market seems to be leveling off just as such movies are getting ''better,'' i.e., slicker in finish, more professional in quality. Although a few of the hucksters are going in for kinkier, more perverse sex, the watchword in the ranks of ambitious pornographers is still quality, on the assumption that superior celluloid eroticism will drive the trash out. Some of the arty features do well on the charts, but the dynamics of the porn box office are complicated.

Leslie Bovee and Linda Wong on a promotional tour in 1976.

The feature length 35mm porn film—not to be confused with the 8mm ''loop'' or other arcade fare—is principally made for heterosexual audiences, which began to respond in significant numbers in 1972 to Gerard Damiano's *Deep Throat* and the Mitchell Brothers' *Behind the Green Door*. While a few homosexual features like Wakefield Poole's *Boys in the Sand* (1971) have attracted attention outside the gay community, most are technically inferior, often mere 8mm loops spliced together, and do not generate the publicity or the profits of the straight genre. No hard-core feature has come close to matching *Deep Throat*'s reputed gross of over $25 million; moreover, the glossy type of today is typically budgeted at several times *Throat*'s cost of $25,000. Leaving aside the unique qualities of Damiano's film, its strange chicness, and possible shifts in public taste since, the challenges confronting the porn producer aiming at popularity are two.

The first is the uncertainty of adequate national distribution. Porn distribution networks are sketchy, potentially subject to federal legal intervention, as in Memphis, threatened by new zoning ordinances in major cities, dominated in most regions by the Mafia—probably in some ratio to the disruption of circulation that was a consequence of the 1973 Supreme Court decision giving regulatory powers over pornography to local communities, a decision sometimes said to have accelerated underworld involvement with feature films—and undercut by extensive pirating of prints. Bill Osco, whose *Mona* (1970) was the first hard-core feature to be promoted nationally, circumvented some of those problems by forming his own distribution company, General National and the

Alice in Wonderland (1976).

Mitchell Brothers followed suit, though less successfully, with Cinema Seven. Holding the lines open against legal contests and conservative outcry is a continuing worry, and Osco, who now shoots soft-core, has proposed a two-tier rating system with a hard ''X'' and a soft. General National is currently pushing Osco's *Alice in Wonderland,* a soft-core spoof of Lewis Carroll spiced with just a taste of explicit oral sex. As one of *Variety's* top-grossing films of 1976, *Alice* exemplifies the second challenge to the hard-core industry, the proliferation of quasi-respectable soft-core sex films.

The simple ''nudies,'' the breast-fetish Russ Meyer epics, the nipples-and-teeth daughters-of-Dracula gothics, and the violence-suffused sleaze like *Ilsa, She-Wolf of the SS* sidestep distribution resistance because they do not contain explicit sex and doubtless encroach on the hard-core feature's potential audience. Nevertheless, that rivalry can be discounted as having long been a constant. Besides, the most inept film-maker can rely on a hard-core patronage for his hard-core—the predominantly male, overwhelmingly urban (New York City alone has 62 hard-core theaters) group which delights in the explicit regardless of quality—the so-called ''raincoat brigade.'' Should he have aspirations, the producer must aim at a larger middle-class audience of couples who take in an occasional porno if it is touted as good or campy. For this reason, he measures his feature against classier competition, on the one hand, the fluff like Just Jaeckin's *Emmanuelle* (1974) and *Story of O* (1975), soft-core smash imports that weave lush settings, lush bodies, and pretentious plots into ersatz sophistication, and on the other, the superromantic heavies like Bertolucci's *Last Tango in Paris* (1973) or Barbet Schroeder's recent *Maitresse* (1976), which link sex and sensibility in decadent alliance. Both types employ abundant nudity and simulated sex, sometimes with boldness, but because the first is pretty, the second ''intellectual,'' neither fosters guilt in the viewer, or so the argument goes (''X was never like this,'' the ads for *Emmanuelle* burbled). Whether such films are the real competition is beside the point, for the glossy porn entrepreneur thinks that they are. Bent on financial and critical success, on respectability, in short, he embellishes. Greater length, more developed plots, and higher technical values are expensive, of course, and the chances are increasingly against earning back heavy costs.

To a degree, the domestic pornographer gets his revenge against the Jaeckins and Bertoluccis by carrying the battle to their homelands. Surprising as it may seem, given Scandanavian supremacy in the 8mm field, America is now porn feature merchant to the world. So rampant is the penetration of foreign markets that [in 1975] Germans protested the influx of Yankee features in the streets of Munich.[3] It has been legal to exhibit porn features in the Federal Republic since 1974, but only in ''private'' clubs, of which there are large chains. That restriction and the German public's fondness for semi-erotica about the sexual awakening of schoolchildren—a sort of *Bildungsfilm* reflex—has forestalled the gearing up of a hard-core feature industry there. Instead, the PAM chains simply screen American imports. The case has been different in France. Once Gaullist prudery had been overthrown, French film-makers quickly accumulated a surplus of explicit features, in 1975 exporting samples like Jean-François Davy's *Exhibition* (a hit at the New York Film Festival), Frederic Lansac's *Pussy Talk,* and R. Pieri's *Candy's Candy.* That year, it is said, sex films accounted for one quarter of all French movie production.[4] Bewildered, the Giscard government at first tried to make a profit and to protect it against American traders: it imposed double taxation on porn, seized an additional twenty percent of the gross, and subjected American imports to a $60,000 duty. Even so, of the porn features exhibited in France during 1976, 32 percent were American-made.[5] At the end of 1976, worried about the country's image, the French Minister of Culture moved toward outlawing its own porn for foreign distribution by denying export licences. Should that trend continue, Americans will have clear sailing, at least until the Japanese get going.

The marketing of Jonas Middleton's latest film, *Through the Looking Glass,* illustrates the American pornographer's strategy. A veteran producer-director (his 1973 *Illusions of a Lady* enjoyed a vogue among aficionados), Middleton raised his hefty $200,000 budget from respectable sources and assembled a cast of fifty, large for the genre. Well-publicized in *Playboy* and *Penthouse* before release, it opened with ads that read, "A film that is aimed at the same sophisticated couples market that was attracted to last year's 'Emmanuelle.' " By any standard, *Through the Looking Glass* is arty, if not always tasteful. After sixteen weeks on *Variety's* Top-Grossing chart, it had brought in almost $600,000. By contrast, *The Lollipop Girls in Hard Candy,* some scruffy footage in 3-D, in eighteen weeks racked up $1,000,000,[6] in part because of wider distribution. Middleton's gross is hardly spectacular, although it will probably increase steadily (old porn films never die), but so will the gross of the junk film. On the other hand, Middleton's backers presumably will receive a percentage of the book tie-in; Dell published the novelization of the script. Moreover, Middleton shot *Through the Looking Glass* in one hard-core and two soft-core versions so that he could distribute to three types of audience (hard X, soft X, and R). Next he sold the rights to exhibitors in Denmark and Greece, to Rizzoli for circulation in Portugal and Italy, and at last report was dickering with the Japanese and other nationalities. At the Cannes Film Festival this year, Middleton will offer his film in 35mm, 16mm, and video-cassette to foreign purchasers. Apparently the overseas connections are lucrative, for he has announced that his own Mastermind Films (NYC) will co-produce his next venture with his Danish distributor, Panorama Film A/S (Copenhagen).[7]

In addition, Middleton has another "partner"—the U.S. government. With varying degrees of effectiveness, American Customs routinely blocks hard-core feature imports (the most celebrated example was the seizure of Oshima's *In the Realm of the Senses* on its way to the New York Film Festival in 1976), but, unlike France, the U.S. does not restrict films shipped abroad. The ironic result is a virtual protective tariff that is financially significant: the U.S. is not only the largest producer of porn films but also the largest consumer. In the absence of statistics, it is probably accurate to say that Middleton and his colleagues contribute to a favorable balance of payments. Selling overseas is also a hedge against a lackluster market in America.

With some exceptions, most notably Derek Ford's *Diversions* (Britain, 1976), probably the best porn feature ever made, the top-drawer American product has the edge over the European. Now that Arriflexes and Panavision cameras have replaced handheld Bolexes, it is quite polished and likely to become more so, as professional crews continue to gravitate to the porno sets from television. The affinities with video are strong, especially in the relationship between director and producer; the latter exercises considerable control in both media. Thus, a Summer Brown, a doyenne of American entrepreneurs, can direct *China Girl* (1974) or produce *The Joy of Letting Go* (1976) with equally elegant effect. It is much too soon for auteur treatments of porn directors, but enough time has passed for individual styles like Brown's to evolve. The most discernible is that of Alex de Renzy (*Sweet Agony, Femmes de Sade*), who decorates his sets in Early San Francisco Bordello and shoots in wide angles that take advantage of them. Radley Metzger (*The Private Afternoons of Pamela Mann, The Opening of Misty Beethoven*), who once confessed that *his* favorite director is Michael Powell (*Red Shoes, Stairway to Heaven*), is lavish with locations and skilled at staging polymorphous-perverse sexual couplings. Dexter Eagle *(Temptations, Blonde Velvet)* focuses tightly and manipulates plots exuberantly. Amanda Barton *(The Passions of Carol, Midnight Desires)* balances explicit intimacy with good humor.

Frank Rich has pointed out in the *New York Post* that a middling effort like Philip Drexler's *Oriental Blue* (1975) is "structurally on a par" with *The Prisoner of Second Avenue* and makes better use of urban locations than *Sheila Levine Is Dead and Living in New York*.[8] Lest they be praised overmuch, however, it should be noted that whatever the talents lavished on porn, so far their shades of blue do not add up to a coherent spectrum. Craft and crudity war: if a director achieves silky, poetic cinema tones or choreographs bodies balletically, he will blow the continuity or fail in something else. Below the top level, all porn features are dogs, and there is little point in picking best of breed. Even the slickest share faults: scenes held too long, excessive close-ups of genitals, jerky editing, under-lighting, out-of-sync sound tracks. No American porn flick has yet managed a big-studio look.

That does not prevent the pornographers from trying. Middleton has stressed the literary origins (a Russian short story) of *Through the Looking Glass,* has said that, with his adaptation, he is "trying to upgrade the genre . . . and get into a sophisticated" plot, and prefers to call the result a "psychological thriller, supernatural sex, not really a porno."[9] Borrowing from literary modes is popular. Among other recent examples are Armand Weston's *Expose Me, Lovely* (1976), Metzger's *The Opening of Misty Beethoven* (1975), and Barton's *The Passions of Carol* (1974), which respectively rip-off Chandler's *Farewell My Lovely,* Shaw's *Pygmalion,* and Dickens' *A Christmas Carol.* Spoofing of literary or other targets—as in, say, *The Pleasureable Sins of Reverend Star* (1976), which laughs at the Korean Sun Myung Moon—is properly within an honorable tradition, satire having been a function of pornography over the centuries. Unlike these other examples, however, Middleton's is a serious attempt to submerge the sex in symbolism, to offset blatant intimacy with psychologically redeeming importance.

Through the Looking Glass is competently photographed in excellent color, splendidly scored, and occasionally adept in its treatment of its graphic if not original (one reviewer remarked that Middleton must have been "frightened by Fellini") treatment of incest and madness. Major porn stars like Jaime Gillis, Kim Pope, and Terri Hall handle most of the sex, but the leading lady is Catherine Burgess, also known as Cary Lacey when she appeared in *Expose Me, Lovely* and as Catharine Earnshaw (Burgess must have been frightened by Emily Brönte) in Bob Gill's *The Double Exposure of Holly* (1976). A former mannequin for *Vogue,* Burgess has joined fellow models Kristine De Bell *(Alice in Wonderland),* formerly of the Eileen Ford Agency, and Dominique St. Pierre *(The Joy of Letting Go),* from the stables of Halston and Courrèges, in this final refuge of narcissism. Presumably they and the endless stream of new starlets hope for celebrity, but the chances of becoming the next Marilyn Chambers (now about to appear in *Rabid!,* her first "dramatic" role) are slim. The Screen Actors Guild still ignores porn. Georgina Spelvin, who made the journey from Radio City Rockette to star of *The Devil in Miss Jones,* has had her troubles in Memphis. Linda Lovelace, save for an occasional Las Vegas date, is in eclipse. Andrea True *(Illusions of a Lady)* has turned rock singer on the strength of "More, More, More" (Buddah Records), and Bree Anthony, stalwart of countless features, has metamorphosed into Sue Richards, publisher of *High Society* magazine.

Because the raincoat brigade—the economic underpinning of the industry— tires quickly without new performers, the scouting for talent renders female careers short. As nubility gives way to coarseness, which happens abruptly, as if a Dorian Gray syndrome were operative, the women drop out, drift into related work, such as writing columns for *Cheri* or *Screw,* or wind up in production. Producing, casting, and directing now occupy Darby Lloyd Rains, Sandi Foxx, and Tina Russell. Ex-performers are valuable because they know their way around sets, have studied the best camera angles (perhaps the most important aspect of the feature), and can give pointers to novice crews. In some respects, this personnel feedback is reminiscent of the early days of the cinema, when actors like William S. Hart became directors churning out formula westerns. Like any formula genre, the porn feature is highly self-reflexive, so that, in a sense, it forever turns back upon itself to make obeisance to the tradition from which it derives. To a degree, this tradition has been fed by the nudies of the late fifties and early sixties—Radley Metzger, for instance, came to hard-core from a career of them *(Camille 2000, The Lickerish Quartet)*—but its true roots are the stag films, the silent, flickering black and white image unreeling in thousands of American Legion and fraternity halls of the past.

The stag film itself survives as the ubiquitous 8mm loop, staple of arcade peep-shows in the urban tenderloins of the nation, where it continues to pollinate the feature by crossbreeding. Performers and cameramen support themselves between gigs by making loops (John C. Holmes, of the massive penis, has appeared in over two thousand) which, conversely, provide training for the larger screen. Yet the newer form leans on the older in more profound ways. Many early features were narrative compilations of stag films, the best being De Renzy's *History of the Blue Movie* (1970), or quasi-documentaries on the shooting of stags, a format which persists, so that even today a sizable percentage of features are "about" the making of pornography. Such a scheme not only permits a rapid, credible disrobing and bedding of performers, but also adds the *frisson* of voyeurism within voyeurism as the "real" camera follows photographers filming the action. Central to any hard-core film is the presence, pictured or implied, of a camera intruding on intimate behavior. Perhaps more than is the case with any medium save television, this consciousness of the lens is essential to its appeal and is the chief reason why features keep touching old bases. In *China Girl,* for instance, Oriental villains video-monitor the sexual peccadillos of prominent scientists; in *The Double Exposure of Holly* (the title is significant), video-tapes of her trysts ruin a haughty, unfaithful wife; in *Blonde Velvet,* a spy ring blackmails diplomats by means of concealed cameras, and at the end, the spy-mistress says that she will turn the tapes over to Dexter Eagle, the actual director of the film—such twists are commonplace and respected as indices of deliberate artifice.

To say, then, as do critics and not a few aesthetically inclined producers, that the hard-core feature requires more subtlety, is to forget that camera convention. Given the porn movie's reason for being, the depiction of actual sex through the violation of public and private taboo, the camera's presence is always blatant whether its focus is ethereal and gauzy or grainy and harsh. The intrusion always shocks. Over seven decades, the stag film has evolved formulas and clichés to cushion the impact, and they have been transmuted into patterns within the feature film as well. Frequently lamented by the critic as boring, the cushioning devices are crucial: popular belief to the contrary, sex has not lost its mystery or its power, and without the cut-out characters and the erotic templates, film pornography would probably be intolerable to those who enjoy it most. Protective on the one hand, restrictive on the other, but ontologically necessary in either case, the conventions help to explain why it is so difficult for a pornographer aesthetically to improve his product in any meaningful sense.

It might be argued that the more the porn feature departs from the form of the early stag, the less erotic it is, that the greater length of the former, for instance, robs it of the appeal of the latter, whose brevity is less likely to bore the audience. If the silent film is "the most voluptuous art form ever devised," as Jack Kroll has said,[10] then the mere addition of sound may be a liability. Certainly collectors have been discovering that old stags have considerable charm. Vintage porn offers eroticism aged and layered, lacquered in fading sepia tones of nostalgia. Its age confers a kind of innocence and blunts its threatening aspects—it seems quaint beside the graphic, convention-lacking celluloid which unreels in the peep-shows of the seventies. And yet, the early stags are reminders that sexual fantasies change but little.

The compilations of male and female sexual fantasies currently flogged in magazines and books also suggest that people are turned on by similar scenarios. Ascribing archetypicality to them is unnecessary, especially since it is impossible to decide whether the fantasies derive from an actual mental set or from cultural—and pornographically traditional—influences. At the very least, these fantasies are chestnuts to be prized for whatever warmth they bring to pornography. Given greater importance on a psychic scale, conventionalized fantasies may literally shape the individual's sexuality, sometimes with such urgency that he seeks to mesh fantasy and reality in highly ritualized behavior, like acting out iconographic S–M scenes with others so inclined. For the less driven, those content with a moderately rich fantasy life, pornography may feed and frustrate needs.

The storehouse of pornographic tradition contains multitudes, from simple penchants for garter belts and anachronistic lingerie to complex erotic situations, most of which replicate endlessly in the feature film. The principal difference between the 1924 stag *Slow-Fire Dentist* and the 1974 feature *Dental Nurses* is that the first jokes about drills, cavities, and anesthetized females silently for only twelve minutes, while the second requires a talky ninety. Fluid as it is, the human libido can attach itself to virtually anything, but generally wish-fulfillment seeks standard constructs, so that the characters in stags and features are stereotyped. Historically, stags have been weighted toward lower-class tastes, partly because they were shot illicitly on farms, in basements, and in dingy hotels, partly because they were aimed at a blue collar and lower-middle-class market. Stealthy encounters between nondescript males and obvious prostitutes gave way to greater definition of male roles, most of them demotic, if not exactly variations on D. H. Lawrence's gamekeeper: window washers, grocery boys, bell-hops, salesmen, plumbers, janitors. Gradually, as stags spread more widely, middle-class roles developed. Lust-crazed doctors, dentists, students, teachers, artists, and photographers seduced or were seduced by randy females, who fall into less succinct occupational roles: the love-starved librarian, the repressed schoolteacher, the nymphomaniac housewife, the female executive yearning to be dominated, and so on. By and large, stags were democratic, their theme that passion recognizes no class boundaries.

Although early (1968–1972) features made use of similar characters and themes, recent attempts to enhance the genre have fastened on decadent aristocrats in elegantly perverse settings. To an extent this trend suggests that domestic pornographers are distancing themselves from native American vulgarity by drawing on Victorian English and French erotic vocabularies. From another perspective, it suggests the survival of the Las Vegas Syndrome, so called after a cultural attitude prevalent in the fifties, which approved lavishly mounted nude extravangazas for big spenders able to vacation in Nevada but condemned strippers in home-town bars for beer drinkers who had to take their pleasure where they found it. Class-conscious taste still leads critics to distinguish between, say, Bob Chinn's well shot "Johnny Wadd" series (*Liquid Lips* [1976], *Tell Them Wadd is Here* [1976]), which relies on performers in average occupational roles, and Damiano's *Story of Joanna* (a loose adaptation of *Story of O*) or *The Opening of Misty Beethoven,* both of which involve moneyed types gone degenerate. In *Misty Beethoven,* the female lead is played by an actress named Constance Money, to suggest affluence. As we have already noted, that film derives from *Pygmalion,* and its success is at least partly a function of the congruence between Shaw's plot line and an ancient porn formula in which an older male educates a young girl into sexual knowingness. Despite their efforts at novelty, Metzger and Damiano respect conventions.

Pseudo-elegance also governs *Through the Looking Glass,* whose protagonists are members of the horsey set, yet parts of that film are extremely distasteful. When Middleton tries to jettison formulas, he is usually grotesque. For example, figures coated with paint or excrement cavort in surreal sequences representing a tormented psyche. Strictly speaking, there is not much actual sex, so that Middleton's intent loses itself between slickness and coarseness, but his film is superior to most of the trash turned out by the industry. At that other extreme, hacks like the aptly pseudonymous "Oscar Tripe" *(Come Fly with Us, The Love Bus)* eschew formulas and conventions in favor of gritty improvisations of non-stop sex routines. The result is cheap grubbiness.

Equally mistaken are the amateurs who load their scripts with sententiousness. Prominent in the repertoire of pornography are humorous formulas that have evolved to balance the natural gravity of sex and to encourage defensive laughter: the beauty who actually is a man in drag, the Milquetoast who turns out to have a monstrous organ, the woman who resists conquest because she has venereal disease, which she reveals after her seducer has scored, and many others of equal age, almost all of them turning on "expected" surprise. *Deep Throat* was a smash in this country partly because of the then-freakish talents of its fellatrice and partly because of its amusing surprises. Damiano combined a classically comic porn formula revolving around a wacky, sex-mad doctor with a parody of the American fetish for the perfect orgasm and the sententiousness it attracts in the marriage manuals. When Lovelace finally does learn to manipulate the "clitoris in her throat" through fellatio, Damiano punctuates her orgasms by cutting to frames of bursting rockets, waving flags, and stirring music. About the only thing missing from the exaggeration is Ernest Hemingway intoning "The earth moved."

Cathedral tones and Lawrentian paeans to physicality, couched in terms that insist that sex—usually masquerading as affection—is its own justification, are no substitute for formulas. Paradoxes dwell at the heart of porn: the hard-core film may tug at male romantic sensibilities just as straightforwardly as *True Confessions* and *Popular Romance* pull at those of females, yet out-and-out pornography has little to do with love, and there is no reason why it should. Given the imperatives of eroticism, objectification—the reification of desire beyond affection or even good sense—is essential. Pornography must continually assault barriers and menace taboos, whose power is dependent on the individual viewer, else it cannot be erotic. Eroticism flows from a vision of the irresponsible, the wild, and the anarchic and crystallizes out of super-saturated fantasy. Like myth, like dream, pornography accomplishes its intent through glimpses of the unlikely, occasionally the unspeakable, made flesh—or made object.

The function of formulas in pornography is to allow audiences to traverse a seamy side of life without being defiled by it. Vladimir Nabokov once remarked that pornography has no style, just content; and, while the contention has application to some filmed pornography—e.g., modern loops that concentrate on extreme perversion without any buffering convention—it does not acknowledge traditional formulaic devices. In Westerns, stereotypes and clichés unite in well-proved recipes to shield the viewer's sensibility from the aggression inherent in that genre. The cowboy hero never draws first, never betrays a friend, never harms a woman, but having observed those codes, may slaughter his enemies with impunity. The Western's conventions legitimize violence, permit anarchic behavior in the midst of a society that values order, though to be sure the typical frontier setting is still raw and not yet fully socialized. Like the gun-fights which take place on the edge of civilization in the Western, sexual encounters flourish on the frontier of socialization in the porn flick. Because our culture has rationalized violence more than it has sexuality, the Western's formulas are better defined and more rigid, yet pornographic formulas also legitimize anarchy otherwise unacceptable in an ordered society and are probably even more essential. Just as conventions offset the brutality of a .45 slug ripping through a chest in the shoot-'em-up, so they offset the visible invasion of flesh in the porn film, where the impact of penetration, measured by social opprobrium, is even greater (the usual response of a first-time viewer of hard-core is "Omygod! They're actually doing it!").

Liberal pieties have little to do with the real business of the porn film, the creation of an arena in which someone dominates and someone submits. In our culture, that is what eroticism comes down to, as we are continually reminded by authors as diverse as Norman Mailer and Gael Greene, Henry Miller and Erica Jong. In a recent letter to the correspondence column of *Club* magazine, a patron of porn features wrote that he doted on just that aspect: "It's a sort of reflected glory thing I guess. When I see pictures of John Holmes' superb 12" dick in full erection I feel proud of my sex: it's like my team winning at football." If this Nixonian metaphor of sex as stadium sport is amusing, it does offer insight into fantasies commonly purveyed in films, some of which are decidedly macho. Depending on the film, male stereotypes can range from redneck to sophisticated stud. Ludicrous on the one hand, dead-serious on the other, the supermasculine types doubtless appeal to dark shapes in balconies across the country. And yet, contrary to received wisdom, not all features—nor stags, for that matter—depict satyriatic males. Reversed roles are equally common, for otherwise there would be no need for an arena. Fairly typical is the insatiable goddess, a part played with verve by Jennifer Welles *(Honeypie, Sweet Cakes),* New York's reigning porn queen, a Marilyn Monroe look-alike, who dyes both her tresses and her pubic hair, and who exhausts every male she meets.

Such females are more than a match for their male antagonists, however well endowed. Indeed, the larger the penis, the less personality the male usually possesses. Holmes and his colleagues are mere pegs on which nothing hangs, sperm banks and little else, whereas the women are the focus of attention. Should the female appear initially as colorless, once her desire is unlocked she will take on grandeur that threatens to overshadow the male: Temple Drakes are always more interesting than Popeyes. To celebrate a penis is to release ambiguities similar to those that result from putting a woman on a pedestal: the male becomes objectified, a toy, devoid of personality, vulnerable, with only his organ standing (maybe) between himself and anonymity, in a position roughly equivalent to the cowboy who has only his gun to defend himself from extinction. The pornographer assumes that the mystery of sex can be compelled to reveal itself if all the normal attributes of individuality can be stripped from the participants: that the encounter will be more primal if both parties to the act (the male as well as the female) can be transformed into objects.

Fear is the other side of domination; it sharpens the tension which shapes the pornographic response. Female sexuality endangers male order. That is the reason why the *Club* correspondent's metaphor is not inappropriate. As with football, as with high-noon showdowns in Laredo, as with primitive rites, there must be rules, formulas and codes and clichés, to circumscribe and contain potential anarchy. Without them, the prospect is anxiety. While these formulas may not offer what Susan Sontag calls "moral resonance," they do provide moral protection, at least of a sort, in that existential moment toward which pornography strives.

Still, where they are in force and germane, formulas alone cannot even the odds. Clearly, many porn features degrade women. Equally clearly, many do not, simply because the female must at least sometimes be the male's equal or his superior in order that their encounter be significant. Now more and more often directed by women, heterosexual hard-core films are obviously oriented

Fifi Watson in *Mona, the Virgin Nymph* (1970).

toward males, but the sexuality they carry must be ratified by females. The Western hero can kill his opponent in a duel as long as both agree to the conditions. The male porn protagonist can perform any sexual act with a female, but if he is operating within conventions—and of course he may not be—only with her explicit or implied consent. He may seduce or overpower her and be justified when she responds with a passion equivalent to his own: she must acknowledge the thrust of her own sexuality, which abates the guilt of the male. Crude exceptions notwithstanding, within a formulaic scenario, the male may not rape a female—unless he is depicted as deranged—without it being clear that she "really wants it." If he does, the conventions dictate a bad end for him. In this regard, the traditional values endorsed in the porn flick are remarkable. Poetic endings are common: the brutal male will be punished, the unfaithful wife will return to her husband, the nymphomaniac will find happiness with a Marlboro man, the irresponsible Don Juan will fall hopelessly in love. After anarchy has been indulged, order prevails in the final frames. Love—manifest as a coming to one's senses or as a forsaking of eroticism— not infrequently triumphs.

The formulas which encapsulate the vision of unleashed sexuality presumably can be satisfying in themselves. In his essay on wrestling, Roland Barthes has observed that the stereotypical activity of that sport bores the casual spectator but holds nuance and subtlety for the aficionado. Monotonous to some, the sexual couplings in films are like wrestling holds seen a hundred times before, valuable to the initiated precisely because of the minute variations on the familiar. Robert Warshow has made a similar point concerning the self-reflexivity of the gangster film. Originality in that genre, he says, "is to be welcomed only in the degree that it intensifies the expected experience without fundamentally altering it." The genre "appeals to previous experience of the type itself: it creates its own field of reference."[11]

Erotic formulas, however, differ in important ways from those in Western or gangster films. Like happiness, eroticism is at best measured in moments. Buried deep or carried near the surface of the psyche, our particular fantasies are colored by respect for certain powerful taboos, against which we calibrate those moments. While we ordinarily violate those taboos mentally, in secret, as expressions of our personal sexuality, some of these forbidden longings we share with others. Formulaic patterns fix, compress, and intensify such fantasies: they become models for erotic moments. That does not mean that the individual cannot enjoy spontaneous arousal or experience serendipitous moments, just as the prevalence of formulas in pornography does not rule out novelty. It probably does mean that people respond to certain patterns of behavior more readily than to others. It is possible that members of the raincoat brigade sit through hours of trash in search of a formula that especially gratifies them. Behind the hokum and the hackwork, they may find moments of eroticism authentic for them, some set that fits, or they may not; but hope would seem to spring eternal, for they return again and again.

What turns one individual on may turn another off. Moreover, pornographic conventions—being partly personal—have not imposed themselves on general public consciousness to the degree that their counterparts in the Western or the gangster film have, although they are surely familiar to the raincoat brigade. Neither the occasional patron nor the average director is necessarily aware of their age or power. The director who thinks he has come up with something new more often than not is merely recycling a pattern long since reduced to repertoire. On the other hand, he may find something so freaky that no formula can make it palatable. Considering the urges of eroticism, the constant need to transgress limitations, psychic chaos may overwhelm any convention. After all, no convention could contain the fantasies of the Marquis de Sade. The material in his works remains fundamentally disquieting.

Recognize them or not, the porn film director cannot escape using some formulas, which are as inherent to the medium as they are to television melodrama: the trick is to use them well. Nonetheless, he faces special problems stemming from the momentary nature of eroticism. Sexual encounters are discrete in themselves, complete in very brief compass. As depicted on screen, acts of intercourse are intended to arouse. The raincoat brigadier may masturbate to orgasm, after which he must wait on another moment and his own physical recovery. Yet not all viewers, least of all those sophisticates at which the quality-minded producer is aiming, require immediate gratification. Even so, virtually every act on-screen culminates in orgasm (a convention itself), and "the little death," ironically, is more final than, say, a killing in a Western. It halts the plot. Successive literal climaxes ultimately weaken dramatic ones. Thus, although a formula may be perfectly tailored to encapsulate the sex in a short stag-film scenario, it may actually undermine the dramatic possibilities of the longer feature by preventing the development of a coherent plot. The very discreteness of the formulas may mandate an episodic form. Acceptance of that notion has made Derek Ford's *Diversions* a very workmanlike film. In it, the heroine fantasizes in vignettes. She imagines herself as a rape victim turned vengeful toward males, a captive of lustful Nazis, a photographer's seductive model, a pretend prostitute, and so on, all of these roles being tied together in her consciousness. With such an approach, pacing becomes paramount, and Ford excels at it. Thus far, no American director has employed similar techniques so well or caressed clichés so lovingly.

Beyond such special considerations, the pornographic feature director must deal with his formulas like directors in other conventionalized genres. If he does not use the conventions, the audience will not enjoy the security of the familiar, behind which lurks the mystery of sex with its risk of confusion. If he uses them too slavishly, without novelty or whimsicality, the result will be predictability and boredom. Nowadays, with money and talent at his disposal, some director should theoretically be able to shoot the porn equivalent of a *Shane* or a *Stagecoach*. Until that occurs, the porn feature will receive neither careful critical attention nor extravagant box office rewards.

NOTES

 1. Addison Verrill. "Parisi Sees Porn Market Off, Now Averages $150,000–$300,000," *Variety,* 9 June 1976, p. 42.
 2. "Assert Pornopic Market Still Big," *Variety,* 19 January 1977, p. 1.
 3. Hazel Guild, "Germany's United Church Assn. Rolls Drive Vs. Porn Pix, Books," *Variety,* 9 June 1976, p. 44.
 4. "France Discovers Porn," *Oui* (April, 1976), pp. 82–91.
 5. "International Sound Track," *Variety,* 30 March 1977, p. 32.
 6. "50 Top-Grossing Films," *Variety,* 23 February 1977, p. 9.
 7. "Mifed Murmurings," *Variety,* 10 November 1976, p. 28; "U.S. Porn Producer Goes O'Seas for 'Fresh Faces, More Natural Attitudes,' " *Variety,* 24 November 1976, p. 23; "Soft-X and Hard-R Versions of Porn; Adopt 'Smart' Tactics," *Variety,* 16 March 1977, p. 5.
 8. Frank Rich, "Movies: Sex Is Just a Four-Letter Word," *The New York Post,* 6 September 1975, pp. 14, 40.
 9. Jonas Middleton interviewed by Alex Bennett, on "Midnight Blue's America," Channel J, Teleprompter TV, New York City, 2 October 1976.
10. Jack Kroll, "Voluptuous Silence," *Newsweek,* 10 January 1977, p. 65.
11. Robert Warshow, *The Immediate Experience* (Garden City, N.Y.: Doubleday Anchor Books, 1964), p. 85.

FOUR/MOVIES AND THEIR TIMES

MAINSTREAM AMERICAN CULTURE HAS evolved through a variety of periods of change and development. Each period, whether it lasts for just a few years or for decades, seems to have its own particular character. Because movies have traditionally been made in such great numbers and therefore have had short and immediate public lives, movies take on the tenor of their times. And because movie-makers have always known that, to be successful, their product must satisfy the values and tastes of their specific audiences, movies often provide one of the best ways to understand elements both visible and hidden in the people of different cultural eras.

At times, certain types of movies emerge that capture the feelings and thoughts of the period. In other instances, a single film seems to sum up the entire experience of a generation. The essays in this chapter demonstrate both of these tendencies.

The 1930s in America were years of economic hardship. Social drama films of the time stressed the virtue of hard work and pulling together toward a common reward. Other films offered a fantasy world of escape from the strident realities of everyday life. Both types of films tell us at least as much about the audience as about the subject matter on the screen. Thomas Pauly's article on *Gone with the Wind* and *The Grapes of Wrath* demonstrates how both realistic films about rural economic hardships and romantic films centering on dreams of bygone times sum up the fears and frustrations of urban moviegoers at the end of the 1930s.

Brian Murphy, in his article on 1950s monster movies, illustrates how genres peculiar to a specific period demonstrate some of the obsessions of that era. He describes how the films reveal public fears of science, foreign powers, atomic energy, and conformity with such depressing consistency that we should look at the 1950s not as a golden era of simple, pleasant lives but rather as a twentieth century ''wasteland'' filled with boredom and repression.

No specific genre unites the films in Vivian Sobchack's study of certain 1970s films, ''The Violent Dance.'' What marks all of the films in her essay is their renditions of violent death in gory yet often poetic detail. Sobchack's approach to her subject, like Murphy's, is a reflection based on personal experience. In Sobchack's writing, however, we experience along with her an attempt to explain culturally why she and millions of other 1970s moviegoers were fascinated by movie content that common sense and rudimentary good taste both suggest would normally be repulsive.

Finally, John Yates takes up an analysis of two 1970s films, *Godfather* and *Godfather, Part II*, to suggest contemporary American attitudes toward the family. Like the other articles in this chapter, ''The Godfather Saga'' clearly shows that, although people have always gone to the movies to be entertained, we apparently have need to be ''entertained'' by reflections of our fears, failings, and discouragements, as well as by our hopes and triumphs.

Gone with the Wind and The Grapes of Wrath as Hollywood Histories of the Depression

THOMAS H. PAULY

Popular culture of the later Depression years was dominated by *Gone with the Wind* and *The Grapes of Wrath*. As novels, these two creations topped the best seller lists during 1936, 1937, and 1939. Interest in both works was then renewed in early 1940—perhaps even reached its greatest peak—when both opened as movies within weeks of one another (*Gone with the Wind* on December 15, 1939, and *Grapes of Wrath* on January 24, 1940). Though both were tremendous box office successes, their critics responded to each quite differently. While the reviews of *Gone with the Wind* strove to top one another with accounts of all the gossip, glitter, and money involved in the making of *Gone with the Wind*, those discussing *The Grapes of Wrath* stressed the outstanding quality of the film itself. "No artifical make-up, no false sentiment, no glamor stars mar the authentic documentary form of this provocative film," asserted Philip Hartung in his review of *The Grapes of Wrath* for *Commonweal*.[1] Similarly, Otis Ferguson was confident enough of the dissatisfaction *Gone with the Wind* would bring that he postponed going,[2] but he opened his review entitled "Show for the People," "The word that comes in most handily for *The Grapes of Wrath* is magnificent . . . this is the best that has no very near comparison to date."[3] Despite the overwhelming critical preference for Ford's movie, however, it won only one Oscar (Best Director) in the 1940 balloting, whereas Selznick's extravaganza swept all the major awards in 1939 except one (Best Actor). Clearly, the latter film was the people's choice. At issue here was an intense, unacknowledged debate over what the age preferred in its movies. In an era fraught with intense sociological upheaval, *Gone with the Wind* seemed consciously intended to project its audience into a realm of sentiment and nostalgia beyond the confines of actual experience. As Lincoln Kirstein complained in the opening paragraph of his scathing review for *Films:*

> . . . history has rarely been told with even an approximation of truth in Hollywood, because the few men in control there have no interest in the real forces behind historical movements and the new forces that every

new epoch sets into motion. *Gone with the Wind* deserves our attention because it is an over-inflated example of the usual, the false movie approach to history.[4]

Implicit in these remarks is a charge often leveled against the movies produced during this era. Critics and historians of the cinema repeatedly call attention to Hollywood's striking reluctance to address itself to the problems of the Depression. Nothing, they point out, could have been further from the bread lines and the deprivation photographed by Dorothea Lange than the social comedies of Lubitsch, the slapstick of the Marx Brothers, and the polished dance routines of Fred Astaire and Ginger Rogers. Nonetheless, as Andrew Bergman has asserted and then persuasively demonstrated in his book on films of the Depression, *We're in the Money,* "People do not escape into something they cannot relate to. The movies were meaningful because they depicted things lost or things desired. What is 'fantastic' in fantasy is an extension of something real."[5] In other words, the "dreams" the audience is said to have demanded, those for which they spent the little extra money they had, were not mere illusions or abstractions but exciting, imaginative articulations of their greatest hopes and fears, their deepest doubts and beliefs. On this score, *Gone with the Wind* possesses a significant measure of both historical validity and importance. The fact that it was far and away the most successful film of the decade probably had less to do with the glittering surface that so annoyed the critics than the common ground it shared with *The Grapes of Wrath.* Though it was less daring and less accomplished than Ford's work as an artistic creation, *Gone with the Wind* was similarly preoccupied with the problem of survival in the face of financial deprivation and social upheaval. Both movies also demonstrate a nostalgic longing for the agrarian way of life which is ruthlessly being replaced by the fearful new economic forces of capitalism and industrialization. By way of extension, both reflect an intense concern for the devastating consequences of these conditions upon self-reliant individualism and family unity, two of America's most cherished beliefs. In each case, however, serious concern for these implications is dissipated into indulgent sentimentalism so that the audience's anxieties are alleviated rather than aggravated.

Even if the script had been available, *The Grapes of Wrath* dealt with issues that were too familiar and too painful to have been made during the early thirties. Yet, in deciding to produce a movie of this controversial novel at the time he did, Darryl Zanuck was sufficiently concerned about the specter of the Depression that he decided to mute and even eliminate some of the more charged aspects of Steinbeck's social criticism.[6] As Mel Gussow has explained, "For Zanuck, *The Grapes of Wrath* and *How Green Was My Valley* were not really social documents but family pictures of a very special kind; movies about families in stress.''[7] Thus, the movie's emphasis falls upon the sentimental aspect of the conditions confronting the Joads. At the outset, this takes the character of the loss of a home, which deprives the family of its essential connection with the land. Tom's initial return assumes the character of a search for a place of refuge from the suffering and hostility he has been forced to endure in prison and on his truck ride. That everything has changed is made clear by his encounter with Casy; but the full impact of this upheaval is registered only when he beholds the vacant, crumbling house in which he was raised and hears Muley's distracted tale of how his reverence for the land has been desecrated. "My pa was born here," he insists; "We was *all* born on it, and some of us got killed on it, and some died on it. And that's what makes it ourn. . . ."[8] Equally striking in this regard is the later scene where Grampa asserts, "I ain't a-goin' to California! This here's my country. I b'long *here*. It ain't no good—but it's mine,"[9] and then underlines his points by distractedly gripping his native soil.

   In dramatizing the intense suffering these people experience, these lines

John Carradine, Henry Fonda, and John Qualen in *The Grapes of Wrath* (1940).

serve the more important function of locating its source. The former agrarian way of life predicated upon man's intimate attachment to the land has given way to an economy of industrialization with its efficiency, practicality, and inhumanity. For Tom and his fellow farmers, there is no possibility of retaliation. The fury that drives Muley to take up a gun produces only frustration and helpless dejection because there is no enemy to shoot. The man on the caterpillar turns out to be his neighbor who is trapped by the same problem of survival. The machines that level their homes, like the foreclosures which are delivered in dark, sinister automobiles, cannot be associated with particular individuals; they are the weapons of a system devoid of both personality and humanity.

The Man: Now don't go blaming me. It ain't *my* fault.
Son: Whose fault is it? . . .
The Man: It ain't nobody. It's a company. He ain't anything but the manager. . . .
Muley (bewildered): Then who *do* we shoot?
The Man: . . . Brother, I don't know.[10]

Deprived of the only home he has known, Tom Joad joins his family in their quest for a new one. However great may be their need for food and money, keeping the family together, Ma Joad makes clear, is the most pressing concern. She sees that nourishment involves the spirit as well and in the face of the increasingly depersonalized world confronting her, the shared concerns of the family offer the only remaining source of humanity. These become the basic issues by which the audience measures the significance of the ensuing trip to California. As Ford dramatizes them, the policemen who harass the Joads, the strawbosses who dictate to them, the thugs who break up the dances and union gatherings are, like the handbills that bring them to California, products of a sinister conspiracy beyond human control. They combine with the inhospitable landscape encountered to create an environment in which the family is unable to survive. Grampa and Gramma die before the destination is reached; Connie cannot stand up to the punishment inflicted upon him and flees; Casy is killed by the growers' hired guns; having avenged Casy's death, Tom is forced to flee for his life.[11]

The Grapes of Wrath, however, is more than a mere drama of defeat. The futility of individualism and the breakdown of the family furnish, in the end, a distinct source of optimism. Having witnessed the miserable living conditions in which the Joads have futilely struggled to endure—the filthy tent in the clapboard road camp, the concentration of starving people in Hooverville, the gloomy squalor of the cabin at the Keene ranch—the audience is now introduced to a utopia of cooperative socialism which has been as scrupulously

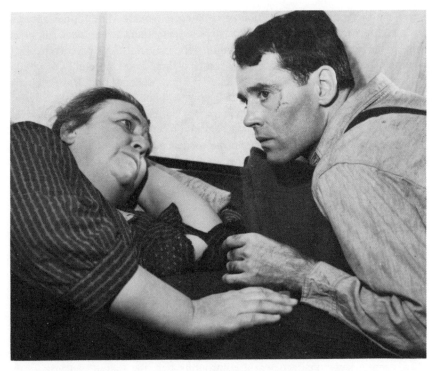

Jane Darwell and Henry Fonda in *The Grapes of Wrath* (1940).

sanitized of communism as it is of filth. In contrast to the derogatory view expressed earlier in the movie, working with the government is shown to offer a more valid prospect of salvation than fighting against the prevailing conditions; at the Wheat Patch camp, the spirit of Tom's involvement with Casy is realized without the self-defeating violence and killing. Here, as George Bluestone notes, the Joads find "a kind of miniature planned economy, efficiently run, boasting modern sanitation, self-government, cooperative living, and moderate prices."[12] Here, people work together with the same automatic efficacy as the flush toilets. Cleanliness nourishes kindness, the caretaker explains with the serene wisdom of his kindly confident manner (does he remind you of FDR?).

Even the language has been changed to accord with this new society; one finds here not a shelter, a house, or a home, but a "sanitary unit." Though this community has been conceived to accord with the depersonalized society outside its gates, it has also incorporated a basic respect for human dignity. It is a world characterized by its Saturday dance with its democratic acceptance, its well-controlled exclusion of the forces of anarchy, its ritualistic incorporation of the outdated family into a healthy new society—a new society which would actually be realized only two years later in the "comfortable" concentration camps for Japanese-Americans during World War II. Above all, the Wheat Patch camp episode affords a bridge to the "new" ending Zanuck was moved to write for his movie.[13] As Tom and the Joad truck return to the outside world and strike out in different directions, they have no idea where they are going, but they all have renewed hope that they can find salvation just by being with "the people."

> Rich fellas come up an' they die, an' their kids ain't no good, an' they die out. But we keep a'coming. We're the people that live. Can't nobody wipe us out. Can't nobody lick us. We'll go on forever, Pa. We're the people.[14]

Such conviction, Zanuck concluded, was not to be thwarted by the "No Help Wanted" originally indicated in Nunnally Johnson's screenplay,[15] so he gave them an open road—which, appropriately enough, leads off to nowhere.

The Grapes of Wrath is a fine movie, but it is considerably flawed. Furthermore, for all its "documentary" technique, it is badly distorted history. Its depiction of the plight of the migrant worker contributes considerably less to our understanding of the conditions of the Depression than its suspicion of big business, its manifest agrarianism, and, above all, its sentimental concern for the breakdown of the family. Given the striking commercial success of the movie, one cannot help wondering what it was the public went to see—an artistic masterpiece, a direct confrontation with the reality of the Depression, or its handling of the above concerns. Of the three, the last was perhaps the most important, for this was the one striking point of resemblance between it and the biggest box office movie of the decade. *Gone with the Wind* succeeded as well as it did in large part because it so effectively sublimated the audience's own response to the Depression. For them, the panoramic shot of the Confederate wounded littering the center of Atlanta was not a matter of fact but of feeling. All concern for the scene's historical authenticity simply vanished in the face of its dramatization of the sense of helplessness and devastation they themselves had experienced.

Amidst these circumstances, Scarlett's subsequent return to Tara bears a striking resemblance to Tom's homecoming, in her quest for refuge from the adversities she has endured. Yet her expectation is shattered by the same scene of desolation that Tom discovered. For her, also, there is the same decaying ruin in place of the secure home she formerly knew. Tom's encounter with Muley seems almost a rerun of Scarlett's even more painful confrontation with her father, whose demented condition strikingly illustrates the magnitude of change resulting from the war's upheaval. As in *The Grapes of Wrath*, this breakdown in the integrity of the family is associated with the destruction of an agrarian way of life, which strikes at the very core of Scarlett's emotional being. The burned soil of Tara that Scarlett grips in the concluding scene of Part I is fraught with the same significance which attended Grampa's similar gesture in *The Grapes of Wrath*.

Gone with the Wind (1939).

Scarlett's response, however, marks an important point of difference. Unlike Tom Joad, who took to the road and sought to survive by working with his family, Scarlett resolves to be master of her destiny. Her moving declaration, "As God is my witness . . . I'll never be hungry again," pits her will against the prevailing conditions. Her determination is such that she not only antagonizes the remnants of her family but she also exploits them; having slapped Suellen, she proceeds to steal her prospective husband, Frank Kennedy. Nonetheless, her actions are prompted by some of the same motives that carried the Joads to California.

In the characterization of Scarlett is to be found most of the complexity that *Gone with the Wind* possesses. As the reviewer of the *New York Times* ob-

served, "Miss Leigh's Scarlett is the pivot of the picture."[16] Were she merely
a bitch or strong-willed feminist, the appeal of this movie would have been
considerably diminished. In order to appreciate the intense response she elicited
from the audience, one has to understand the particular way in which Scarlett's
return to Tara and her subsequent commitment to rebuilding it qualifies her
initial assertion of independence and results in a tragic misunderstanding that
brings her downfall. In the opening scenes of the movie, Scarlett wins the
audience's sympathy for her determined spirit of rebellion. It is she who provides critical perspective on the glittering world of plantation society. Tara and
Twelve Oaks, with their surrounding profusion of flowers and lush background
sweep of countryside, are as magnificently attired as the people who congregate
there and therefore are perfect settings for the featured scenes of dressing and
undressing, posturing and strutting. The main function of women in this world
is providing ornamental beauty. The illusion of grace and elegance they sustain
is predicated upon a harsh standard of propriety, a painfully tight corset. Parties
become major moments in their lives in helping them to achieve their ordained
goal of marriage, but their area of decision is limited to the choice of a dress or
hat. Since the threat of a rival is the only war they can be expected to understand, they are all herded off to bedrooms to freshen their appearances and
restore their frail energies while the men debate the future of the South. Given
the stifling confinement of this role, Scarlett balks. Like the other women, she
entertains a vision of marriage and consciously attends to her appearance, but,
unlike them, she is determined to act on her wishes. Thus, while her rivals
retire according to the convention of the submissive female, she slips down-
stairs to confront Ashley in the belief that he will not be able to resist her
assault.

The war, which pre-empts Scarlett's fight for Ashley, dramatically affirms
these and all the other deficiencies of this society, but as a "lost cause," it also
forces Scarlett to determine her highest priorities. At first, she displays only a
selfish interest; its tragedy is for her a source of gain in relieving her of an
unwanted husband. However, the flames of Atlanta which occasion a nightmare of emotion as they destroy the Old South, illuminate a new romantic
potential in Scarlett's deepening relationship with Rhett. During their flight,
their affair of convenience, predicated upon the same spirited, but pragmatic,
individualism which alienates them both from plantation society, achieves a
new level of interdependency in the intense feelings they exchange and share.
Having been stripped of her gentility, her vanity, and finally her self-
confidence, Scarlett is reduced to her greatest moment of need. At this point,
Rhett's selfishness, which reveals itself to have been basically an emotional
shield, also gives way. For the first time, both reach out for something greater
than themselves. The result, however, is not a common understanding. Rhett

proposes a marriage and a new future, only to discover that Scarlett prefers to retreat to the past. Survival, she has come to believe, lies in the red earth of Tara. Rejected, Rhett goes off to fight for the cause. Thus, the situation which brought Rhett and Scarlett together propels them along separate paths in search of ideals which ironically the war is at that moment destroying. Though they survive to marry one another, the decisions forced by the war constitute an insurmountable breach which the conclusion of the movie simply reaffirms, as Rhett goes off to Charleston in search of "the calm dignity life can have when it's lived by gentle folks, the genial grace of days that are gone," while Scarlett heeds her father's words calling her back to Tara.

In his concerted effort to reproduce the novel as thoroughly as possible, Selznick felt that the increased emphasis he accorded to Tara was one of the few points of departure. "I felt," he explained in one of his memos, "that the one thing that was really open to us was to stress the Tara thought more than Miss Mitchell did."[17] For him, Scarlett's character was grounded in Tara, in agrarianism and the family, just as the identity of the Joads was. Yet, in according it much the same meaning, he dramatized its tragic consequence quite differently. Scarlett's vow never to be hungry again as she grips the burned soil of Tara at the end of Part I moves the audience with its stirring determination, but this vow is severely qualified by the scene's logic. Quite simply, Tara, or "terra," cannot provide the nourishment she requires.[18] The turnip she ravenously devours and then vomits is strikingly emblematic of Tara's true value. In the first place, the fact that the earth is red is an obvious signal that the soil sustains crops with great difficulty. Without the slaves and strong-willed owners, Tara is not even capable of generating enough capital to pay its taxes. The main reason for Scarlett's determination to return to Tara, however, transcends all these considerations. Tara is home—its essence is to be found more in the echoing sound of her father's voice and the heart-tugging strains of Max Steiner's music.[19] For her, Tara is the sphere of her father's influence, a refuge where matters were firmly under control and she was treated with tolerance and indulgence.[20] Yet this is equally foolish, for she discovers that her father has been broken by the war and now relies on her for the consolation she has expected him to provide. Nowhere are the disadvantages of Tara revealed more dramatically than in the buckboard visit of Jonas Wilkerson whose association with the new economic forces supplanting agrarianism recalls the nameless men of *The Grapes of Wrath* in their sinister cars.

Since money has become the only source of power, Scarlett must seek beyond Tara for survival. Scarlett appears to marry Frank Kennedy to pay the taxes on Tara, but she obviously sees that he is associated with the prospering forces of industrialization. Consequently, in becoming his wife, she really becomes a businesswoman. These conflicting allegiances to Tara and to her lumber mill place Scarlett in the paradoxical position of shunning the role of wife and mother in order to uphold her passionate commitment to family and the home. Her identification with business and its ruthless practices now loses her the audience's sympathy, yet, because she never understands the character and consequences of what she is doing, she proves more tragic than villainous. Her determined quest for the greatest margin of profit is not to be understood as her predominant aim. Much more essential is her desire that Tara be rebuilt. To do so is not only to eliminate the desperate state of poverty to which she had been reduced, but also to restore the spiritual strength of her family home. Only the audience, however, comprehends the hidden cost. Frank becomes her lackey and her marriage no more than a working partnership. She herself becomes a social pariah. Most important, Scarlett begins to die from emotional starvation, as her business absorbs her energies without providing any of the attention and compassion she has always craved. The sorrow she drowns with liquor following Kennedy's death is neither anguish nor a pained sense of confinement—it is a strange lack of feeling.

Once again, Rhett comes to offer her salvation. Despite his manifest contempt for propriety, Rhett's invasion of her privacy and his cynical proposal of marriage are joyfully welcomed, because they offer Scarlett an opportunity to escape her business and enjoy her own home. Unfortunately, the seeds of her undoing have already been sown. The self-reliant determination of her struggles has rendered her temperamentally incapable of filling the role of the devoted wife she would like to be. Rhett's gifts—the house and even Bonnie—all simply deprive her of the thing she needs most—a challenge. For this, she returns to Ashley, whose embodiment of the devoted husband she must destroy in order to win. Her visit with the dying Melanie causes her finally to realize this, as well as the fact that Rhett is a much worthier ideal. Sensing her folly, she rushes home to find that he has indeed become unreachable. As a mother without a child, a wife without a husband, Scarlett is left by Selznick at the end of the picture turning to a home she can inhabit only in her dreams. The famous concluding line of the novel, "tomorrow is another day," is almost drowned out in the movie by the emotionally charged flashback scene of Tara with Gerald O'Hara's words echoing in the background.[21] Thus, Scarlett stands at the end a strong-willed individualist in possession of all the wealth the audience could imagine, yet no better off than they because of her inability to realize her impossible dream of a happy home and a loving family.

At the height of the Depression, thirteen million workers were unemployed. People who had enjoyed marked prosperity during the twenties suddenly found themselves struggling just to stay alive. Equally troubling was their inability to comprehend the reasons for this devastating reversal. As Leo Gurko has observed, ''The decade of the thirties was uniquely one in which time outran

Clark Gable and Vivien Leigh in *Gone with the Wind* (1939).

consciousness . . . the misery of the country was equalled only by its be-wilderment.''[22] The absence of checks and balances in the market place, which was supposed to provide the ordinary citizen with opportunity, seemed only to be making the rich richer and the poor poorer. Everywhere, big business seemed to be prospering. The general lack of knowledge about those who ran it or how it operated simply added to the pervasive belief that these companies were somehow profiting at the expense of the suffering individual. Similarly frustrating was the helplessness and loss of dignity caused by unemployment. No longer was the working man able to fill his expected role as head of the household. Either he could not support his family or he was forced to strike out on his own in order to do so. Consequently, his traditional source of consolation now only contributed to his distress. In the cities, where these problems were most acute, the idea of "getting back to the land" seemed to offer a ready-made solution. As Broadus Mitchell explains:

> In the cities, unemployment emphasized crowding, squalor, and cold; the bread lines were visual reproaches. In the country, on the other hand, was ample room. Further, in the cities, workers won bread by an indirect process which for some reason had broken down. But life in the rural

setting was held to be synonymous with raising family food. The thing was simple, direct, individually and socially wholesome.[23]

This solution, of course, turned out to be most impractical. Yet it reveals the direction in which the people's anxieties were working. Coming at the end of the Depression as they did, *Gone with the Wind* and *The Grapes of Wrath* appealed to viewers who had lived through this ordeal. Both succeeded in large measure because they so effectively tapped the emotional wellsprings of this urban audience which was their chief patron. Repeatedly, the viewer found himself confronting these same troubling issues; but they were presented in such a way that he was reassured that everything would work out just as he hoped it would. At the same time, neither could have been as compelling had this sentimentality not been treated with a subtlety and understanding notably lacking in similar films like *Our Daily Bread.*

NOTES

1. Philip T. Hartung "Trampling Out the Vintage," *Commonweal 31* (February 9, 1940), p. 348.
2. Otis Ferguson, "Out to Lunch," *The Film Criticism of Otis Ferguson,* ed. Robert Wilson (Philadelphia: Temple University Press, 1971), pp. 280– 81.
3. Otis Ferguson, "Show for the People," *Film Criticism,* p. 282.
4. Lincoln Kirstein, "History in American Films *(Gone with the Wind)*" in *American Film Criticism from the Beginnings to Citizen Kane,* ed. Stanley Kauffmann (New York: Liveright, 1972), p. 372.
5. Andrew Bergman, *We're in the Money: Depression America and Its Films* (New York: New York University Press, 1971), p. xii.
6. For a discussion of these deletions, see George Bluestone, *Novels Into Film* (Berkeley: University of California Press, 1971), pp. 156– 161. Warren French discusses other important differences between the novel and the film in *Filmguide to The Grapes of Wrath* (Bloomington: University of Indiana Press, 1973), pp. 22– 27.
7. Mel Gussow, *Don't Say Yes Until I Finish Talking: A Biography of Darryl F. Zanuck* (Garden City, N.Y.: Doubleday, 1971), p. 95.
8. Nunnally Johnson, *The Grapes of Wrath,* in *Twenty Best Film Plays,* ed. John Gassner and Dudley Nichols (New York: Crown Publishers, 1943), p. 338. There may be minor variations between these quotes and the actual movie since this filmscript is not the final version.
9. *Twenty Best Film Plays,* p. 345.
10. *Twenty Best Film Plays,* p. 338.
11. The movie, for some reason, doesn't include Noah's desertion, though the scene was apparently filmed.
12. *Novels Into Film,* p. 165.
13. Mel Gussow reports that Zanuck wrote Ma's speech which concludes the film, p. 92.
14. *Twenty Best Film Plays,* p. 377.
15. *Twenty Best Film Plays,* p. 377.

16. Frank Nugent, *"Gone with the Wind," The New York Times Film Reviews: A One Volume Selection* (New York: Arno Press, 1971), p. 185.
17. David O. Selznick, *Memo From David O. Selznick,* ed. Rudy Belmer (New York: Viking Press, 1972), p. 212.
18. Despite this meaning which emerges from the dramatized pronunciation of Tara, the plantation was most probably named after the famous hill in County of Meath which for centuries was the seat of the ancient kings of Gerald O'Hara's native Ireland.
19. The Tara theme song, which echoes through the movie, subsequently became a popular song entitled, appropriately enough, "My Own True Love."
20. To some extent, Scarlett's failure to find a satisfying husband can be traced to the fact that none was able to measure up to the image she had of her father when she was a young girl.
21. For its demonstration of the quintessential spirit of the Hollywood ending, the recent four-hour ABC-TV special on "The Movies" concluded with this scene.
22. Leo Gurko, *The Angry Decade* (New York: Dodd Mead & Co., 1947), p. 13.
23. Broadus Mitchell, *Depression Decade: From New Even Through New Deal 1929– 1941* (New York: Rinehart & Co., 1947), p. 107.

Monster Movies: They Came from Beneath the Fifties

BRIAN MURPHY

"Enough to break a man." Also sprach Norman Mailer on that curious and little-loved decade, the 1950s. In America, at any rate, the 1950s were a guilt-ridden, frightened, paranoid time: they were, in an anachronistic word, up-tight.

Literature had to do with running away, with retreating: there was the case of poor, sad Holden Caulfield. Politics had to do with incredibly boring men like Eisenhower and Dulles or with incredibly evil men like Joe McCarthy, who at the time were too droning and fat-faced to make even their evil interesting. Pop music had to do with simpering, weak, meretriciously sentimental ballads. And movies seemed to have to do with nothing at all: there were absurd 3-D things and spectaculars like *The Robe,* but except for some technical advances (if that's what you want to call 3-D, Cinerama, Cinemascope, Vista-Vision, etc.) Hollywood seemed to be doing nothing at all. One can think of thirties' gangster movies and forties' musicals, but it is difficult to think of any kind of film which is characteristic of the fifties.

But there is, curiously, a kind of film which is more characteristic of the fifties than any other kind of film is characteristic of its time (even, perhaps than the spy films of the sixties): they are certainly not memorable, although they do seem to have a subculture of aficionados now; they are, of course, monster movies. The difficulty is to decide just what a "monster movie" is. Monster movies have been considered a part of the more general genre of the horror film—quite rightly—and as part of the general genre of the science-fiction film—also quite rightly. What makes the fifties' monster movies a species unto themselves is the combination of the two forms—the horror and sci-fi—and the ideological purpose to which they were put in that age, that age which was enough to break a man.

Ivan Butler, in his little book on *The Horror Film* (Barnes, 1967), says that the first of the kind was *The War of the Worlds* (1953), but he is really talking about a different kind; he is, in fact, talking about science-fiction films, generally, and such films are practically as old as the cinema itself. Fritz Lang was making them in the twenties; Orson Welles was adapting them for radio; and novelists are enjoying a considerable sci-fi fashion these days. In the novel, certainly, science-fiction has come of age; and Kubrick's famous *Space Odyssey* shows that the form can be treated seriously in films. The usual characteristics of sci-fi are obvious enough: there is often inter-planetary space travel, a setting in the distant future, and a consideration of the implications of technological advances. While there is no one purpose to be found in sci-fi novels or films, the aesthetic advantages of the form center around the idea of *possibility*. The sci-fi writer says, in effect: Consider man. Remove him from his environment in time and place, and let us see what happens to him. Kubrick used the form to explore the idea of infinity (as did the film *The Incredible Shrinking Man*), to take man even beyond Lord Byron's mountain top. And sci-fi generally can have that kind of purpose, a most Romantic one: take man literally to the top of his form and see what happens. Sci-fi used more modestly in the simple form of futuristic novels or films can show man as a political or social disaster—*1984* and *Brave New World* spring to mind. And there are countless possibilities in between: C. S. Lewis used science-fiction to demonstrate the eternalness of Christianity; Colin Wilson, in *The Mind Parasites,* to elucidate and propound "phenomenology," the extremely complex philosophy of Edmund Husserl. Generally, this is the kind of thing novelists like Bradbury and Asimov are doing today—seeing what this "piece of work," man, is like.

Now, the fifties' monster movies did not do this kind of thing badly: they did not do it at all. Their general form might have been the form of science-fiction, but there were, for one thing, far too many elements of the horror film. The

The Blob (1958)

horror genre, of course, in literature and the cinema, is even older than science-fiction. The novel of horror (the "Gothic Novel") dates from Walpole and Radcliffe in the eighteenth century, that is, almost from the beginnings of the novel itself. The horror film comes into being with the cinema itself: Ivan Butler dates the earliest as a one-reel *Frankenstein* made in 1910. The Gothic novel and the horror film are more difficult to generalize about than science-fiction, because both have a longer history and have been put to such different kinds of purposes and, finally, because the aesthetics of horror are suitably mysterious. The Gothic novel and the horror film seem to have one general kind of purpose, however: to bear witness to Hamlet's famous remark that "there are more things in heaven and earth, Horatio, than are dreamt of in your philosophies." From the point of view of the reader or spectator, the most obvious effect is sensation—the exquisite thrill of being frightened, thus reminding oneself that one is, after all, alive. But, of course, fright alone is not the earmark of the horror film or Gothic novel: adventure novels and suspense films achieve the same kind of effect: there is fright without horror, for instance, at the end of *Sorry, Wrong Number*.

The essence of a horror film is that it deals with the mysterious, the eerie—and it is generally agreed that the most effective kinds of horror are not patly explained—like Henry James's *The Turn of the Screw* (brilliantly filmed as *The Innocents*). But more usually there is a kind of "explanation" in the very substance of the material—the legend of the vampire or the werewolf or the specially created legend of Doctor Frankenstein's famous monster (created in films, it should be pointed out, for purposes very different from those of Mary Shelley's). We suspend our disbelief and enter a never-never land (rarely the future, the present, or the clearly specified past) which is governed by absolutely inflexible laws: men turn into werewolves only but always on nights of the full moon; vampires always dislike garlic, cast no reflection in mirrors, and can be destroyed only by having their hearts pierced with a wooden stake; and it is the nature of Frankenstein's monster that he can never, never be destroyed. It is a curious phenomenon, really: horror's never-never land is bearable because it is so entirely rational. These hideous "things," unexplainable by our philosophies, are things we want to believe in because we do not want to accept the prosaic philosophy of the materialist, but we cope with these "things" by making them run according to laws infinitely more exacting than those capricious laws which govern the nervous structure of an atom.

The monster movies of the fifties use elements of both forms in a very stylized way. They are like early nineteenth-century operas, really, in their degree of structural stylization—or, to take a more contemporary simile, as Kingsley Amis has shown, they are like the stylization of a James Bond novel. One reason for the rigorous stylization of the form is that it was put to a rather limited social purpose; another reason is that the form was so oddly restricted in time—to the almost exact temporal boundaries of the fifties. Now, more than ten years after the end of the fifties, even the Japanese seem to have stopped making monster movies, and with a couple of exceptions, only the Japanese made monster movies after 1960. Consider the following highly selective but representative list:

1950	*The Thing (from Another World)*
1953	*The War of the Worlds*
1953	*Them*
1953	*The Beast from 20,000 Fathoms*
1953	*It Came from Outer Space*
1955	*It Came from Beneath the Sea*
1956	*Godzilla* (Japanese)
1956	*The Invasion of the Body Snatchers*
1956	*It Conquered the World*
1960	*Gorgo* (British)
1962	*The Day of the Triffids*
1964	*The Earth Dies Screaming*

Kevin McCarthy in *Invasion of the Body Snatchers* (1956).

Films which seem to be superficially like the fifties' monster movies—such as *The Earth Dies Screaming*—are really very different: for one thing, they are all either more thoughtful or much more pessimistic or, of course, both. At the other end of the list, one finds Howard Hawks' *The Thing*, which is a genuinely original film and which clearly, because it struck a cultural nerve, began the spate of monster movies. With one exception it has all of the essential elements of the fifties' monster movies: a team of U.S. military-scientific types discover, precisely, a "thing" and must use all of their military and scientific knowledge corporately to destroy the monster; the film ends with a question mark (as many of the later monster movies literally end, not with a "Fin" but a "?"): we were successful this time, but next time . . . ?

The Thing was an original film in its combination of the materials of science fiction and Gothicism: there is the mysterious and eerie atmosphere; there is the science fiction questioning about the nature of reality: man confronts something he has never had to confront before, a new creature, a new problem, and the response means, in a sense, a new man. It would be hard to think of any films before *The Thing* which possess quite its combination of materials, and there is nothing easier than to think of countless films after it which have all the elements except setting: the fifties' monster movies changed location after *The Thing;* those first discoverers of alien life found it in an almost mythical, Nordic setting near the North Pole; then the monsters moved closer to home: American cities were in constant danger of destruction from a variety of monsters throughout the fifties.

The only film which one might think of as a prototype for the fifties' monster movies is *King Kong* (1933; and feebly echoed in 1949 in *Mighty Joe Young*). But Kong is not the Thing or the Beast or It, Kong is not new; he is old. In facing him, man becomes not a changed new being; he becomes a changed old being. The monster movie ends with a question mark; *King Kong* ends with Robert Armstrong reciting the film's epigraph about "beauty and the beast," an old, old proverb. Kong's destruction—in the famous Empire State Building scene, which certainly did provide a key image of catastrophic climax for the fifties' monster movies—was, naturally, greeted with relief, but the triumph was choked by an odd and oddly affecting combination of remorse, guilt, and nostalgia: Kong was more a victim than an agent of evil, and he never had a chance against either the planes which shot him down from the Empire State Building or the beauty of Fay Wray. Nostalgia is, I suppose, the strongest final emotion which *King Kong* renders: Kong was our last link with our primitive past; Kong was primitive in his destructiveness and in his love; he was something like Wordsworth's "Nature" which we have lost, have given away; and we turned him into a sideshow freak and then, because of the complexity and density of our civilization symbolized by the then-recently built Empire State Building, we had to kill him.

If Kong represented something primitive which we had to lose, the monsters of the fifties represented something new, something we had never encountered and of which we were simply terrified. These days, apparently, the only available monsters are on *Sesame Street* and those monsters presumably show children that even their awful fantasies are good, are part of us, can be, shall we say, assimilated. The children who watch *Sesame Street* see monsters who recite the alphabet and crunch cookies; those "things" can be, in other words, coped with: we don't have to be afraid; Gordon and Susan and Bob are so smart and nice—nothing to be afraid of; they have the situation well in hand.

The point is that, in the fifties we were not so sure that the situation could be gotten in hand at all. Maybe the premise of the fifties' monster movies is, man isn't, after all, strong enough to cope with the "things." The fifties' monster movies are founded on a premise of fear, and this is what makes them so radically different from usual horror movies. In the Frankenstein and Dracula and Wolf Man movies, we wanted to be frightened—partially because our world was rather prosaic—and we wanted the mysterious poetry of horror. In the fifties, prose itself became horrifying, and the response was, certainly not poetry but more and more prose; and the more scientific, the more it sounded like computerized jargon, the better, the more reassuring.

It is obvious that fifties' monster movies call forth little of the affectionate nostalgia that, say, thirties' horror movies do. One reason is that the monster movies are, generally, not very good movies. There are some exceptions, but very few; and, in any case, most people afflicted with cinematic nostalgia like to recall *kinds* of films rather than specific films, a thirties' musical, a Charlie Chan movie, even "British comedies." It would seem a true enough rule that a kind of film, in order to be remembered well, has to achieve a reasonable level of excellence in its formal internal consistency. This is what the fifties' monster movies were never able to do.

One cause of this general weakness of monster movies is the poverty of the language. Poverty of language turned the U.S. moon flights into bores because no one, except a few journalists, could think of any compelling way to talk about them. There is a similar aesthetic problem in monster movies: they deal with interesting problems and even Great Issues, but it is nearly impossible to remember anything that is said in them. The case is very different with horror movies; there one finds a kind of pop poetry, a specially created and specially charged language which celebrates the world of the mysterious, the eerie, the horrible. Who can forget Count Dracula curtly answering a young lady who says that it is nice the Count has bought an old London house so that there can be some nice improvements made? Who can forget that Lugosian accent and horrible look in the eye as the Count chants:

> There will beee
> No
> Improve-
> ments.

The best of such films managed to be both creepy and funny. The opening of the *Bride of Frankenstein* is an excellent example; when Mary Shelley explains to her husband and to Lord Byron that her story should have another ending, even she is frightened in the telling. The scene is marvelously comic and at the same time splendid in its preparation for the fright to follow. The fifties' monster movies lacked not only a language of their own: they lacked, as well, any humor.

What the monster movies did accomplish, however, was a rendering of the special kind of fear which ran deep in the bone of the 1950s. *The Thing* makes this fear perfectly plain: there was a new world after World War II. There was a world which was just beginning to understand the significance of that atom bomb: in 1946 or so a pop singer could happily chant, "You're my Atom

Bomb Baby''; the realization took a little while; by 1950 there were fears of a
new and still more horrible war; by 1950 the phrase ''Iron Curtain'' contained
such horrible poetry that one yearned for prose; in the 1950s it seemed that all
America was tunneling through its bowels to build bomb shelters, and theolo-
gians argued about the morality of shooting a radium-contaminated neighbor at
the door of your family's private shelter; generally, one's thinking was eschato-
logical; doom seemed imminent.

Kevin McCarthy in *Invasion of the Body Snatchers* (1956).

The fifties' monster movies dealt with this kind of doomridden eschatologi-
cal fear. The tension which carried the better movies along involved the thrill
of fancying the world's extinction and the nervous hope that we were, maybe,
strong enough and smart enough to stave off that extinction—if only for just a
little while longer.

The monster, therefore, is not the principal character in a monster movie—as
Kong is very much the main character of *King Kong*. The monster is the
symbol of what we have to fear: it is not fear itself; it is the horror of what we
have done, scientifically and militarily, to bring the world to the brink of

destruction. Now, in the 1970s, we feel free to question the value of scientific progress (the suffocation of polluted cities does seem a rather high price to pay for scientific and technological advances) and more than question the morality of the U.S. military (My Lai was the *coup de grace* to the image of the U.S. soldier as the man, who, while saving the world from evil, dispensed understated wisecracks and invigorating Hershey bars). But in the 1950s, while sensing the potential disaster that the (naturally, crudely imagined) scientist and soldier might bring about our heads, we asked the scientist and soldier to save us from that very disaster. Perhaps that is what Norman Mailer meant by saying that the fifties were enough to break a man: in the fifties we didn't trust ourselves. We wanted to be assured that the soldier was good enough and the scientist wise enough to take care of us.

Again, the contrast with a standard horror movie could hardly be more marked. There are no soldiers at all; there is the bungling constable, of course, or the preposterous burgomaster: but these representatives of Society are hopelessly inadequate to deal with the forces of Horror's evil.

But both monster movies and horror films have scientists, or at least quasi-scientific types, as principal characters. The scientist of the horror film is, of course, The Mad Scientist ("Frankenstein, I tell you no human being has the right to . . ."). He is a descendant of Faust who will sacrifice anything to go beyond the boundaries of knowledge itself. He is a perversion of the scientist, of course, and his usual foil is often his own young scientific assistant who draws back in time to save his own soul. More than a scientist, though, he is a mystic who defies all conventional modes of thought. We respond to him (amused, tongue-in-cheek, of course) because he represents possibility—like, curiously, the more orthodox sci-fi films—the possibility of what man just might do and become. He is a kind of pop Lord Byron, and we delight to follow him up to his strange mountain peak, peopled with strange beings, shrouded in swirling mists, and infused with magical, if primitive, wonder.

In the 1950s, reality itself, as it were, took us to those mountain peaks; and, appalled, we wanted to be led back down to the flat lands. So we hired Frankenstein's assistant, and all those well-mannered, sensible assistants who kept regular hours, had degrees from MIT and nice girl friends, to talk to us in sensible language (i.e., scientific jargon), to assure us that things were really going to be all right, to take us down from those damnable, accursed, goddam *scary* mountain peaks.

Consider the manner of the descent in a rather good film which is a superb example of the monster movie form. (An even better film, *The Invasion of the Body Snatchers*, is a brilliant variation on the theme rather than a statement of the theme itself.) In 1954 (just about the height of the fashion for monster movies) appeared *Them*. It has all the ingredients. The setting is contemporary

America, an America which is marvelously "ordinary," "normal," "nice." It is an America in which teenagers might do crazy things like drive funny cars too fast or neck on deserted roads—but, of course, they didn't wear beads and flowers or bomb post offices. The tranquillity of this scene is broken by an isolated disaster—some strange doings someplace: maybe a lone, night watchman is found murdered in such a way as to suggest death by most unnatural causes; and maybe his body has been contaminated by radium. At any rate, one of the sheriff's deputies or one of the bored local cops thinks that maybe they ought to call a "prof" at a nearby research station. There is an investigation. More killings. Reports—often by frightened teenagers lately necking (an obsessively recurring motif). Then a whole town realizes the danger, and there is, for a moment, panic and an absolutely uncontrollable fear.

So, in *Them,* as in all monster movies, we turn to scientists and soldiers. They blur together, in fact: was it James Arness or James Whitmore who was the scientist? Well, there was a girl (Joan Weldon)—the busty assistant scientist (quite de rigeur), and in *Them,* we were allowed to see a great deal of her because she had "scientific knowledge" in "insect pathology." Presiding over all was the wise, elderly, unthreatening, and reassuring Edmund Gwenn. The scene in which he gives a scholarly discussion about the habits of ants was marvelously effective. The monsters, everyone knew, were giant ants; and, in order to deal with the obvious havoc they could wreak, we listen to a fatherly scientist begin at the beginning and, well within the clearly defined boundaries of science, tell us what we need to know.

Enlightened, James Arness and James Whitmore (and the busty specialist in insect pathology) go to do battle with Them (note the impersonal, paranoid, accusative form of the pronoun with no mentionable antecedent). The battle is a huge one—and yet curiously parochial: it involves all of America but only America. On one side are Them, those giant ants. Where did they come from? Scientist Gwenn explains that they are "mutations" which were the result of the first atom bomb explosion in 1945. Moreover, these mutations will proliferate in the way ordinary ants will, so the result will be, of course, catastrophic. There is only one fit adversary, and that cannot be some solitary Frankenstein's assistant or brilliant writer, some mere *individual:* no, the only fit adversary for such an enemy is the Government of the United States of America. So, Arness and Whitmore are backed up by all the resources of the Government, scientific and military, operated by an inevitable "open line to Washington."

One consequence of such battle lines is that the country is absolutely unified. In the face of such an enemy as Them, Americans respond nobly: they do precisely as they are told. The ants are discovered nesting in the sewer system of Los Angeles. Whitmore and Arness and the busty pathologist get to work. But what about the panic-stricken citizens? An announcer goes on the radio and

James Arness and Joan Weldon in *Them* (1954).

the television air waves to utter a sentence which echoes through all the monster movies and which, indeed, echoes through all the fifties: "Your personal safety depends upon your cooperation with the military authorities."

As a film, *Them* succeeds admirably in making such a sentence thoroughly convincing. The triumph in the film is, of course, the destruction of Them: it is a triumph of science and the military and the country itself. The film makes the triumph powerful enough by showing the pathos of private agonies. The climax of the film involves the search for the ants in the Los Angeles sewer system. But there are children playing in there someplace, and in order to save the children, in a brilliantly done scene with stunning technical effects (those bloody ants *are* frightening), James Whitmore has to die horribly. Well, that is the cost: the individual perishes so that the country as a whole (convincingly symbolized for the moment in the children trapped by Them) might survive and return to what it wants so desperately—a nice, safe world in which teenagers drive hot rods and neck a lot. The last lines of *Them* are spoken by Edmund Gwenn as he muses on this "atomic age," this—the very last words of the film—"new world."

It is not a very brave new world, and it is a new world which no one wants. But it is a new world which we, in actual, appalling fact, *have;* and there is no getting out of it. Those beasts and things—Them generally—are awfully real; and, it seemed, we could deal with them only by going back to the very people who spawned them: the scientists working "in full cooperation" (such an important word, that "cooperation") with the military.

Of course, very, very few of the monster movies ever achieved the kind of conviction which gives *Them* its strength. Most of them are scarcely worth remembering or talking about. *The Invasion of the Body Snatchers* has justifiably received a revival of interest because it is so convincing in its rendering of paranoia: the image of people, your postman, your policeman, your wife, being taken over by an alien force was rendered with horrible and frightening conviction. But *The Invasion of the Body Snatchers* is in almost all ways a special case; for one thing, it has no visible monster. And it is with just that problem— of making the monster an adequate symbol for the kind of fear that the film deals with—that most of the monster movies floundered.

There wasn't much anyone could do with *The Astounding She-Monster* (1957). The film begins with some blather about our nuclear age and its crises and ends with a message taken from the body of the She-Monster about how some outer-space type thinks that earth has developed sufficiently (the myth of Progress was still then embraced) to join in interplanetary fellowship. Of course, the radium-contaminated She-Monster proved to be a singularly ineffective messenger.

A more ambitious film was *The 4-D Man* (1958), directed by Irvin S. Yeaworth, who made monster movies, evidently, daily. What is mildly interesting about this film is that the monster is the scientist himself—actually, one of the scientists. There is a bad, even Mad, scientist, then. He is the brother of a Good Scientist. The Good Brother is appalled by his younger brother when the younger brother says, "Maybe I like having the power to do something no one else can do." The Good Brother, horrified, wants to know: "Is this why I sent you to school—to become a *mystic?*" The younger brother is given a job; at the lab people say things to him like "Welcome aboard" and talk about "the team." But he proves to be a bad sort because he won't really join the "team": he likes to keep a lock on his locker and indulge in all sorts of privacies. The Good Brother is a perfect team man: he knows the score; and he knows that there is no place for the kind of willful, perverted individualism that his brother increasingly comes to represent. Finally, of course, the individualist goes bonkers, and his own brother, true to the team, and assisted by a busty assistant, must destroy his brother, root him out, and excise him like the horrible cancerous canker that he clearly is. The world is, after all, a team, and we're all going to play ball, by God, according to the rules, or with the full cooperation of the military authorities we'll have to take positive action.

The form peters out with the fifties (except in Japan, of course) in idiocies like *How to Make a Monster* (1958), the very premise of which is that the vogue for monster movies is over: not quite soon enough. And it peters out with feeble jokes like an early Steve McQueen film called *The Blob* (1958), which even has a bouncy title song called "Be Careful of the Blob." It's old Irvin S. Yeaworth directing again, and most of the film has to do with that nice normalcy of the teenagers vs. the Blob. There is panic, and even though the military are not called in, the small town must function as a unit to save itself. Then the military arrive to take away the now-frozen and harmless Blob. As long as the Arctic stays cold, we are safe: this is one of the films in which "The End" dissolves into a question mark.

One assumes that the Arctic, being what it is, will in fact stay chilly for some time yet. But what hideous monsters might lurk beneath its frozen surface? Ah, in the fifties, we really understood the opening of "The Waste Land":

> April is the cruellest month, breeding
> Lilacs out of the dead land, mixing
> Memory and desire, stirring
> Dull roots with spring rain.
> Winter kept us warm, covering
> Earth in forgetful snow, feeding
> A little life with dried tubers.

That was all we wanted: "a little life," covered by snow, if necessary. We thought we understood this new age, and we thought that we knew how to deal with it. We were wrong, of course, in most of the ways in which we tried to deal with it, but we weren't so entirely wrong about the kind of world it was — and still is. Oh, yes, in the fifties we really understood "The Waste Land": we lived in it.

The Violent Dance: A Personal Memoir of Death in the Movies

VIVIAN C. SOBCHACK

Violence and death do not only sell movie tickets today; they also are the source of countless arguments, safely confined to paper, to panel discussions, to cocktail parties. What is all that technicolor blood doing to our Youth? Are we a nation of voyeurs? Can the movies make us callous, unfeeling? Are the films innocent, merely presenting to us something which is already there? Is today's movie violence reflective of some phenomenon presently existent in our society (good, "honest," documentary revelation like *The French Connection*), or is it teaching us to regard blood and death with a blasé aplomb we would not otherwise acquire in our own insular lifetimes? Answers to these questions often boil down to whether one believes that cinema is reflective or affective, mimetic or cathartic. At any rate, issues such as these have been worried about and nosed over until one's response becomes, at best, gentle boredom and, at worst, calculated oversight.

Violence and death have always been with us in the darkness of the theater. They were there before I became a regular moviegoer in the late 1940s and will be there long after I have bloodlessly expired in bed or been juicily run down by an aggressive taxicab. They've always been there, as familiar as the smell of popcorn; and yet the violent deaths I remember from long ago—the deaths which have stuck to my ribs, so to speak—are rare. It certainly was not because I was shielded from the horrors of the screen. The first film I ever saw was *Bambi* and his mother's death before the forest fire was a movie experience I'll never forget. Little sobs, including my own, rose in the audience; animated or not, the violence of that fire and the death of a mommy were real. Saturday and Sunday matinees followed—triple features plus ten cartoons—and the cinematic fare I grew up on consisted of little else but violence: Errol Flynn, Tyrone Power, Stewart Granger ran their enemies through and through, themselves suffered the rack, the Spanish Inquisition, and the slings and arrows of assorted outrageous fortunes; Joel McCrae, Randolph Scott, Audie Murphy said they hated guns but used them expertly, made their opponents dance to the graveyard or the scaffold in the name of decency and law and order; John Wayne and his battalions bombed, machine-gunned, and grenaded their way to Bataan and beyond, tearing themselves on barbed wire, dragging useless but precious left legs after them like so many sacks of mail from home.

Was it simply that as a child I had no intimations of my own mortality? Those deaths certainly never had the impact of the one in *Bambi*. (Perhaps I unconsciously believed that only mothers could die.) I watched those scenes of piracy and gunfighting and war with a great deal more forbearance than I gave to the gratuitous love scenes at which we all groaned in pubescent unison, but they didn't really touch me as did *Bambi* or the violent films I see today. Was it merely childish hubris that kept me essentially unmoved and only marginally fascinated by the deaths I saw in what were supposed to be fairly realistic movies? I think not. I feared and cowered before death in the horror films; I believed in Dracula and Frankenstein and Vincent Price. Death by fang, claw, and hot wax were very real to me, while bullet holes and stab wounds never once caused my steps to quicken on my way home from the theater.

Perhaps the violent deaths I saw in those somewhat representational films were *too* realistic to move me to an awareness of my own fragile flesh. For one thing, they were often expertly concealed in a Breughel-like *mise en scene,* similar to one of those puzzles we tried to solve on rainy days: There are twenty-three rabbits hidden in this picture. Find them! Death came swiftly, noisily, and in the midst of confusion—on the decks of pirate ships, in the circle of covered wagons, over the teeming battlefield. As in real life, no one told us precisely where to look and by the time we had found the locus of interest, a character or two had already neatly keeled over. The long shot, the panoramic view, kept death far from us and that was real. The bullet holes were too small to see well; the sword wounds were always on the side facing away from the camera. Sitting in the theater, it was as realistically futile for us to crane our necks to see—really see—as it was when we passed an automobile accident in the car and my father refused to slow down in the name of good taste. In this sense, those movies (and I'll include most of the domestic variety up through the mid-sixties) were indeed realistic. Real violence happened far away, neatly in the straight columns of a newspaper, safely confined in the geometric box of a television set.

As in the films I saw when I was growing up, real violence occurred quickly, giving neither the participants nor the spectators much time to abstract themselves from emotion, time to examine and explore and perhaps comprehend the internal mystery of the human body. Of course, in these films, we did have the drama of anticipating death, a drama usually not present in reality: the long ticking seconds before the shoot-out, the tense crawl over rough terrain. But death itself was quick; the camera didn't extend the last bleeding seconds of the antagonist's life, nor did it linger on the carnage. Death was acknowledged in these films, but not inspected. Too few of us in the audience (our parents included) felt threatened enough by the presence of death and violence outside the theater to need the comfort of a microscopic inspection of it on the screen.

Although it was talked about, violence was not yet an everyday occurrence, a *civil* occurrence; it was not yet a time when we feared not only the incomprehensibility of death but the incomprehensibility, the irrationality and senselessness, of man as well. Death in the movies may have been quick, but it was dramatic, meaningful. Those who died did so for a reason. In those days, we didn't even think in terms of assassination (something that happened to Lincoln and livened our history books up a bit), or about junkies, madmen, snipers. We could be pretty certain (who even doubted it?) that the clean-cut kid next door *was* a clean-cut kid. Our relationship with violence and death in those Saturday movies was the same relationship we had with them in life. They happened to someone else and were mildly titillating, mildly disturbing.

Intimations of what was to come—given the right climate, the right circumstances and environment—were revealed in our youthful attitudes toward blood. In another sense, those movies were unrealistic; they didn't satisfy the very human curiosity that only children cared to voice in those safer times. They never told us what we wanted, albeit hesitantly, to know: the color and the texture of blood. All of us children, superficially satisfied with the realistic limitations of movie violence, worried our cuts and picked our scabs and wondered at the rich red that coursed through our insides and occasionally came to the surface. Blood was something we were rarely given enough of on the screen—it oozed rather than spurted, it was most often black or a rusty Cinecolor. Even in medium close-up (the man-to-man shoot-out or duel, the pink traceries of a whip-lashing), I can't remember a single movie death which fired my imagination as much as the bright red blood from my own finger. Then as now, we humans attempted to hide from the frightening reality of our fragile innards by believing in the strength of plastic and supermarkets. Yet we were fascinated, as we have always been, by blood and tissue and bone. Snowden's secret (c.f. *Catch-22*) is everyone's secret. In the late forties, however, and in the fifties and early sixties it was a bit easier to keep that secret; everyone was comfortably mum.

Then, suddenly it seemed, in the mid-sixties, there was blood everywhere. We didn't have to go to war to find it—or stretch our necks to peer at it on the highway. Blood appeared in living color in more and more of our living rooms. And it was there all around us in the streets, is still there. Politicians became surprisingly more than caricatures; they became mortal. People who looked and lived exactly as we did shot at us from water towers, slit our throats, went berserk, committed murder next door. Even children died and supermarkets— meats neatly packaged and displayed to exorcise the taint of the slaughter-house—were no longer havens of safety and sanity and civilization. No place, however ordinary, was safe; blood ran in busy streets, on university campuses, in broad daylight, everywhere. We were all threatened and terrified, all potential victims of our not so solid flesh and some unknown madman's whimsy.

Public figures splattered against our consciousness: John Kennedy, Martin Luther King, Malcolm X, Robert Kennedy, Governor Wallace. Little men with strange other-worldly lights in their eyes took up arms against anonymity: Charles Whitman, Richard Speck, Richard Hickock, Perry Smith, Charles Manson. Students, police, and the National Guard fought it out on university campuses where the most burning issue when I went to college had been whether we had the right to wear Bermuda shorts to class. None of the blood spilt was picturesque or patriotic. Death by violence became a possibility for all of us because it lacked sense and meaning much of the time; there was no drama and catharsis. The blood in our lives had nothing of art or distance about it and we all felt personally threatened. Each one of us could die, each one of us could bleed, each one of us had to consciously acknowledge the secret which Snowden so shyly concealed in his flak suit—we all had pink and vulnerable guts.

One can hardly think that someone's careful calculations somewhere in Hollywood read fear in all our faces and saw our hunger for the seeming security of knowledge, our yearning to find meaning in the senselessness of random

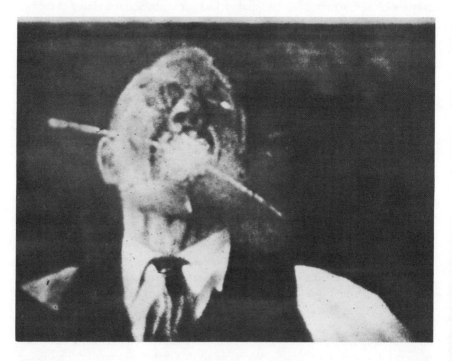

Bonnie and Clyde (1967).

violence. Films which had previously spoken to our unconscious desires and fears (see, for example, Robert Warshow on the gangster films of the thirties or R. H. W. Dillard on the horror film), like Topsy, "just growed." And in the fear-ridden sixties and seventies, it has been no different.

There always is, of course, a first film—the film which transcends its surface intentions and burns into us some unstated message with the intensity not of an arc lamp but of a laser. *Bonnie and Clyde,* released in 1967, was just such a film. Although it was not the first film to overtly bathe itself in blood, it was the first one to create an aesthetic, moral and psychological furor. Uneven in tone yet brilliantly conceived, it fired our imaginations not merely because it was a good film, but because it was the first major film to allow us the luxury of inspecting what frightened us—the senseless, the unexpected, the bloody. And most important, it kindly stylized death for us; it created nobility from senselessness, it choreographed a dance out of blood and death, it gave meaning and import to our mortal twitchings.

There has always been violence and death in the cinema. But the cinematic phenomenon in the films of our decade which is new and significant is the caressing of violence, the loving treatment of it by the camera. The most violent of deaths today is treated with the slow motion lyricism of the old Clairol commercials in which two lovers glide to embrace each other. The once abrupt drop into non-being has become a balletic free fall. This, of course, is what has incensed those who fear for the nation's children and the nation's morality. Making death and violence "beautiful," they suggest, may seduce all of us into a cheerful acceptance of gore, may whet our aesthetic appetites for more and more artful and prolonged bloodletting, may even cause us to *commit* violence. After all, *The Wild Bunch* and their victims died so gracefully. Sonny's body was a poem in motion when he was machine-gunned to death in *The Godfather. A Clockwork Orange* kept our toes tapping to the tunes of rape and beatings. *The French Connection,* while certainly not musical, possessed a staccato tempo which was brutal and bloody.

I suppose that what bothers the moralists most is that these films are selling, are popular, are even critically acclaimed. The idea that we are a nation of voyeurs is indeed disturbing. Our Wednesday and Saturday night outings to see blood and gore while we eat buttered popcorn is disturbing. But then, being human has always been disturbing. People are no more corrupt, no more voyeuristic than they were in the days of my childhood. But we are certainly more fearful. And it is this fear, rather than peeping-Tom-ism, which has caused violence to almost literally blossom—like one of Disney's time-lapse flowers—on today's movie screens.

Fear has made even the most squeamish of us take our hands from our eyes. We still are afraid of violence and blood and death, but we are more afraid of

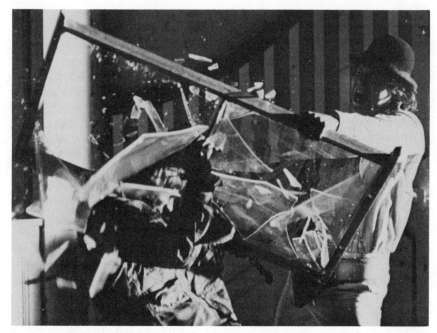

Warren Clarke in *A Clockwork Orange* (1971).

the unknown—particularly when it threatens us personally and immediately. Even those of us who couldn't stand the sight of blood at one time find our desire to know and understand blood stronger than our desire not to see what frightens and sickens us. In a time when we seemed safe, not immediately threatened, we could ignore our fear and indulge our squeamishness. Today, this is hardly possible.

After many viewings of the film, I still cannot watch the scene in Dali and Bunuel's *Un Chien Andalou* in which a woman's eyeball is slit by a razor. I have read about it, heard about it, but I have not seen it. I cannot keep my eyes open; I have tried, but I physically and mentally cannot do it. The content of that scene is violent and bloody (although in black and white), and I am deeply afraid to watch it, to know it. On the other hand, I sat motionless and wide-eyed through *Straw Dogs;* my eyes refused to leave the screen for even a moment. I can remember my husband wanting to leave in the middle (he said his arm had fallen asleep and we had already watched *The French Connection*). I didn't want to go; I didn't want to miss anything. If that sounds voyeuristic, in essence it wasn't. I got no pleasure at all out of watching *Straw Dogs*. I felt extraordinarily tense, upset, sick. And yet I could not leave the theater until the film was over, even at the expense of a family argument. For some reason, it seemed to be a matter of life and death—mine—that I stay.

What is the difference between my responses to the two films? Both play upon hidden fear in the audience. Both have moments of extreme violence. Why should I be able to watch one but not the other? The answer lies, I think, in the qualitative nature of the violence involved. I don't have the pressing need to see a woman's eyeball slit by a razor; seeing it will do nothing but disturb me. And this particular violent action—although terrifying with or without its

Ken Hutchinson, Dustin Hoffman, and Del Henney in *Straw Dogs* (1971).

Freudian implications—seems to have little to do with my life as I live it every day. I am not afraid of someone slitting my eyeball while I passively submit. Watching that scene, in other words, is not going to instruct me; it is not going to reveal to me something that is terrible but which I need to know. The nature of the violence in *Straw Dogs* is different. It may not be treated surrealistically, but it is not totally realistic either. (One remembers the little tailor in the fairy tale who wore a sash that proclaimed "Seven at One Blow.") Yet the violence in *Straw Dogs* touches contemporary nerves in a way that *Un Chien Andalou* doesn't. It involves the kind of violence that one fears now, today. Sickened, terrified, I *had* to watch the film. I had to learn and know what I fear and, however painful the experience was, for the moment I found a certain security in the fact that I had not backed away from instruction. In short, I was doing my homework—trying to learn how to survive. David in that movie was much like myself, the people around me. We all just wanted to mind our own business and yet found ourselves, our homes, our lives, threatened by people and things which plainly didn't make sense, weren't at all rational.

Popular films have always given us—the audience—what we want; otherwise they would not be popular. Today (just recently twenty-seven bodies were unearthed in Texas), we want to know blood and death. Although we retain little of the optimism which sprang from the Age of Reason, we still believe, even if it's half-heartedly and hopelessly, in knowledge, enlightenment. Knowledge is the magic which will save us; cataloguing will restore our crumbling sanity; inspection will cure our anxiety. Blood and tissue, death and killing, rape and beating don't please us, don't titillate us, can't be glibly compared to the centerfold of *Playboy*. Yet we have the clear and present need to know them, to have them made significant rather than senseless, to have them dramatized. Hence the slow motion, the lingering look at physical agony, the tongue-in-cheek treatment of brutality, the indecent amounts of blood. Our films are trying to make us feel secure about violence and death as much as it is possible; they are allowing us to purge our fear, to find safety in what appears to be knowledge of the unknown. To know violence is to be temporarily safe from the fear of it.

Of course, our belief in our sophistication, our comprehension of violence lasts about as long as it takes to walk from the theater to the subway or to the car—and sometimes not even that long. We quickly realize that the orgies of blood on the screen have told us nothing really *useful*. Our fear returns and makes us return to the theater to see more, hoping against hope that we will finally understand.

Our world has changed from the world of the forties and fifties and early sixties. And a world is changed by people. Yet the individual moviegoer today is not really much different than he was a decade ago. When I was a child, it was considered in bad taste to look at blood and talk about death. It wasn't "nice." Adults politely and tactfully avoided the issue because it was possible to avoid it; only we children, lacking manners, refused to hide our fascination with mortality. Today, manners and niceness are too small a social device to cover up the fear and actuality of imminent violence.

At the drive-in, I can see my three-and-a-half-year-old pajama-clad son become disturbed at the bloody and violent coming attractions, disturbed in a strange but very human way. He wants to know why and how. He stops eating his popcorn and wanting to drive the car. He leans forward from the back seat and carefully watches the screen. He becomes even more inquisitive than usual, running a high fever of fascination and questions. He is too young to be personally threatened by the particulars of the violence he sees (the death of Bambi's mommy *would* make him howl), but the blood on the screen seems to sing out to his blood. He may not know it, but he does have intimations of mortality. We, his parents, share his uneasiness but don't tell him to hush. We don't tell him his curiosity is not nice. We sit there in the car, a contemporary family, united with all those other adults and children in their cars by a desire to know.

In the past, we also wanted to know blood and violence but were afraid to ask, found it inconvenient, unnecessary for our day to day survival. Today, we are afraid *not* to ask. It seems our very lives depend upon the answers we get. The movies today merely reflect our search for meaning and significance—for order—in the essentially senseless. Drama can give us that meaning and order through form, through style. What frightens us in our daily lives is not only the possibility of personal violence, but the omnipresence of the chaos which surrounds contemporary violence, the fact that we may die for no other reason than that we were there to be killed.

The films today which stylize death and blood (and I can't think of many which don't) paradoxically reflect our fear of chaos but also create order. The senselessness and purposelessness, the randomness of real violence is certainly upheld in the content of current movies. In *The French Connection,* for example, a young mother walking her baby in the park is accidentally shot, commuters on a subway train find themselves the victims of something they cannot comprehend. Current films reflect our fear for our lives, our fear that no matter how uninvolved we may be, we are all potential victims of accident, that our deaths will horribly have no meaning at all. Yet, the very presence of random and motiveless violence on the screen elevates it, creates some kind of order and meaning from it; accident becomes Fate. If we should get shot minding our own business, if we should be mowed down accidentally, at least we have seen it on the movie screen, have felt—along with a theater full of people—for the hapless victim. And we also have realized that there was some reason even if the poor bystander who fell to the pavement didn't know it: the cop had to catch his crook. Even in films which are not lyrical in their presentation of violence and do not use the mannerisms of a Peckinpah, death—when it comes to Everyman—is given a nobility simply by its presence on the screen, its acknowledgment by the camera. These films reflect our fears, but also allay them.

All the current movies, then, which deal with violence say something important, if not particularly helpful. If we are to die for no apparent purpose, they seem to say, at least we will die with style, with recognition. We will create our own purpose and reason *as* we die; style will give our senseless death some sort of significance and meaning. The *form* of death in the movies today—the way the camera treats it—allows us to find some brief respite from our fears. The moment of death can be prolonged cinematically (through editing, slow motion, extreme close-ups, etc.) so that we are made to see form and order where none seems to exist in real life. The movement of the human body toward non-being is underlined, emphasized, dramatized and we all become Olympic participants of olympian grace. We can also see ourselves on the fringes of the frame, falling by the wayside, but falling *in the movies*. We may be horrified by the senselessness of violence and death, but we are also lulled and soothed by the possibility that there is—for all of us—a moment of truth, a moment of drama. We can believe, if only briefly, that even the most senseless and violent and horrible of deaths has at least a form, an internal order, and therefore a meaning. Those bloody and brutal films which appear on our theater screens today perform, for us all, a kindness.

Godfather Saga:
The Death of the Family

JOHN YATES

"Right under the surface of this film," said Francis Ford Coppola of his movie, *The Godfather, Part II,* "is a loose metaphor for America itself. Like Michael, we all have blood on our hands." That statement, from *Time* magazine, represents the standard American judgment of *The Godfather* and its sequel, and, indeed, of most art that has anything to do with America. Americans are obsessed with being American; they see a reflection of what they are, a metaphor for the country's essence, in even the most oblique reference to the place.

Not that I'm in any position to tell Coppola he's wrong about his movie, nor that he's wrong at all. On a fairly obvious level, American corruption is what the two movies are about. Coppola's mobsters constantly refer to themselves as "businessmen." The meeting of the heads of the families in *Part I* mirrors the meeting in *Part II* of Michael, Hyman Roth, and Batista with the heads of the various U.S. corporations. "We're bigger than U.S. Steel," Roth boasts later to Michael. It is clear that size, and the ruthless will to do anything to achieve that size, are the only differences between U.S. Steel and the Mafia. The business of America is business, as Calvin Coolidge said; it's what the country is all about, and that core is rotten in *The Godfather*.

But an American work, produced after Vietnam, about America's rottenness, is a commonplace. Michael's line to Kay at their reunion in *Part I*, about politicians killing just as blithely as his father, is, after Vietnam, no jarring insight to an American audience. If the two movies said only this, then their significance could really be no greater than that of Mario Puzo's novel. The movies are about American corruption at about the same level as they are about gangsters. Had they gone no deeper than that, they would have been artistic failures.

The Godfather, Parts I and II, are at their deepest level a brilliant revelation of the family, how it worked through the generations, and how it now falls apart. In *Part I,* Coppola and his actors create a real, living, breathing world. Coppola presents his world with what Pauline Kael calls an open camera; everything is shown, the detail is absolutely convincing, and it is convincing because the viewer is allowed to take it all in naturally, without comment by the director. Watching the movie, you know that this is how life is. The director reveals; he does not preach.

Coppola reveals a family, in that first grand scene of *Part I,* engaged in the most familial of rituals, a daughter's wedding. The scene is a picture of tradition, and not merely Italian tradition, but the tradition of the West. The man of respect in the community gathers his neighbors around him, to observe the relinquishing of the care of his daughter to another man, her husband. Implicit in this act is the key to the Western family, the subservience of the woman to the man. The woman bears and tends the children in the home, and the man is strong for his family, to protect them and his home from a hostile world. This is how things work in *Part I;* all the action takes place in this framework.

Even the violence and brutality of Don Corleone's criminal empire fit within this family framework. To call an organization that deals in murder and revenge a "family" is not hypocritical at all. Indeed, it evokes the very origin of the family, that primordial time when anybody or anything that threatened a man's home was beaten to death with a rock. Don Corleone's family is a throwback to that violent time when the family existed primarily for mutual protection. The modern American world in which the Don's family operates has become more subtle in its hostility, just as modern businessmen have become more subtle in their ruthlessness. But Don Corleone's lack of subtlety in response to this world makes him more the businessman, more the family man, not less. He is an archetype, not an aberration.

Posed wedding photo in *The Godfather* (1972).

Michael's interlude in Sicily underscores this fact. For a few moments, the Sicilian scenes seem to be a flashback from the wounded Don's bed on Long Island into his past, and in *Part II,* they might have been. In *Part I,* however, they serve as a picture of the world from which Vito Corleone came, and in which his son Michael operates just as he did. It is a world, existing in the present, that is not too different from the primitive world that spawned the original family. Men walk in the countryside with shotguns over their shoulders. Fathers jealously guard their daughters' virtue. People's wives are blown to bits by their enemies. Men must protect their families. There is no gap between this cruel Sicilian world in which Vito was born and the same world Michael walks through sixty years later. The same rules apply. The family stays together, in Sicily and in America, because it must.

And thus the beautifully accurate family scenes in *Part I.* Don Corleone dances a last dance with his daughter at her wedding. With a father's dignified indirection, he reproves Sonny for undermining the family's show of unity in the meeting with Sollozzo. Sonny plays head of the family in his father's absence, without ever quite pulling it off (''Yeah, don't talk business at the dinner table!'') The Don transforms himself into a retired grandfather figure, puttering around the study as Michael issues orders, giving way to the new generation, but remains, alone with Michael, the anxious father, worried that his son may have neglected some essential detail. Michael, with a son's patience, assures him that the details are taken care of, that the dreams he dreamt for Michael will come at last to the family. Don Corleone dies in the sun, in his garden, with his grandson thinking it's all a part of the game. It is. The game goes on, the rules are in force, Anthony will become a man in the same rich, brutal family tradition in which his grandfather, and his grandfather's grandfather, became men.

Before Anthony takes his first communion, the game is over. The world of the wedding party in *Part I* is, as in the Tahoe party at the opening of *Part II*, in chaos. Throughout *Part II*, there is a terrible sense of things falling apart. Murders, executed with cruel efficiency in *Part I*, are clumsily botched in *Part II*. Panic sweeps the city of Havana as the government collapses before the rebels. Frankie Pentangeli stumbles drunkenly through the Tahoe party crowd, an outraged figure from another time, completely lost in a shiny, new world. The waiters call a Ritz cracker with liver "a can of peas," the family in-laws don't understand Italian, and the closest the band can come to the old songs is "Pop Goes the Weasel."

The most distressing and fundamental sign of change in *Part II* is evident in

Posed first communion photo in *The Godfather, Part II* (1975).

the women of the family. Connie neglects her children and hops from husband to husband. Fredo's wife gets drunk and falls all over other men, humiliating her husband and his family. These crimes are most disturbing because they are crimes against the institution of the family, committed by those on whose obedience the family depends. If women leave the home, the very reason for the family is gone, there is nothing left for the men to protect, the bottom has fallen out. Kay's abortion is a horrible, unnatural blow directed at her man, to whom she owes her security. She murders Michael's son. Seeing no threat to their safety in comfortable affluent America, the wives strike out on their own, away from the traditional family and the domination of men. "These dagos are crazy when it comes to their wives," Fredo's wife babbles. "These wops treat their wives like shit." Connie, her pale Anglo lover at her side, proclaims, "Michael, you're not my father."

Michael's father would fare no better in this new world than Michael does, and that is Michael's tragedy. For Michael, it is clear that the most important thing, the only thing, is to establish what his father would have done in a situation and follow that lead. "Tell me something, Ma," Michael asks his mother, "what did Pop think—deep down in his heart?" As his family crumbles about his ears, Michael can only respond as his father responded, in another world. His success at following his father's lead, and the devastating inadequacy of Vito's example as a model for action in Michael's generation, is clearly established by the jumps between the two men's stories.

The scene switches back and forth repeatedly from a family scene in Vito's young manhood to a family scene in Michael's time. Michael gazes at his sleeping son before he leaves Tahoe for Miami, and the scene fades to Vito, in a 1918 tenement, gazing at his first son in the same ancient way. Michael returns to Tahoe, demanding to know if his aborted fetus was a son, and again we see Vito watching, as the infant Fredo is treated for pneumonia. Vito returns from the murder of Fanucci to his family stoop, saying, "Michael, your father loves you very much," and in the next scene an adult Michael returns to a frigid home, his son's toy car buried in the snow, his wife sewing in an empty room.

Technically Michael stands up well against his father's example as head of the family. He is as patient with the drunken Frankie Pentangeli as Vito is with the ignorant landlord Roberto, and he is as ruthless in his treatment of the enemies of the family. Don Ciccio, the man who killed Vito's father, is, if anything, less of a threat than the sick, powerless Hyman Roth. But the system of revenge demands both men's deaths, and neither Vito, nor Michael, hold back in their fierce dedication to the system.

Connie acknowledges this in her return to the family at her mother's death. "You were just being strong for all of us the way Papa was," she tells

James Caan, Marlon Brando, Al Pacino, and John Cazale in *The Godfather* (1972).

Michael. By now, however, Michael knows that his strength is his family's doom. He knows how hard it is in his time to emulate his father. "It's not easy to be a son, Fredo," he says in the banana daquiri scene in Havana, and there is real empathy in that statement. He and Fredo, as sons in the family, must follow their father. Fredo fails, Michael succeeds, but both are destroyed. Michael, unlike Fredo, suffers the terrible fate of awareness. He must watch himself die without being able to do a thing about it. "He was being strong," he says of his father, "strong for his family. But," he asks his mother, "by being strong—could he lose it?" The old woman doesn't understand. She tells him he will have other children. "No," Michael pleads, "I meant lose his family." "But you can never lose your family," she answers from another universe.

"Times are changing."

These are conservative movies that Coppola has made, conservative in the noblest sense. They apologize for nothing in the past, and hide nothing. Nor do they pretend that the past could or should have survived. But they mourn its passing. They mourn a time when human contact and union were somehow possible, even if only in a limited, rigid family group. They mourn a time when personal liberation hadn't locked us all in our own individual cells. They mourn a time when our fathers loved us very much.

FIVE/MOVIES AND THE CONTINUING HUMAN CONDITION

MOVIES ARE NOT ONLY A REFLECTION of our cultural present and immediate past; they can also be seen as a refraction of the human condition through time. In our humanistic search for cultural links between peoples and ages, movies can aid greatly in our attempts to understand what it is that we share in common—in other words, the human condition.

While we may not always find ourselves in sympathy with the view of the human condition provided to us in movies, and while the view may be more the result of a strong director's or producer's vision than a mirror of society (as Maurice Yacowar points out in his essay on private versus public visions of film-makers in this section), films on the whole do tend to be fairly accurate representations of human desires and needs. They also tend to show us the world as it ought to be rather than, strictly speaking, as it is.

The four articles in this chapter attempt to establish links between the ages in exploring aspects of the human condition that are timeless. Frank McConnell, in his essay on *The Creature From The Black Lagoon,* suggests that, while the 1950s might well have been the breeding ground for such a cultural phenomenon as this film, its message of what lies beneath the lagoon is a message about the basic human sexual condition. Alice and Roland Sadowsky, together with Stephen Witte, illustrate how an apparent nostalgic look at the 1950s in *American Graffiti* is in reality an epic tale retold, this time in the garb of our recent past. Charles Rutherford takes a close look at a beautiful film, *Sounder,* and convincingly shows us the film's classical roots. Finally, Maurice Yacowar pinpoints the dichotomous world of contemporary film which parallels that of all art—the public vision and the private vision exist side-by-side in contemporary culture, as has been the case in all cultures.

Movies have been and continue to be a kind of cultural glue, adhering the cultural present to the cultural past in subtle, strong, and significant ways. When we participate in movies, we are really participating in ritualistic story forms which inform us of the continuing human condition.

Song of Innocence: *The Creature from the Black Lagoon*

FRANK D. McCONNELL

As the popular film, and popular culture generally, become more and more a subject of serious academic interest, we are likely to be treated to more and more thoughtful excursus upon those works which many of us enjoyed, years ago, in the cool unthinking darkness of Saturday afternoon. Not that this multi-leveled coming to light is at all a bad thing: on the contrary, it is one of the healthiest signs of the continuing life of our culture—and of the critical mind which depends so desperately for its own life *upon* that culture. And reading the criticism of a Leslie Fiedler or a Parker Tyler, or the brilliant "pop" fictions of a Thomas Pynchon *(The Crying of Lot 49)* or a Brock Brower *(The Late Great Creature)* is, for a generation trained to be abashed about enjoying films later than *Potemkin,* itself a kind of liberation. But there is a danger in the meeting of academicism and pop culture: one implicit in the phrase, "pop," itself. The danger is, simply, that critics—and their readers and students—might too easily forget that pop culture is, after all, *culture*: that, on its own terms, it is no less serious, and potentially no less moving, than the culture which produced an Ovid or a George Herbert. Those Saturday afternoons—how could we deny it?—were wonderful. But we cannot, should not, go back there; and a criticism which tries to, which turns a serious appreciation of their films into an excuse for returning there, is actually ducking the duties of the more complex and dangerous fun of which, at their best, they were a prophecy.

The film I wish to discuss is, in its way, a parable of this problem, a fable for pop critics. In histories of the horror film, Jack Arnold's 1954 *Creature from the Black Lagoon* is most often regarded as a late and degenerate variant of the Frankenstein motif, a fast-buck piece of sensationalism, a "B-picture" even by the standards of a B-picture genre. There is, certainly, something ludicrously adventitious about the existence of the "gill-man": he is neither a monstrous threat to society (the scientists have to go to the Lagoon to be terrorized by him) nor an extra-terrestrial threat to the world at large (vulnerable, unlike his oriental cousins Godzilla and Reptilicus, to bullets and spear guns). And the charge of silliness may well apply to Arnold's sequels to the first film *(Revenge of the Creature,* 1955; *The Creature Walks Among Us,*

1957), although those productions, too, are not without their delights for the horror aficionado.

The original *Creature,* though, is a far better—and far more important—film than has yet been recognized. Much more than such relatively celebrated efforts as Don Siegel's 1956 *Invasion of the Body Snatchers* or Howard Hawks-Christian Nyby's 1951 *The Thing,* it is definitively a film of the 'fifties, that curious and psychotic decade of American life we seem, in the 'seventies, to be rediscovering with an affectionate and horrified smile. In terms of his popular success—an index of quality frowned upon, sometimes with good reason, by serious film critics—the Creature has established himself along with Dracula, Frankenstein's monster, and the Wolfman as one of the staples of the National crop of fear. I refer, of course, to the series of plastic monster-models produced in the mid-'sixties, with great success, by Aurora Plastics, Inc., which officiated the canonization of the Creature. And I also invoke the fact, unverifiable but obvious, that *any* moviegoer between twenty-five and thirty-five, while he may not recognize the provenance of the Man from Planet X, the Thing, or the phrase "seed-pod," will unquestionably know, upon sight, from what movie comes a photo of the gill-man. The Creature, against all odds of believability, official recognition, and, even, possibly, artistic quality, has *made it.* It behooves us to ask why.

The tradition of horror in the cinema, as we are coming to realize, is one of the oldest and most continuous of cinematic genres. That this is so should really surprise no one with even a minimal acquaintance with the imaginative life of the West, since terrifying tales are among the most ancient and most persistent stories in our inheritance: perhaps, indeed, in the inheritance of the human subconscious. A psychic history of culture, in fact, could be written very efficiently from the morphology of its monsters: the history of those personifications of the void which successive generations have selected as their central nightmares. Roy Huss and T. J. Ross' anthology, *Focus on the Horror Film,* intelligently classifies "varieties" of horror into "Gothic" (or supernatural), "Monster Horror" (mechanical men, zombies, etc.), and "Psychological Horror" (the terrors of dementia). It is a convincing catalogue for the history of film and, indeed, for the history of literature since the romantic era, developing from the Satanic villains of the Gothic tale through the demonic puppets of Mary Shelley and Dickens into the frozen mental landscapes of Kafka and Beckett. But these phases of horror are not *stages,* at least not in an evolutionary sense. According to the particular needs for fear of a given age, any one of the "later" phases of the monster may revert or collapse into a more primal incarnation of the unspeakable, though perhaps overlaid with the trappings of contemporary, "scientific" verisimilitude. Each era chooses the monster it deserves and projects: and all of them are, in their terribleness, blood brothers.

The Creature from the Black Lagoon is a significant case of this. For during the 'fifties, surely the most dominant form of the monster was the alien invader, the hyper-rational saucerman, or the subrational insect mutant, whose threat was not so much personal violence as an insidious, fiendishly cold undermining of the normally (i.e., bourgeois-American) human. I have already mentioned *Invasion of the Body Snatchers* and *The Thing*—both of which exploit the "undermining" of civilization by vegetable life. There are also such classics of 'fifties apocalyptism as *The Day the Earth Stood Still* (1951), *The Man from Planet X* (1951)—in both of which the alien is, ambiguously, well-intentioned but stung to malevolence by human mistrust; *Them* (1954), *Tarantula* (1956), and *The Beast from 20,000 Fathoms* (1953), where the alien is a fearful result of nuclear alchemy; and *This Island Earth* (1955), *Earth Versus the Flying Saucers* (1956), and *Not of this Earth* (1957), "true" types of the evil-bug-eyed-invader movie.

Sociologists and psychoanalysts of the film have for a long time now been making clear the political paranoia underlying these movies: their deep connection with the McCarthyist fear of the subtle Red Menace, with the threat of a massive and nefarious Fifth Column infesting the entire fabric of American society, and (in the case of the gigantic reptilian or insect mutations), with the fear of The Bomb. Raymond Durgnat's splendid essay on *This Island Earth* in *Films and Feelings* may conveniently stand, as example and consummation, of such readings.

But, valuable as these interpretations are, they do not explain the peculiar power of the Creature and lead one to suspect, therefore, that the Creature himself might lead us to a more efficient insight into the life of the decade. He is, as I have said, neither alien invader nor atomic mutant: he is, as one of the scientists observes in the film, "an evolutionary dead-end," a manfish who has, simply and absurdly, survived the eons since his race was spawned. He survives, furthermore, *because* he is the Creature *from the Black Lagoon*—an out-of-the-way South American inlet where time has stood still. His very existence, in other words, is the origin of his peculiar horror. Unlike any other monster one can think of, he is the result of no cause, neither accident nor devilish science nor the supernatural: he simply *is*, primal and eldest, and the outrage he generates is the curse only of those unlucky enough to discover his existence. The story begins with the discovery, by an archaeologist, of a claw-fossil belonging to one of the Creature's ancient race. And the action of the film, then, is the story of what happens to those who seek out—and seek to capture—the primal secrets which are *there* all along in the innocence and blandness of their unharassed privacy.

In what, then, does the terror of the Creature's being there (almost exactly in the sense of Heideggerian *Dasein*) consist? To answer this is to analyze the tightly-conceived plot of the film and to realize, first of all, that, within that plot itself, the Creature is almost as adventitious as he is in the larger tradition of horror-monsters. For while most films in the genre involve some (usually sketchy) love-interest between the young scientist—evil or benign—and the horror's intended female victim, in *The Creature from the Black Lagoon,* unusually and brilliantly, the love-story all but displaces the horror element of the plot. This is for the very good reason, I shall suggest, that the love-story is *another version* of the horror-plot.

After the discovery of the initial fossil, a team of scientists take a small boat to the remote Black Lagoon, hoping to locate more fossils and establish a definite date for their find. The team, besides the mandatory old sage and a pipe-smoking, middle-aged establishment figure, consists of Mark (Richard Denning), David (Richard Carlson), and Kay (Julie Adams). Mark is a brilliant and ambitious young archaelogist, already with a string of important discoveries behind him and anxious to consolidate his fame; David, his assistant, is a more reflective, sensitive, and as yet unproved man; and Kay, Mark's colleague and girl friend from childhood, is beginning to fall in love with David— much to Mark's chagrin. It is in terms of this triangle, Kay's instincts, Mark's possessive jealousy, and David's uncertainty and self-doubt, that the action will develop. And, as the Creature gradually emerges into the center of that action, we see him—perhaps subconsciously, but inevitably, crucially—as a strange symbol and projection of the murderous sexual tension. For *The Creature from the Black Lagoon* is a daemonic pastoral, and its titular monster is, if anything, an almost allegorical vision of sexual terror.

I do not mean to identify the Creature as that shibboleth of critical over-simplification, a "phallic symbol": he is much more than a sublimation; he is a realization of the psychic violence of the phallus itself. He is a *gill man,* a man-fish, a dweller in the aboriginal bath of the world's youth, a rigid swimmer in the generative fluid. I have mentioned that he is one of the most recognizable, memorable of monsters. And surely part of the reason for this is that his make-up is exactly in tune with his deep-structure function in the plot: simply, his now famous head *looks* like a penis. And his behavior in the film, an ambiguous meld of canniness and sheerly instinctual reaction, is not a "symbol" as much as it is a hieroglyph, an icon for the infinitely variable but single-minded urging of the libido.

The Creature's identifying locale, furthermore, as is usual for pastoral, is central to his meaning. The "Black Lagoon," physically, at least, is hardly black at all. Only a few of the film's scenes take place at nighttime, and the Lagoon itself is, as both Kay and David note, lovely—deceptively deep, still waters. The Lagoon's blackness, then, is a matter of its depth—on the naturalistic level of the plot—or of the preconsciously "black," on the symbolic level of the film. For the "*Black* Lagoon," in this sense, invokes inevitable associations of the cloacal: which, as we now know, has strong implications—particularly in the maturely infantile world of the pastoral—with the genital. The very word, "Lagoon," in the popular mythology of American art, has an inevitable tinge of the exotic and erotic about it—via innumerable lovesongs and Dorothy Lamour; imagine the tonal difference in a Creature from the Black Lake or the Black Estuary.

Two years after the *Creature,* Fred Wilcox' *Forbidden Planet* was to earn a justifiable but overblown reputation for its evocation, within a science-fiction context, of Shakespearian pastoral and "the monster from the Id," projected and finally abhorred by its physicist-Prospero. The great advantage of the *Creature* both as art and as socio-political history, is that it represents a confrontation, not with a futuristic monster from the Id, but, in a timescape contemporary to the decade which spawned it, with the *Id itself.* If *Forbidden Planet* is, as many have insisted, Hollywood's *Tempest, The Creature from the Black Lagoon* is its *As You Like It:* less perfect, less profound, even, in a sense—but ultimately richer, truer to generic form, and more *humanly* inclusive.

To go to the Black Lagoon, then, is to return to the primal sink, the nursery site and origin of the species' sexual jealousy. The Lagoon is a place, like all true pastoral places—Arcadia, Arden, Shangri-la—of clarification and terror. And, in this respect, the casting of the *Creature* is a marvel of subtlety and wit, for, throughout the first part of the film, we simply do not know with whom our sympathies are to lie. Granted that the Creature himself is phallus-fascination and phallus-fear, *whose* fascination and fear is he? Richard Denning and Richard Carlson, Mark and David, are two of the most perennial starring leads of all 'fifties B-movies, and thus present a serious dubiety of identification to the viewer. If Mark is sometimes overbearing, David is sometimes too feckless: they even *look* alike, complicating their sexual contest with overtones of sibling rivalry, older against younger brother. And Julie Adams, as Kay, may also—though less predictably—emerge as the dominant member of the trio. Ms. Adams was, simply, one of the sexiest leading ladies that Hollywood managed to produce in the 'fifties, a tantalizing combination of chippie and girl-next-door (the raped schoolteacher in *Blackboard Jungle,* the standoffish school-nurse in *The Private War of Major Benson),* at once statuesque and approachable. In the *Creature,* as sexual motivation for both horror and psychodrama, she is usually photographed—with great good sense—from below and in a one-piece bathing suit.

David (Carlson) emerges at the end of the film as our agent of identification, but not without a good deal of vacillation on the part of the storyline. Even before that, though, the film establishes itself as what we might today call a "sexist" tale, that is, a tale about the warfare *for* Kay, which never, however, takes into account Kay's own emotions in the matter. Bound to Mark by nostalgia and loyalty, she is bound to David by the stronger tie of love. And, in fact, once she admits this tie, the central action of the film can begin, for her function is simply *to love,* and the problem of Mark and David is how to come to terms with the promise and threat to their masculinity of her decision.

After the characters enter the Lagoon, their rivalry and mutual tension becomes increasingly explicit; that, after all, is what pastoral landscapes are there for. The culmination of the first (non-monstrous) part of the film is, surely, the scene—almost absurdly obvious for a generation of Freudian cineastes—where David and Kay, pledging their love on the deck of the ship, are interrupted by Mark, preparing to dive for gill-man fossils, armed with flippers, oxygen mask, and spear-gun. Mark makes a pointed demonstration of the spear-gun's power by firing it into the ship's mast and then gruffly commands David to prepare for their dive. He has become, visually and psychologically, a mirror-image of the archaic monster who will destroy him.

This scene is terribly important, since it establishes for us the nature of the sexual warfare between David and Mark. Possession of Kay is, in reality, only a strategic objective in that war, since the real issue at stake is the nature of manhood itself. Who shall have, finally, the courage to appropriate to himself the energies and violences of the libido? to be, in other words, a *man* for the decade? Both David and Mark—siblings, twins, co-scientists—are good, job-oriented, middle-class rationalists exploring the cloacal-genetic Lagoon, and their contest is a *Kulturkampf,* a definition of what sort of "manhood" their culture will tolerate or sanction. Mark, as owner of the murderous phallic spear-gun, as "older brother," begins with the upper hand; but this itself is a tipoff, since, at least in fiction, upper hands are always dealt to be called. So the Tale of the Monster will, among other things, chasten his individualism and ambition, leading us to recognize in gentle, self-effacing David the waited-for dragonmaster of the Eisenhower decade.

Immediately after the spear-gun scene comes the central—and surely the most famous—passage in the movie, Kay's swimming excursion in the Lagoon. As Kay swims at the surface of the water, the Creature, making his first extended appearance, swims only a few feet below her, his body exactly synchronized with hers, looking up at her. It is a wonderfully balletic sequence and one of the most striking allegories of sexual desire in the history of the art. For the Creature certainly *does* desire Kay, and all the more intensely since he is, himself, a highly abstract, nearly "disembodied" projection of that desire in David and Mark. He is, to repeat, that force which men face only in the simplified world of the Lagoon, which civilization, indeed, refuses to let them face.

The great horror-film analogue for this situation, of course, is King Kong's lust for Fay Wray. But *King Kong* (1933) is a far more conventional, perhaps simpler, exploitation of erotic panic. The giant gorilla, after all, is not a projection of the psyches of the film's two male leads, the slick showman-entrepreneur and the rough-edged but human sea captain. He is, as innumerable commentators have pointed out, himself a pathetic, all-but-human victim of that rage for beauty which is man's cross and crown in this tradition of mythology. *Kong* assimilates, then, to the uncounted retellings of the Beauty and the Beast story, from James Whale and Cocteau to Claude Chabrol's brilliant *Le Boucher*. *The Creature*, however, as I have already suggested, belongs to the older, sterner archetype of the dragon and the dragon-slayer. In that archaic contest, we recognize the ultimate stakes to be the recreation of the world, through control of the anti-human, instinctual chaos which the dragon incarnates—and which the hero must slay in himself before meeting his apocalyptic adversary.

As the film develops, the Creature manages to kill three of the crew and, escaping from momentary capture, to maim another. Mark, the assertive, sexual, and intellectual bully, insists on staying to capture or kill the monster—insists, in other words, upon being the simple hero which the archetype demands, on *mastering* the penis-fear of the Creature and thus establishing his right to Kay. David, however, is kinder. He realizes that the Creature is himself an innocent monster, provoked only by human intrusion, as he realizes that his older-brother adversary, Mark, is the prey of emotions over which he has no control. After the last attack, though, supported by the remaining crew, David insists that the ship leave the Lagoon, for the safety of all. Nor can it be accidental that that last attack is the maiming of the middle-aged, establishment figure of the team (Whit Bissel), whose judicious yet still-productive place in the microcosmic society of the science-ship needs now to be filled.

It is the first time in the film David has usurped Mark's authority and a decisive—though not a final—moment in his struggle for manhood. For *The Creature* is, psychosexually, a much subtler movie than many recent "serious" films in the same area (to take one among many, Schlesinger's *Sunday, Bloody Sunday*). David's *public* assertion of control must be supported by a more difficult, privately won self-assurance. And the film, without ever suggesting the least dramatic agony in the character of David, brilliantly projects that struggle, with a tact almost like that of medieval allegory, in its final movement.

To a psychoanalyst, the young David's early, forced assertion of dominance might well lead to a kind of sexual paralysis, an uneasy stand-off between the adult and the adolescent within him. In terms of the movie itself—and of a long tradition of Western allegory—it is not enough to escape from the phallic Creature and all he represents: he must be faced, and faced maturely. How appropriate, then, that, as the ship, under David's command, begins to sail out of the lagoon, the crew finds the exit channel has been blocked *by the Creature.* Exit and entrance channel, one should say, since it is an exit from the clarified world of erotic drives in the Lagoon and an entrance to the "real" world of grownup life: a real *limen,* a threshold, with all the associations Freud, Jung, and Jack Arnold are capable of giving that word.

"Crossing the threshold" is the traditional duty of initiates and, in our own culture, of bridegrooms about to take on the full rights of manhood. No less so for David. For to cross this threshold is at once to overcome the final terror of the Creature, to establish his professional/societal usurpation of Mark, and to win his intended bride, Kay. If the film, as a whole, has been on one level a parable of occlusions to sexual maturity, this last movement is beautifully (physically, *filmically*) its culmination and resolution.

In order to remove the blockade the Creature has placed across the channel, Mark and David once again go under water, but now with David directing operations. Once they are below, the Creature, predictably enough, attacks, grabbing Mark. And now David takes the spear-gun, already established as the emblem of Mark's self-confidence, to save his partner. The transfer of power, made socially on the deck of the ship, is now being ratified in the Lagoon-world. And it is important to note that David seizes the spear-gun, as he had seized power, out of a kind of higher selflessness, a primarily *corporate* sexuality and psychic maturity.

But this, too, is not enough. There has to follow the climactic test upon David, his confrontation with the Creature himself. In the well-known sequence that follows, the wounded Creature summons the strength to take Kay from the ship, through his secret underground passage, into his own subterranean lair. David, of course, follows: and by now, in this film, we are not surprised to see the re-emergence of such an archetypal motif as the night-journey through the labyrinth (cf. Theseus searching for the Minotaur, Aeneas in the Underworld, Leopold Bloom in Nighttown). To meet the Creature face-to-face is to meet, in a preternaturally violent atmosphere, the *full* terror of maturity; and it is thus a brilliant touch that the Creature wrests away from David his spear-gun, robbing him of any of the mechanical attributes of manhood in a terminal—sexually, an apocalyptic—crisis. But David, to the end, is a corporate hero. As he has sacrificed his own *rite de passage* to the good of society, so society intervenes to complete that rite for him. He stands his ground, facing the unspeakable gill-man. And, in an ending that can only be called *civitas ex machina,* we find that the other crew-members have followed him through the labyrinth, and shoot—though they do not kill—the Creature, driving him away, back to the Lagoon, so that they, David and Kay, may rejoin the daylight world to which all pastorals, ultimately, lead back.

A strange film, a strange blend of insight and inadvertence, of the archaic and the post-industrial. And, I suggest, a film, a work of art, which like all major works of art makes sense only by making sense of its age. *The Creature from the Black Lagoon* confronts, as frankly as 'fifties reticence will allow and more subtly, perhaps, than 'sixties and 'seventies frankness can manage, the tangled skein of sexual, social, and violent impulses out of which politics is made. It is a horror story whose true theme is the refusal of heroism, a story of battle against the monstrous almost without battle. And, as such, it makes deeper sense of those other 'fifties monster movies I have mentioned. For beyond the political, anti-communist implications of the seed-pods in *Invasion of the Body Snatchers* or the withered, desiccated saucer-men of *Earth Versus the Flying Saucers,* we glimpse in *The Creature* the central evasion of energy, the central fear of the life-force itself which underlay the witch-hunts and HUAC purges. Philip Wylie, in his celebrated attack on McCarthy in *Generation of Vipers,* identified the real power of the charismatic Senator as an extension of the timidity and protracted adolescence of "Mom-ism." *The Creature* helps us see—beautifully, in every sense of the word—how right Wylie was.

In a film of the year before *The Creature,* Samuel Fuller's 1953 *Pickup on South Street,* one can see the traditions of the thriller and the *film noir* undergoing a metamorphosis into the political shadings of the decade: the enemy has become The Enemy, the mysterious and incredibly resourceful Fifth Column, and the hero's battle against the crooks has become Richard Widmark's quest for the ability to love Jean Peters. Arnold's film gives us the same transformation, but from the other side of the spectrum. If the thriller was turning into sexually-timid romance, the sexually-timid romance of the horror film was also turning into political thriller, in a more subtle way. David's wet-suit in *The Creature,* at least symbolically, is made of grey flannel. Like Hugh Marlowe in *Earth Versus . . .* , Rex Reason in *This Island Earth,* James Whitmore in *Them,* and John Foster Dulles in the Suez crisis, or Eisenhower in Vietnam, David fights only when provoked by the eruptive terror of the insidious, the anarchic, the asocial. And his fight, although it may seem an entry into maturity, is in reality a struggle to *maintain* the innocence, the happy consciousness of a man who knows his place in the system and comfortably functions therein. The threshold becomes a circle, the labyrinth the maze of a standardized I.Q. test.

This is what I mean by insisting that the Creature, unlike other and earlier versions of horror, is almost *not there.* He is *what threatens:* but it is an abyss glimpsed only in three-quarter profile. One is not surprised to discover that the horror film, after its late heyday in the mid-fifties, should take two quite different lines of development from anything that had gone before. The Roger Corman Poe-cycle, featuring Vincent Price, is almost a non-horror genre; Price is usually cast, not in the role of villain, but of perturbed and deranged *victim* of forces too awful and too complex to be even visualized (*House of Usher,* 1960; *The Haunted Palace,* 1963). It is as if he were at once David and the fearsome Creature. The nostalgiac revivals of Dracula and Frankenstein produced by Hammer films, on the other hand, represent a kind of vision of America from abroad that insists, like British rock of the 'sixties (The Beatles, The Who, The Rolling Stones), upon rediscovering, in a continental context, the true roots of the American vision of the abyss. Their great popularity in the States, like the successes of the rock groups, are in fact a testimony to the persistence of those dangerous visions, even throughout the relative doldrums of the Eisenhower and Kennedy years.

But to say this much is, perhaps, to read *The Creature* as a failure of the imagination; and that, definitively, it is not. The film, brilliant in its truth to its own form and era, is also a landmark in the psychic history of the horror film. Song of innocence it may well be; but, in its final (unintentional?) implications, it is not only an exploration, but a criticism of those monsters our younger selves found fit to tremble at. And, in the sad, abandoned figure of the Creature himself, we may read an equally powerful, maybe even more compelling, version of that insight into the tragedy of the human denial. . . .

It is what Saturday afternoon was really *about,* and its darkness is central to whatever of light we may have since achieved.

The Epic World of
American Graffiti

ALICE SODOWSKY, ROLAND SODOWSKY, AND STEPHEN WITTE

"Where were you in '62?" ask the posters advertising *American Graffiti;* and the film does take its audience back to a time which many remember as "the good old days." But the movie imports more than mere nostalgia for a past: it explores the consequences of technology upon an age that still has the need to understand experience through a mixture of epic, myth, and romance patterns. *American Graffit's* achievement—or near-achievement—is that it gives us a chance to satisfy this need, to find these patterns, in a mundane, all-too-familiar mechanized world.

The mythic land of *American Graffiti* is a country of city streets under the false day of relentless lights, of youths who live on wheels, where even the waitresses are on roller-skates and where all are electronically linked through the pulsating beat of their radios. The music (of the spheres?) is broadcast by Wolfman Jack, the mysterious surrogate god of this neon wasteland. Among its inhabitants are a few adults who are shadow figures, aliens briefly encountered with hostility or indifference by the true "citizens" of this country: the police have the rear axle of their car torn off; John Milner calls a cop an obscene name in contemptuous dismissal; the Moose Lodge members of the arcade are naive about Curt and consequently are robbed; in the airport scene, Curt and Laurie's parents are mere props who simply say goodbye. The only adult who tries (ineffectively) to reenter this country is a high school teacher who betrays his official trust by meeting one of his female students in an alley just after giving Curt some sententious advice about going away to college. There is, however, an adult who remains ambiguous. She is the elusive blonde in the white Thunderbird, a woman who may be a prostitute, or the wife of a jeweler, or both, or neither. Silently mouthing, "I love you," she is a vision of beauty that Curt has seen through the double windows of the parallel cars. She is the dualistic symbol of romance and seduction, a figure of great appeal yet associated with societal decadence.

Defining the topography of this mythic country are the patterned streets of Modesto, California, which stretch into mazes of vibrating lines and harsh colors ending on one side at the wooded lake area where couples attempt to make love and where, as the story goes, the Goatman kills people. On the other side, however, a route extends beyond the boundaries of the country. It is Paradise Road, where two climactic actions occur: John Milner defeats the challenger from another town here, and Curt's last view of Modesto is of this road as his plane carries him away.

Within this closed "universe" moves John Milner, duck-tailed driver of a chopped and channeled '32 Ford, the fastest car in town. John is the epic hero of *American Graffiti's* society: he is the idealization of its code of conduct, the gloomy (because of his Beowulfian sense of his own impending doom) upholder of the "traditional" values of the high school set, the foremost of the Mel's Drive-In knights who, not unlike those of Arthur's Round Table, start out on their quests for adventure from the circular curbs of this Burger-and-Coke Camelot and return to recount their deeds, always accompanied and comforted by the omnipresent, seemingly omniscient voice of their local deity, Wolfman Jack. John's legs are too long for his torso, so that his walk is almost absurdly graceless; he cannot stand, but slouches against car fenders and walls, thumbs in pockets or belt-loops. Only when he dons the "armor" of his squinting, visor-like hot-rod coupe does he assume heroic proportions; like his literary antecedents, Milner is nothing unless encased in his battle dress. Only once—when he rescues Toad from the car thieves—does he act heroically without his armor, and in that scene the inept hoods are also "out of uniform," that is, not automotively accoutered.

As the representative *par excellence* of the social order, Milner must be prepared to accept all challenges from suitably formidable opponents, opponents who intrude on the domain (i.e., the "main drag" streets of Modesto) and thus threaten the honor (essentially, the jejune "manhood") of the society. So it is when Bob Falfa appears on the drag in his hot '55 Chevy and begins issuing challenges with the proper heroic decorum; when a gum-popping girl he has picked up entunes "Ain't he cute?" through her nose, the "epic battle"— the drag race—becomes inevitable.

John cannot carry the entire burden of the hero in *American Graffiti*, however, because he is limited. He is capable of feats of derring-do only within the physical-social sphere of his "world." It remains for Curt, the anti-hero, whose consciousness increasingly includes more than John can comprehend, to reach beyond the apparent bounds toward a spiritual goal, symbolized by the woman in the Thunderbird. Curt is neither wholly within nor without the order: he drives a rickety Citroen, an obviously weak link to John's souped-up world. But, despite the ambiguity of his relationship to the society, of which Curt alone seems aware, he is accepted and even esteemed by its members, as though they somehow sense his importance, as a kind of societal *Vates,* a poet-prophet, to them. John is his rough but sincere friend; a former girl friend still has affection for him; even the "Pharaoh Gang" members eventually solicit his companionship after first threatening to kill him.

John and Curt's adventures during the night differ essentially in that John, having long since passed all initiatory tests and having no further ambitions, needs nothing and learns nothing. For Curt, everything is preparatory: the high school hop merely amuses him, and he leaves, while another member of the peer group, Steve, remains—an action foreshadowing the fate of the two characters which is so mechanically proclaimed in the "epilogue" of the film. Curt engineers an abrupt leave-taking from a former girl friend while Laurie entices Steve to stay behind; in league with the Pharaoh gang, Curt sabotages a police car then tactfully rejects them; he talks face-to-face with Wolfman Jack while the rest speak of the disc jockey as an other-worldly figure. Unlike Curt's destiny, John's is heroic in the society's terms because it is identifiable; Curt's "destiny" has some parallels with John's but is unheroic because it is beyond the society's ken.

Curt and John, then, are hero and anti-hero around whom the episodes leading to the climactic drag race and Curt's departure revolve. John's rescue of Toad from the two thugs, his preliminary race with Bob Falfa, the issuing of

Mackenzie Phillips and Paul Le Mat in *American Graffiti* (1973).

challenges and counter-challenges, and the encounter with the cop are trivial activities from an adult's point of view or perhaps from Curt's, but, given the values of the world as John knows them, the episodes take on significance and thereby qualify as epic-heroic actions. In this sense John is not unlike the western gunfighter caught in a time and place by his role, sensing his own doom and unable to escape it. Curt's actions against adult or alien "enemies," such as the cops and the Moose Lodge members, are significant within the order; but he recognizes the meaninglessness of those actions. Reinforcing the idea of triviality within the system is Toad, who, like the original braggadocio, dons armor for which he is unfit and parodies—and thus cheapens—the actions of the real hero. Furthermore, Toad's too-eager acceptance of an armor for which he is unsuited prepares the audience for the stark announcement of his disappearance in the Vietnam War.

Complementing the sterile aimlessness of the blacktopped kingdom are the relationships between the knights and their ladies: Toad and Debbie, John and Carol, Steve and Laurie, Curt and the blonde in the Thunderbird. One sees mirrored in these relationships facets of the dehumanizing mechanical world: Toad must lie about the number of vehicles he owns to attract Debbie, and John in his super car can get Carol to leave only after pretending he is going to rape her. Steve and Laurie's relationship is the most visible and permanent, however, because it is they who remain and from whom a new generation of knights will spring. But they, too, are objectified in terms of the machine. They are first seen in Steve's Impala talking about the future. Framed by the car window, Laurie tells Steve, between mouthfuls of french fries, that he should not leave Modesto. Her reasoning is defined by the car's enclosure, narrow and cramped and omitting any possibility for change or expansion. Their final reunion is brought about by Falfa's car wreck. Only Curt, whose "lady" remains apart, is finally able to realize that no fulfilling human relationship can exist in the Modesto universe.

Curt and John make parallel visits into areas which have meanings beyond those which the hero and the anti-hero have previously explored. These areas take on significance because there Curt and John are not accompanied by music and because they cannot come into these places by car. Milner takes Carol to a dark salvage lot, the equivalent of the epic romance underworld, where they walk in the quiet unlit shadows as Milner points out the dented and crushed armors of past heroes. The scene bodes not only Milner's eventual death but also the death of the world which sustains him.

Curt, on the other hand, makes his visit to the radio tower where, if he does not experience an ethereal vision, he at least begins to understand what is amiss in his blacktopped world. Curt "climbs the mountain" in search of Wolfman Jack, the elusive and mysterious disc jockey god to whom all the young knights and their ladies respond and whose music provides the background for all the film's errant adventures. Curt hopes that Wolfman Jack will send a radio message which will put him in touch with the nameless blonde in the Thunderbird. The tower, unlike the salvage lot, is brightly lighted, making it easy for Curt to find its only inhabitant, a corpulent man sucking popsicles. He tells Curt that he is not Wolfman Jack but that he will do what he can to get the message to him. Then, between slurps on his popsicle, he off-handedly advises Curt to leave town. He also offers Curt a popsicle (the wafer of the electronic temple) which Curt, significantly, refuses. As Curt leaves, he overhears the fellow taping a Wolfman Jack commercial and thus learns what no one else in his group knows, viz., that the sticky-fingered man is the pop god of the air. Curt returns from the tower; and although his quest cannot be granted by the turntable deity, Curt will act on his advice, thereby freeing himself from the world in which John Milner is both hero and victim.

Curt's increasingly frantic search for the woman in the white Thunderbird is like the other episodes of the film in that it has meaning only in context, and even there only for Curt's heightened awareness. Given these conditions, she— or the ideal she represents for Curt—gradually acquires a mythic significance;

Wolfman Jack in *American Graffiti* (1973).

she is the Holy Grail of King Arthur's Knights, the romantic Daisy of *The Great Gatsby,* the powerful ring of *The Hobbit*—all of which are associated with the collapse of a society. Thus, Curt's quest is less spectacular but ultimately more profound in its impact than John's adventures; Curt cannot attain the White Vision in Modesto, but he can leave this ''world''; and when he does so, he sees from the airplane window that if he has not yet achieved the goal of his quest he is at least headed in the right direction, away from the neon nights of Modesto and toward the sun of a larger world.

Thus, these gasoline-powered experiences become, as they are translated into time-honored patterns, more than graffiti, more than isolated adventures in nostalgia. In looking at the two protagonists, John the inner-hero, gloomy with a half awareness that he epitomizes the values of a world he no longer can belong to or escape from, and Curt, the anti-hero who is able to leave John's world, we are painfully aware of the kind of society being explored in this film. The land of techno-youth is as depressing a nether world as one could imagine. But the meshing, valid or not, of this four-wheeled world with the patterns in which our ancestors once found dignity and meaning offers us a bit of sanity, allows us to fulfill that singular human need to find form where there appears to be none.

A New Dog with an Old Trick:
Archetypal Patterns in *Sounder*

CHARLES S. RUTHERFORD

In viewing the film *Sounder* for the first time, I was particularly struck by the second reunion sequence (the earlier return of the wounded hound, Sounder, having presaged the ultimate return of the wounded father). Now, as the halting figure moved up the dusty road, Sounder began to whine and bark for the first time since the separation and shooting and then to plunge eagerly toward the man he recognized as Nathan Lee. Here, just as in Homer's *Odyssey,* the faithful old hunting dog is the first to recognize and affectionately greet the returning exile. Reflecting on this correspondence in situation and names (Argus and Sounder) and numerous other parallels, I sensed that the *Odyssey* had been employed to provide a continuing thematic skeleton for *Sounder.*

A subsequent reading of William H. Armstrong's novella *Sounder,* from which the screenplay was adapted, has confirmed this conclusion. In an "Author's Note" to that novella, Armstrong speaks of his first teacher, "a grey-haired black man," who, after the lessons were finished, told stories which "came from Aesop, the Old Testament, Homer, and history." The teacher "talked little, or not at all, about his past. But one night . . . after he had told the story of Argus, the faithful dog of Odysseus, he told the story of Sounder, a coon dog. It is the black man's story, not mine. It was not from Aesop, the Old Testament, or Homer. It was history—*his* history."[1]

Though Armstrong's novella indeed contains the kernel of the epic myth found in the film version of *Sounder,* the film differs greatly from the novella in emphasis and in the specific details of the Homeric parallel. It is not my intention here to record these differences in a fiction-into-film approach. I shall mention them only in passing. It is enough to state that, if the novella, like the old black man's stories, draws upon the Old Testament, Aesop, and Homer, it is the Homeric elements which screenwriter Lonne Elder III has chosen to emphasize in fashioning a screenplay which he characterizes (in a letter to the *New York Times*) as "a story that has as its focus the universality of human dignity and strength in the face of adversity."[2] I intend here to trace the Homeric motifs which lie beneath the beautiful and moving surface of *Sounder,* ultimately lending it the universality which Elder wished to impart.

The Homeric substructure, while it underlies much of *Sounder,* is never allowed to surface, to take over the film. It is constantly held in check as the best known model of a timeless pattern, the motif of exile and return played out within a single family. We view in *Sounder,* as in the *Odyssey,* the strength and cohesion of a family unit, the desperate need for the return of the father figure, and the relentless search for the father by the son. We do *not* focus upon the journey of the father or witness his struggle to return. In other words, we view the action primarily from the point of view of the household in Ithaka: of the mother (Penelope/Rebecca) and the son (Telemachus/David Lee). The action of *Sounder* thus roughly corresponds to the first four books (the "Tele-machiad") and the last twelve books of Homer's epic.

Yet, as in the *Odyssey,* the father is, even absent, the most powerful character in the household from which he has been separated. By the time Nathan Lee Morgan has been shipped off to the labor camp, we have already witnessed the bonds of affection between father and son, and father and mother, and recognized the extent to which the Morgan family draws strength and dignity from Nathan Lee. In the *Odyssey,* which begins with Odysseus already gone, this affection must be shown in retrospect (reported not dramatized), as various characters remind Penelope, Telemachus, and the Ithakans "how like a gentle father Odysseus ruled [them]."[3] In *Sounder,* this bond of love is demonstrated by the camera in such shots as the exchange of glances between Nathan Lee and Rebecca (after the coon hunt and at parting) and by the silent dignity of the handshake between David Lee and his father.

An even more important function is served by the sequence depicting the baseball game, an episode not found in Armstrong's novella. Nathan Lee is technically a reprobate, a thief. He *has* stolen the food. But this sequence clearly portrays his *joie de vivre* and establishes him, beyond the bounds of his family, as a hero among his peers. Here Elder seems to have borrowed the common heroic device of the epic games to demonstrate Nathan Lee's prowess, just as Odysseus' skill is revealed in his titanic discus throw at the court of Alkinoos in Book VIII of the *Odyssey.* The awareness that Nathan Lee is clearly the superior athlete is nicely complemented by the following sequence, the journey home in which Ike, reflecting another common epic device, composes a song celebrating the hero's exploits:

> Speedball, Speedball, baseball is your game.
> Speedball, Speedball, baseball is your game.
> The other team got two,
> Speedball's team got three.
> Speedball, Speedball, baseball is your game.

In response to this, Nathan Lee utters his epic boast: "If they saw me pitch the way I did, they'd hire me just to strike out Babe Ruth." If the following arrest sequence shows Nathan Lee to be a common thief in white men's eyes, the epic baseball game has forced us to view him, by other standards entirely, as a heroic figure in his own community. Conversely, in the *Odyssey,* while we view the greatness of Odysseus' exploits, we are constantly aware of a different point of view—that of Polyphemus or the suitors—which apprehends him in more negative terms.

Janet MacLachlan and Kevin Hooks in *Sounder* (1972).

The deepening of the character of Rebecca, the mother, presents perhaps the most striking difference between novella and screenplay. In Armstrong's novella, she, like all the other characters, is nameless; very little of the action focuses on her. Yet, in the film, Rebecca plays such a central role that Cicely Tyson was nominated for an Academy Award as best actress. Certainly, the expansion of the role of Rebecca is related to Elder's employment of the *Odyssey* myth. She is the Penelope figure who keeps the household going while the father is away. We frequently witness Rebecca doing domestic tasks (shelling walnuts to sell, preparing meals, washing clothes). Moreover, if Penelope shuns the suitors' advances, Rebecca is no less disdainful of the meager offerings of the white men with whom she must deal, telling Sheriff Hill, "You got you a low-life job, Mr. Sheriff," telling Mr. Perkins that the family will get the crop harvested, without Nathan Lee if necessary, refusing to take consolation from the words of the preacher ("Is that a blessing, Reverend?" she asks), and, finally, adamantly refusing to accept Perkins' praise for a job well done. If Rebecca is not actually besieged by suitors while Nathan is away, she is forced to deal with representatives (Sheriff Hill, Mr. Perkins) from a powerful society alien to her own, a necessity she manages without compromising herself. Yet even Penelope's very plight is suggested in an almost frivolous manner at one point in the film. When David Lee arrives at Mrs. Boatwright's house to enlist her aid in finding his father, he is momentarily unable to find her; as he stands on the porch calling, we hear a radio from within her house droning a soap opera: "Over and over you've been asking me to marry you," says a woman's voice. "I'll marry you this very day." Finally, Penelope's device to fend off the suitors by weaving (and undoing) Laertes' shroud is obliquely suggested in *Sounder* when Nathan Lee finally returns. Rebecca is sitting on the porch sewing.

It is, however, in the character of the son, David Lee, that the Homeric myth makes itself most strongly felt. He is the Telemachus figure who, in quest of his father, passes the threshold from youth to early manhood. The boy is the focal point of Armstrong's novella and only fails to dominate the film because other characters have been deepened, not because his part has been diminished.

From the film's opening sequence, the coon hunt, the son is identified with the father. A visible bond of affection and a common experience bind their fortunes together. Even their names—David Lee and Nathan Lee—are so similar as to cause minor confusion at the outset when Rebecca utters one or the other. The confusion is intentional! The two are not meant to be separated; their identity is fused. The education and maturation of the boy depend directly upon his relationship to his father. This is emphasized at the outset when David Lee rationalizes their empty-handed return from the coon hunt in the words of his father: "You miss some o' the time what you do go after; but you miss all o' the time what you don't go after." To this, Nathan Lee replies, "Now, who says I didn't put my mark on you, boy?" Just so Telemachus is told repeatedly in the first four books of the *Odyssey* that in speech, cunning, and appearance, he bears the mark of Odysseus. Yet, at the beginning of the *Odyssey,* Telemachus is not his father's equal; he is an untried youth, sheltered by his mother and his nurse, Eurykleia, who asks him, "Dear Child, whatever put this into your head?/Why do you want to go so far into the world—/and you our only darling?" [4] Just so, David Lee is not his father's equal at the outset, as he finds out when he chides his father about missing the coon with his "big shootin' rifle.'' Nathan Lee puts him in his place firmly, telling him, ''Don't make funny with your daddy, boy!''

It is only with the departure of the father that the son begins to assert himself. Rebecca leaves for town to see about Nathan Lee with the injunction to Josie May and Earl: ''David Lee's in charge now, and you do just as he tells you.'' The next shot shows David Lee aping his father, chopping wood, the last domestic chore at which we had seen the father. Then we see David Lee feeding his brother and sister, symbolically taking over the function of his absent father, putting food on the table.

The crux of the Homeric parallel, in the film as in the novella, lies in the boy's actual search for the father, a journey which is also a search for his own identity. Telemachus is stirred to go off in search of his father by Athena, first in the guise of Mentes, then of Mentor, an old sea captain who rounds up a crew and outfits a ship for the boy. This function in *Sounder* falls to Mrs. Boatwright (boat-wright), who finds out where Nathan Lee is being held and, in a semi-comic sequence, tries to instruct David Lee how to get to the Wishbone Labor Camp. The camera reveals that the boy's subsequent journey is of epic proportions, showing him on the road in different terrains, at different times of day, and in different weather conditions. It is also obviously an educational journey, one upon which he ''finds himself'' even if he does not find his father. What David Lee learns at Miss Johnson's house about Harriet Tubman, Crispus Attucks, and W. E. B. Dubois (in the film's only intrusive, contrived moment) is incidental to what he learns about himself and his own capacity for learning, about his desire for the future.

By this point in the film, David Lee has matured to the extent that he can articulate the central theme of the film, a lesson that the father already knew. This is the function of the moving sequence in the schoolhouse in which David Lee alone supports Clarence's story (about saving his sister from drowning, even though Clarence didn't know how to swim), citing in evidence his own family's experience in working the farm *because they had to work the farm*. Earlier, Nathan Lee had explained his theft to Rebecca very simply: ''I did what I had to.'' His son's realization that one can often perform superhuman feats because there is no alternative serves as an index of the growth that adversity has thrust upon him. At the film's end, the theme will be reiterated by Nathan Lee in recounting the story of the dynamite blast that crippled his leg. He says that he resolved, as he saw the wall of rocks coming at him, ''To beat the death comin' at me.'' And he projects this inflexible determination into the future in his similar resolution to defeat the pain in his leg, *because he has to*.

If the sequence in the schoolhouse shows David Lee's matured self-awareness, the following one at Miss Johnson's house reveals the lingering need to be reunited with his father before his initiation into manhood is com-

Paul Winfield in *Sounder* (1972).

plete. As David Lee stands at the window, looking out into the blackness, he explains that "Daddy always looks out into the dark even when there's nothin' to see. He says 'It's what you hear.' " (That is, it's Sounder, not Argus.) Their ensuing conversation leads up to the boy's anguished cry: "But where's Daddy?" The son's journey and education have proved him worthy of his father, just as do Telemachus' adventures with Nestor and Menelaus; but the education and quest for self-awareness remain incomplete without the subsequent reunion of father and son and the latter's words of praise for the son's exploits. These can come only after Nathan Lee has returned. He tells David Lee, "That was *some* journey you went on, Son." David Lee tells his father that he has cleaned and oiled his father's rifle in his absence (Telemachus removed Odysseus' weapons from the great hall in Ithaka to avoid smoke damage and to put them out of the suitors' reach). The father's final words of praise confirm the son's initiation into manhood: "I sure am proud o' the way you helped your mama keep this place goin'."

Over a decade ago (1959), another film, *Black Orpheus,* also employed a classic myth as its skeleton. Yet, in that film, it was the Orpheus myth itself which was illuminated; the blackness was incidental, merely a function of the film's setting, carnival time in Rio. In other words, *Black Orpheus* employed a mythic archetype placing its emphasis on the archetypal pattern itself, even calling explicit reference to the myth in its title. The emphasis has been reversed in *Sounder*. The archetypal pattern of the *Odyssey* underlies that film, but it is never insisted upon. *Sounder* focuses specifically upon the experience of a black family in Louisiana in 1933, recording the agony, the dignity, and the strength of *that* experience. Yet, by basing *Sounder* upon the mythic archetype represented in Homer's *Odyssey*, screenwriter Elder has indeed emphasized the heroic proportions of that experience; by suggesting the epic dimension latent in the meanest black experience, he has truly illuminated "the universality of human dignity and strength in the face of adversity."

NOTES

1. William H. Armstrong, *Sounder* (New York: Harper and Row, 1969), pp. vii, viii.
2. Lonne Elder III, "Movie Mailbag," *New York Times,* November 26, 1972, p. D9.
3. Book II, 1. 229. Quotations from the *Odyssey* are from the Robert Fitzgerald translation (New York: Doubleday, 1961).
4. *Odyssey,* Book II, 11. 363– 65.

Private and Public Visions: *Zabriskie Point* and *Billy Jack*

MAURICE YACOWAR

Billy Jack and *Zabriskie Point,* two films that are very different, very similar, very different. *Zabriskie Point* comes from Antonioni, of course, a man who needs no introduction; however, his films may. *Billy Jack* comes from the putative "T. C. Frank," Tom Laughlin, known previously for that shrewd and eccentric motorcycle film, *Born Losers.* Highbrow and lowbrow, do the twain ever meet?

Despite their difference in brow, both films express the climate of America in the early '70s. Protest against the war, confident suspicion about the corruption of the police force, life to the rock sound track, the pill and its pregnant freedoms, both films are steeped in the '70s sense of the times and how they've been a-changing.

The films also have common themes. Both depict the radicalizing of a young girl by her witness to the persecution of a young man. In both films, the heroine grows from a life of cynical, uninvolved wandering to commitment. In *Zabriskie Point,* Mark teaches Daria that the desert that to her seemed "peace" is really "dead." When he is killed returning a borrowed plane, Daria visualizes a beautiful destruction of her master's house and all its plastic contents. That vision is a curse. It augurs her commitment to a violent life. As she drives off into the sunset, Roy Orbison sings of a new dawn.

Billy Jack is narrated by one girl, the school-teacher Jean, but centers on the maturing of another girl, Barbara. The first scene in the film is Sheriff Cole telling his deputy that Barbara has been found. Instead of going to meet her, the deputy goes to shoot mustangs illegally with the town boss, Posener; we first meet Billy Jack when he interrupts Posener's hunt. Through Barbara's eyes we first see the experimental school.

At first Barbara is cynical and disillusioned by "all those phony maharishi types who kept telling me love is beautiful and all that bull shit" — "the person hasn't been born that I like." Through her experience with the school, her love for an Indian boy who refuses to take advantage of her, and her filial devotion to Billy Jack, Barbara recovers faith in the human potential, a sense of community, and militance. She loads the guns for the besieged Billy Jack until she is wounded.

In both films, the central figures are set against a backdrop of revolutionary potential. *Zabriskie Point* opens with a black and student debate over revolution: an entire generation stands behind the individual rebellion of Mark and Daria. Similarly, when Billy Jack is driven off to stand trial at the end of the film, the children of the school line the road in a small but firm honor guard, fists raised in the oath of power. Their gesture moves outside the theater to the streets, where a generation of discontent seethes. Within the film, the gesture relates back to Barbara's introduction to the school where her pregnancy was dramatized as the birth of a black Jesus. When Barbara asks him for a "sign before you die," he responds with the black power salute. The erect fist is antithetical to Billy Jack's pacific resignation of his wrists to the handcuffs.

Nor is the revolution restricted to the young. In both films, the hippy spirit crosses generation lines. In *Zabriskie Point,* the crowd of delinquents who strut around Daria, teasing her for "a piece of ass," are a minor-key version of the revolutionary whites on whose debate the film opened. Both groups have a goal, a slogan, but not the potency to achieve it. The ten-year-olds' gang-rape degenerates into a scuffle among themselves, much as the revolutionaries dissolved into a quarrel among themselves over organization. The old man who helps Mark and Daria repaint the plane has the hippy spirit, as he tells Mark: "It's nice to see a young man who shows some respect." Anyone can join the revolution. As the title song tells us, Zabriskie Point is anywhere, anyplace for those who care.

Similarly, in *Billy Jack* the revolutionary school ranges from eleven-year-old Carol to the middle-aged O. K. Koralis. Billy Jack and Jean are of indeterminable age, wise beyond the years that their energy suggests. In the characters of the doctor, Sheriff Cole, and the town citizens who appreciatively visit the school, Older Folks are related to the school's revolutionary spirit and values. Of course, the antagonists have the same range, from old Posener down to young Bernard and his thirteen-year-old whore.

In both films there is a revolution in the wind that blows across generation lines. But the old hippy in *Zabriskie Point* is a hermit; none of the older generation is shown to change his mind in Antonioni's film. In contrast, in *Billy Jack,* the good citizens are shown to change.

In both films, the revolution is shown as a return to primitivism. The dominant motif of *Zabriskie Point* is not the sterility of the desert but its irrigation. The developers plan to pipe in water for their residential project. Daria and Mark refresh the desert in a livelier way, making love in a dried-up river bed.

Zabriskie Point (1970).

Daria's marijuana high gives her the first of her visions in the film; their love is amplified into a community of writhing lovers, bodies taking shape out of the sands of the desert. Later, Daria discovers water flowing out of rock in a cave; the sight of the stone weeping releases her own tears at Mark's death. Where the Rod Taylor people bring plastic to the landscape, Mark and Daria are harmonized to the elements, particularly air and water.

Billy Jack is based upon a series of contrasting initiation rites—further primitivism. Bernard Posener is initiated into two false kinds of manhood. He "grows" from his inability to shoot at the corralled mustangs to a willingness to shoot Billy Jack, and finally to the murder of Martin. In addition to his initiation into the violence of manhood, he is initiated into sexuality. From a failure with Cindy, he progresses to a preliminary rape of Miss 69, to the bad eminence of his rape of Jean, which is the first time he ever "went all the way with a woman," he tells his aptly named cohort, Dinosaur. Billy Jack finally catches him at the peak of his perverse manhood, in bed with a child, a revolver ready at hand.

Billy Jack has two initiations. One is the unceremonious beating he suffers in the town square, a warning he does not heed of what will happen to him if he persists in a violent and solitary confrontation of society. The second is the snake ceremony, where he will either be killed by the snake or become his blood brother, an old Indian rite.

These rites are interrelated. The snake ceremony is intercut with Posener's aiming his blank gun at Billy Jack: "I could do it. I could kill him." At that time, Bernard sights Barbara with Martin, which is the beginning of Martin's end. When Bernard returns to shoot Billy Jack, he comes upon Jean instead. The film establishes a choice between the traditional American criteria for manhood and the old Indian values of passivity and honor.

The improvisatory theater scenes in the film also relate to the primitivism. For the actors swap roles. In the concert at the school and in the street robbery, the actors play the parts of their adversaries. Children play parents and cops; cops play robbers. This modern psychodrama and role-playing—"things that the townspeople could never understand"—has its analogue and source in primitive magic.

Billy Jack articulates the film's primitivism in his vision. He foresees a triumph of the old Indian spirit and values. "Now what the young people of the world are looking for, what the young whites are looking for, is the Great Spirit" of the Indian heritage. Billy Jack himself, of course, is "a half-breed . . . a war hero who hated the war and turned his back on civilization."

As the film looks back to the American Indian for its values, it also detaches itself from the traditional treatment of Indians in film. Specifically, *Billy Jack* at times becomes a rebuttal to the traditional Western. Bernard Posener is a villain for aspiring to the kind of manhood defined in Western films. The Town Council is comical for its Western predisposition in not respecting O. K. Koralis as a naturalized American. The Freedom School is the very reverse of the schools that occur in traditional Westerns, where a calico schoolmarm comes from the East to teach readin', 'ritin', 'rithmetic, and the repression of the ways of the wild. This school—consisting of Indians, Negroes, whites, the young and the innocent and the oversexed and the worldly of all race, religion, hue, and cry—teaches the civilized savages of contemporary America to be wild and free. Whites are taught to be Indians. Lessons are given in barrel-racing and painting old Indian legends. "Being an Indian isn't in the blood," Billy Jack tells Barbara; "it's a way of life." Perhaps there is even a vestige of the Western myth in the priestly celibacy of Billy Jack. "When will Billy find me," a lovely child sings when Barbara asks if Billy Jack and Jean are lovers. The scenes between Billy Jack and Jean have a sad sense of waste about them that grows out of Billy Jack's resolve to go it alone, not to make a romantic commitment to another.[1]

At the end of the film, when Billy Jack is persuaded to surrender to the police and to stand trial, the meaning of the decision derives from the Western tradition again. Billy Jack is refusing the heroic solution characteristic of the Western, the last-gasp siege, the final shoot-out, the suicidal fighting to the end. That—as Jean tells Billy Jack—is the easy way. Instead, Billy Jack accedes to Jean's pacifism.

In this essential contrast between Billy Jack and Jean, the film achieves its finest subtlety. Billy Jack is a man of violent values and actions, but he is capable of keeping them in check. He is capable of delicate sentiments but not free in their expression, as his unattachment to Jean expresses. Jean is capable of violent feelings but stands for peaceful, selfless acceptance. Jean has the courage and strength to build a Freedom School on that alien civilized frontier; Billy Jack has the strength to lend a protective hand to the school but will not settle in. Only at the end, when violence—Bernard's and Cindy's, both—has led to the death of Martin and Barbara's father, does Billy Jack make the ultimate sacrifice for his love and for her principles and her school. He abandons the shoot-out for a public trial, a public hearing. And he sacrifices his freedom. Instead of waiting to be shown "one place where people love one another and don't hurt each other" before he lays down his arms, he recognizes the school as just that place worth preserving by pacific means.

Billy Jack, then, is a film that operates in the context of other films. In contrast, *Zabriskie Point* is rooted in pre-cinematic culture. Although Antonioni has an undeniable filmic genius, his work has a primarily literary base.

For example, Antonioni expresses his regeneration theme in a series of literary references to the mythical phoenix. Daria is driving to Phoenix, Arizona, when the shadow of Mark's plane crosses her car. When Mark repaints the plane, he transforms it into a bisexual bird, which he even calls a prehistoric bird with flaming genitals, like the phoenix.[2]

Another expression of Antonioni's literary consciousness is the theme of language in *Zabriskie Point*. Mark leaves the opening debate because he thinks action is needed, not words. For the bulk of the film, Antonioni would appear to agree. Words are one way the establishment represses the young and the dangerous. So the police officer translates "I am an associate professor of history" to "clerk" and Mark's comic identification, Karl Marx, to Carl Marks.

Daria's radicalizing is in terms of her abandonment of words. Her first appearance in the film is retrieving a book she was reading at lunch time. At the end, in her vision blasting the American dream house, at a climactic point in the balletic explosion, books are included in her curse. But at the moment the books appear, there is a change in the music. The calm ends, and the sound becomes shrill. At the sight of those flaring flowers of page, the viewer must feel discomfort. The image may be more beautiful than newsreel shots of fascist book-burnings, but the idea is the same.

Perhaps the shrillness of the music expresses Antonioni's detachment from his heroine's vision at the point of her curse on books. Antonioni has been using words well and lovingly in this movie. Mark's plane carries the important words: "One," "She-He-It," "Freecome" (happily under the cockpit), "No More War," "No More Words," "Suck Bucks," "Thankx." The first three, of course, point to the phoenix and regeneration themes. In the parallelism of "No More War' and "No More Words," Antonioni recognizes that the establishment uses words to win its wars. Lexically and logically there is "war" in "words."

The establishment doesn't mean the words it uses, so they call a desert Sunny Dunes. "Do you mind telling me who I'm talking to?" Rod Taylor asks Daria's roommate on the phone, but the "do you mind" is a false pretense. The listener understands and calls his bluff. "Yes, I do mind," he replies, says "hello," then hangs up. Mark, to preserve the sincerity of his "thanks," spells it "thankx."

Because the characters' language is not particularly significant, the dialogue is often delivered in an offhand, inaudible, even incomprehensible manner. The important lines ring out clearly, such as Rod Taylor's remark to his clients that "the price of anything is never either high or low except in relation to its potential use." The line refers to real estate but also applies to the revolution, which, however costly, may still prove a bargain.[3]

Though he shows the abuse of words, Antonioni has not lost his faith in words or his pleasure in their use. In *Zabriskie Point,* the word survives the image. The dawn of which Roy Orbison sings, the sum of Antonioni's affection and respect for the beauty, energy, and values of Daria and Mark and their generation, gives the lie to the sunset which is the image. And the song continues against the blank screen long after the spectacle—the violence and the peaceful splendor, both—have disappeared.

So, Antonioni's cultural background and Laughlin's popular filmic one provide a point of distinction between films. As a result, *Billy Jack* is the more accessible film. It does not require a literary education to interpret it; direct reactions to the characters and situations suffice. Indeed, we are not expected to listen to Laughlin's words too closely. Who, for example, is the "tin soldier" of the theme song?

Billy Jack uses the characters' faces more effectively than words. Antonioni's Daria is given an Indian earthiness by her dark skin, bare feet, brown dress and underwear, long hair, and beads, and by the shot of her reflection solid in a window in her boss's house behind the Indian maid. Laughlin plays his faces for paradox. His halfbreed Billy Jack has a Caucasian face, whereas

Tom Laughlin in *Billy Jack* (1971).

the villainous Bernard has a vulpine Indian haggardness. But then, being Indian is a way of life, not a matter of the face. At times, too, Bernard is a reluctant villain; he must talk himself out of his ambivalence. Then his Indian features may express a goodness that his Posener upbringing has spoiled.

Thematically, the films differ by their final images. *Zabriskie Point* has an ethos of permissiveness and indulgence. Mark will buy a gun and then try to beg a free sandwich. A plane is stolen and defaced, a car is borrowed, a job is abandoned, traffic laws are broken, for no reason but our heroes' restlessness. And the end is the sensually delightful spectacle of a house and its contents blown to the heavens.

Billy Jack ends on a more ambiguous image. The film closes on the sight of a line of kids saluting their hero with the black power sign but dwarfed by the huge open landscape. The film has worked out a circumspect preference for Jean's pacifism over the violence customary to the Poseners and occasionally — albeit dance-like—to Billy Jack. Yet that closing image threatens violence. *Billy Jack* has a more hopeful conclusion than the various explosions that closed off *Zabriskie Point, The Bed-Sitting Room, The Wild Bunch,* and *Leo the Last,* all of them independently working around to the same end. *Billy Jack* sends its hero off to a trial, to a public hearing. *Billy Jack* gives its society one last chance before the explosion, before those children grow up with those fists.

One more difference. *Billy Jack* shows people changing their mind. *Billy Jack* has the power to change people's minds. *Zabriskie Point* is a sermon preached to the converted. No one will change his mind about hippies or life or materialism from watching *Zabriskie Point*. Some of us may change our minds about Antonioni or remark how Antonioni has changed his mind—say, from a vision of vanishing humanity to a faith in its regeneration—but the movie won't change our minds about its topics.

Zabriskie Point is a personal film, an exercise in techniques, a personal essay with personal vocabulary. *Billy Jack* is an auteur film, in which the film-maker manipulates the conventions of his genre to express himself through the public language, thereby perhaps manipulating his audience into refined reactions, revised sympathies, perhaps even a change in view.

Watching *Zabriskie Point,* I was horrified to hear the adult male behind me say, ''That's the way!'' when the black student is killed early in the film, and, ''Good for them!'' when Mark is murdered returning the plane. The polarized characterization in the film permits that kind of misidentification with it. Neither Jean nor Billy Jack is ever far enough away from the moral point of the film to permit that much misunderstanding.

Zabriskie Point is a richer, more beautiful, more profound, better film—I am sure Mr. Antonioni would be relieved to hear me conclude. But *Billy Jack* works better as a social summary and a social force.

NOTES

1. As Andre Bazin reminds us, "Love is to all intents and purposes foreign to the Western." *(What Is Cinema?* Vol. II, 1971, p. 151).
2. The resurrection and bisexual themes are confirmed by one of the songs in the film, "Brother Mary."
3. Compare Antonioni's remark about the letter which Jeanne Moreau reads to Mastroianni at the end of *La Notte:*

   The letter gives a precise portrait of the writer. It's a modestly written letter showing how correct he was to think his talent unsatisfactory. Perhaps I shouldn't have had it read so that the words would be understood. ("An Interview with Antonioni," by Charles Thomas Samuels, *Film Heritage,* Spring, 1970, p. 7).

SOURCES FOR THE
STUDY OF
POPULAR FILM

BY LARRY N. LANDRUM

The purpose of this bibliography is to provide the student and scholar with basic sources for the study of popular film and to indicate where further information can be found. The reference section contains the most useful sources for further information, including the completed and projected volumes of the *AFI Catalogue* and information on production, directors, performers, and screenwriters. Standard general sources that contain much useful information about film, such as *Abstracts of Popular Culture, Readers Guide to Periodical Literature, Bibliographical Index, Humanities Index,* and others, have not been included but should be kept in mind when searching for information about specific films, genres, and trends.

This bibliography covers all aspects of popular film, but it focuses on those that have tended to be most fruitful for understanding the relationships between popular film and culture. Sections on analysis and history emphasize such relationships on a more theoretical level, and the section on themes and genres includes most of the work done in genres in the last decade.

References

General

American Film Institute. *The American Film Institute Catalog: Feature Films, 1961– 1970,* 2 vols. Richard P. Krafsur, executive editor. Washington, D.C.: American Film Institute, 1976. Volume 1 lists by title over 5,800 films exhibited in the United States. Data include country of origin, production and distribution companies, date and place of release, length, MPAA rating, credits for production, genre, sources for script, plot synopsis, and subject classifications. Volume 2 includes an index to credits, with biographies, an extensive subject index, and an index to countries of origin.

————. *Catalog. American Films 1893–1910.* New York: R. R. Bowker.

————. *Catalog. Feature Films 1911–1920.* New York: R. R. Bowker.

————. *Catalog. Feature Films 1921–1930.* New York: R. R. Bowker, 1971.

————. *Catalog. Feature Films 1931–1940.* New York: R. R. Bowker.

————. *Catalog. Feature Films 1941–1950.* New York: R. R. Bowker.

————. *Catalog. Feature Films 1951–1960.* New York: R. R. Bowker.

————. *Catalog. Feature Films 1961–1970.* New York: R. R. Bowker, 1976.

————. *Catalog. Newsreels 1908–1920.* New York: R. R. Bowker.

————. *Catalog. Newsreels 1921–1930.* New York: R. R. Bowker.

————. *Catalog. Newsreels 1931–1940.* New York: R. R. Bowker.

————. *Catalog. Newsreels 1941–1950.* New York: R. R. Bowker.

————. *Catalog. Newsreels 1951–1960.* New York: R. R. Bowker.

————. *Catalog. Short Films 1911–1920.* New York: R. R. Bowker.

——. *Catalog. Short Films 1921–1930*. New York: R. R. Bowker.

——. *Catalog. Short Films 1931–1940*. New York: R. R. Bowker.

——. *Catalog. Short Films 1941–1950*. New York: R. R. Bowker.

——. *Catalog. Short Films 1951–1960*. New York: R. R. Bowker.

Aros, Andrew A. *A Title Guide to the Talkies, 1964–1974*. Metuchen, NJ: Scarecrow Press, 1977. A continuation of the work of Richard Dimmitt. The guide is arranged in alphabetical order according to title and identifies the production company and the literary basis for the film.

Batty, Linda. *Retrospective Index to Film Periodicals 1930–1971*. New York: R. R. Bowker, 1975. Indexes nineteen journals. Items arranged by films, subjects and authors of reviewed books.

Bukalski, Peter J., comp. *Film Research: A Critical Bibliography with Annotations and Essay*. Boston: G. K. Hall & Co., 1972. Annotated items appear on pages 29–38. Brief information on rental, purchase, periodicals, and various categories of information on subjects concerned with film study. Books only.

Cawkwell, Tim, and John M. Smith, eds. *The World Encyclopedia of Film*. New York: A&W Visual Library, 1972. A substantial encyclopedia of personalities involved in film-making. Index to films.

Chicorel, Marietta, ed. *Chicorel Index to Film Literature*. New York: Chicorel Library Publishing Corp., 1975. [Chicorel Index Series, Vols. 22 and 22A]. Identifies books that can be divided into several dozen categories.

Cowie, Peter, ed. *International Film Guide*. South Brunswick, NJ: A. S. Barnes, Annual. International film production, trends, people in film-making.

Cyr, Helen W. *A Filmography of the Third World*. Metuchen, NJ: Scarecrow Press, 1976. Brief credits and annotation for over 2,000 films.

Dimmitt, Richard Bertrand. *A Title Guide to the Talkies: A Comprehensive Listing of 16,000 Feature-Length Films from October, 1927 Until December, 1963*. Metuchen, NJ: Scarecrow Press, 1965. 2 vols. Identifies title, author, and genre for the source of some 16,000 feature-length films.

Directory of Films by and/or About Women. Berkeley: Women's Historical Research Center, 1972.

Dyment, Alan R. *The Literature of the Film: A Bibliographical Guide to the Film as Art and Entertainment, 1936–1970*. London: White Lion Publishers, 1975. Annotated bibliographies arranged according to history, aesthetics, personalities, screenplays, technique, genres and types, film and society, the industry, general works, and miscellany. Subject index.

The Film Index: A Bibliography. New York: Museum of Modern Art Film Library and the H. W. Wilson Company, 1941. Important early source for articles in popular magazines as well as film periodicals. Annotations.

Film Literature Index: A Quarterly Author-Subject Index to the International Literature of Film. Albany, NY: Filmdex, 1973 to date. Indexes articles on film from about 240 periodicals according to titles, films, and subjects.

Gerlach, John C. *Critical Index: A Bibliography of Articles on Film in English, 1946–1973*. New York: Teachers College Press, 1974.

Gottesman, Ronald, and Harry M. Geduld. *Guidebook to Film: An Eleven-in-One*

Reference. New York: Holt, Rinehart, Winston, 1972. Partially annotated lists of books and articles on various aspects of film study, with lists of theses and dissertations, museums and archives, schools, equipment distributors, bookstores and publishers, organizations, festivals, awards, and a glossary.

Halliwell, Leslie. *The Filmgoer's Companion.* (Sixth revised and expanded edition.) New York: Hill and Wang, 1977. Each edition of this popular encyclopedia of film becomes more useful as a general reference. Entries on films, personalities, and subjects are informal. Credit entries usually contain brief filmographies.

Heinzkill, Richard. *Film Criticism: An Index to Critics' Anthologies.* Metuchen, NJ: Scarecrow Press, 1975. Index to 41 critical anthologies by Renata Adler, James Agate, James Agee, Hollis Alpert, John Mason Brown, Judith Crist, Raymond Durgnat, Manny Farber, Otis Ferguson, Penelope Gilliatt, Graham Greene, Pauline Kael, Stanley Kauffmann, Caroline Lejeun, Dwight MacDonald, William Pechter, Rex Reed, Andrew Sarris, Richard Schickel, Wilfred Sheed, John Simon, Susan Sontag, Mark Van Doren, Robert Warshow, Herman Weinberg, Richard Winnington, and Vernon Young—through 1973. Arranged by film title with references to critical works.

Index to Critical Film Reviews in British and American Film Periodicals, together with Index to Critical Reviews of Books about Film, comp. and ed. by Stephen E. Bowles. New York: Burt Franklin & Co., 1974. 2 vols. Indexes 31 film journals.

International Index to Film Periodicals, ed. by Karen Jones. New York: R. R. Bowker, annual. Annotated index of about 60 major film journals according to 11 subject categories, with a subject index.

Lee, Rohama, ed. *The Film News Omnibus of Film Reviews.* New York: Film News, Annual. Reviews of fiction and non-fiction films, together with distribution data and awards. Subject index.

MacCann, Richard Dyer, and Edward S. Perry. *The New Film Index: A Bibliography of Magazine Articles in English, 1930–1970.* New York: E. P. Dutton & Co., 1975. Follows the format of *The Film Index,* with subject categories and brief annotations of entries.

Manchel, Frank. *Film Study: A Research Guide.* Rutherford: Farleigh Dickinson University Press, 1973. This is the most competent general guide. Contains eight sections of references identifying book and periodical items on film literature. Annotated filmographies and bibliographies for genres—war (exhaustive), gangster, musical, horror, science fiction, western; stereotyping; themes—the self, conflict with society, family, adult roles, moral and philosophical aspects; literature and dramatic comparisons; the historical period 1913–1919; film history, a brief section of film study. Six appendices: (1) critics and periodicals; (2) film distributors; (3) a list of cautions; (4) Motion Picture Code and Rating Program; (5) further sources: archives, libraries, bookstores, and sources for stills; (6) selected dissertations. Indexes to article titles, article authors, book authors, book titles, film personalities, film titles, subjects.

Manvell, Roger, and Lewis Jacobs, eds. *International Encyclopedia of Film.* New York: Crown, 1972. More comprehensive than Cawkwell (above), the volume includes a brief history, a chapter on color cinematography, and a chronological list of major films. The encyclopedia covers an extensive range of subjects in some depth. Bibliography, checklist of title changes keyed to country of origin, and indexes to films and names.

Michael, Paul, et al., eds. *The American Movies Reference Book: The Sound Era*. Englewood Cliffs, NJ: Prentice-Hall, 1969. Chapter 1 is a brief history of the film through filmographic histories of genres and other topics, while Chapters 2 through 5 cover credits for players, films, directors, and producers; Chapter 6 lists awards. Brief bibliography; name index.

New York Times Directory of the Film. New York: Arno Press, 1971.

New York Times Film Reviews, 1913–1968. New York: New York Times, 1970. 6 vols.

North American Film and Video Directory: A Guide to Media Collections and Services, comp. by Olga S. Weber. New York: R. R. Bowker, 1976. Includes sources reporting from the United States and Canada. Information on libraries and other sources; includes lending and rental information on films and videotapes, the availability of other media, budgets, expenditures, and staff.

Rehrauer, George. *Cinema Booklist*. Metuchen, NJ: Scarecrow Press, 1972. Supplement 1, 1974; Supplement 2, 1977. The most useful guide to critical materials.

Samples, Gordon. *The Drama Scholar's Index to Plays and Filmscripts: A Guide to Plays and Filmscripts in Selected Anthologies, Series, and Periodicals*. Metuchen, NJ: Scarecrow Press, 1974. Locates sources for play scripts, filmscripts, critical essays, reviews, and biographical information in anthologies and periodicals. Arranged by author and title.

Samples, Gordon. *How to Locate Reviews of Plays and Films: A Bibliography of Criticism from the Beginnings to the Present*. Metuchen, NJ: Scarecrow Press, 1976. An annotated bibliography of guides, indexing services, checklists, periodicals, references for synopses, specialized publications, and sources for stills.

Production

Ash, Rene. *The Motion Picture Film Editor*. Metuchen, NJ: Scarecrow Press, 1974.

Balio, Tino, ed. *The American Film Industry*. Madison: University of Wisconsin Press, 1976.

Carmen, Ira H. *Movies, Censorship, and the Law*. Ann Arbor: The University of Michigan Press, 1966. A historical analysis of the actions of federal, state, and local courts and censorship boards, together with appendices of interviews with individual censors, a table of cases, bibliography, and subject index.

Cripps, Thomas. "The Birth of a Race Company: An Early Stride Toward a Black Cinema." *The Journal of Negro History*, 59:1 (January 1974), pp. 28–37.

Daily, Jay E. *The Anatomy of Censorship*. New York: Dekker, 1973.

Edmonds, I. G. *Big U: Universal in the Silent Days*. South Brunswick: A. S. Barnes and Company, 1977. Brief, but valuable, introduction to the early days of Universal Studios. Illustrations, indexes to titles and names.

Ernst, Morris L., and Pare Lorentz. *Censored: The Private Life of the Movie*. New York: Jonathan Cape and Harrison Smith, 1930. A satirical examination of some of the kinds of censorship that were being carried on in the late twenties by various censoring boards across the country.

Fadiman, William. *Hollywood Now*. New York: Liveright, 1972. An attempt to provide a guide to occupational roles in Hollywood, with chapters on the industry, agent, director, star, writer, producer, and the future. Brief bibliography, index.

Farber, Stephen. *The Movie Rating Game*. Washington, DC: Public Affairs Press, 1972. Drawing from his experiences as an intern on the rating panel and his subsequent experiences, Farber argues that the system is hypocritical and arbitrary in its present form. Appendices include a reprint of the MPA code objectives, studio contract stipulations, a list of typical objections, a list of appealed films with judgments, Dr. Stern's rating definitions, and an extract from the original MPP code.

Faulkner, Robert R. "Dilemmas in Commercial Work: Hollywood Film Composers and Their Clients." *Urban Life,* 5:1 (April 1976), pp. 3– 32.

Faulkner, Robert R. *Hollywood Studio Musicians: Their Work and Careers in the Recording Industry*. Chicago: Aldine-Atherton, 1971. A sociological investigation through interviews of the job situation for Hollywood musicians. The author notes typical categories of attitudes and includes thoughts on methodology. Index.

Fernett, Gene. *Poverty Row*. Satellite Beach, FL: Coral Reef Publications, 1973. Informal history of the B independent films from 1930– 1950. Heavily illustrated.

Fielding, Raymond. *The Technique of Special Effects Photography*. New York: Focal Press, 1972. This is the bible of special effects cinematography, covering cameras, glass-shots, mirror-shots, various matte processes, optical printing, arial-image printing, front and rear projection, and miniatures.

Film Book Series. Vol. 1: *Directors*. New York: St. Martin's Press, 1976.

———. Vol. 2: *Screenwriters and Producers*. New York: St. Martin's Press, 1977.

———. Vol. 3: *Technicians*. New York: St. Martin's Press, 1978.

———. Vol. 4: *Actors*. New York: St. Martin's Press, forthcoming.

Guback, Thomas H. "Social Context and Creativity in Mass Communications." *Journal of Aesthetic Education*, 8:1 (January 1974), pp. 65– 83.

Halas, John, and Roger Manvell. *The Techniques of Film Animation*. New York: Communication Arts Books, Hastings House, 1972. Third ed. The most complete book available on animation techniques. This volume covers all standard aspects of animation from conception through specialized forms, with speculation on future development. An appendix contains opinions about the future of animation, math, measurement tables, a list of films cited, glossary, and selected list of books. Index.

Heraldson, Don. *Creators of Life: A History of Animation*. New York: Drake, 1975. Illustrated, bibliography. Informal introduction to the history, technical development of and major contributors to animation. An appendix contains how-to suggestions, lists Academy Awards, contains a brief bibliography, and a list of suppliers.

Hunnings, Neville March. *Film Censors and the Law*. London: George Allen & Unwin, 1967. A comparative analysis of the practices of censors in England, the United States, India, Canada, Australia, Denmark, France, Soviet Russia. With appendices, tables, bibliography, and index.

Levin, G. Roy. *Documentary Explorations: 15 Interviews with Film-Makers*. Garden City, NY: Anchor Press, 1971. A brief history of the documentary is followed by interviews with Wright, Anderson, Cawston, Garnett, and Loach in Britain; Franju and Rouch in France; Storck in Belgium; Van Dyke, Leacock, Pennebaker, the Maysles, Barron, Wiseman, Pincus, Shamberg, and Cort in the United States. Brief bibliography and index to names and titles.

Leyda, Jay, ed. *Voices of Film Experience: 1894 to the Present*. New York: Macmillan, 1977.

Limbacher, James L., comp. and ed. *Film Music: From Violins to Video*. Metuchen, NJ: Scarecrow Press, 1974. Divided into two parts, the first includes brief articles by artists and others, collected into sections on the early days, theories, and commentaries, techniques, scoring dramatic films, film spectacles, arranging classical music for film, and scoring animated films and comedies. The second part amounts to a film list with dates, a chronology of films with production company and composer(s), a composer checklist, and a discography. Index to Part 1.

McCarthy, Todd, and Charles Flynn, eds. *Kings of the Bs: Working within the System: An Anthology of Film History and Criticism*. New York: E. P. Dutton and Co., 1975. Divided into four major sections and an extensive filmography, this is the most useful collection of essays available on minor films and directors. Contents include essays on attitudes toward B films, various directors, films and film genres and themes, interviews with major personalities, and filmographies of several hundred lesser known directors.

Madsen, Axel. *The New Hollywood: American Movies in the '70s*. New York: Crowell, 1975. Impressionistic view of contemporary film production, stars, directors, publicity, and a chapter on Peter Bogdanovich and Francis Ford Coppola. Subject index.

Marcorelles, Louis. *Living Cinema*. New York: Praeger, 1973.

Maremaa, Thomas. "The Sound of Movie Music." *The New York Times Magazine* (March 28, 1976), p. 40. Discusses the changes in contemporary film music with emphasis on the compositions of John Williams.

Miller, Don. *"B" Movies: An Informal Survey of the American Low-budget Film, 1933– 1945*. New York: Curtis Books, 1973. A useful background survey of the low-budget production companies that flourished briefly before the Second World War.

Powdermaker, Hortense. *Hollywood the Dream Factory: An Anthropologist Looks at the Movie-Makers*. Boston: Little, Brown and Co., 1950. Long one of the most influential studies of the Hollywood system and the relationships between film and the public imagination, the author covers most aspects of film-making and experiencing films in what appears to be a common-sense, if circumspect way. Index.

Rovin, Jeff. *Movie Special Effects*. South Brunswick, NJ: A. S. Barnes, 1977. Illustrated history of special effects, with chapters on science fiction, Disney, Harryhousen, and television. Notes and index.

Salt, Barry. "Film Style and Technology in the Thirties." *Film Quarterly*, 30:1 (Fall 1976), pp. 19–32. Important consideration of technical developments and editing techniques in the production of feature films during the decade.

Salt, Barry. "Film Style and Technology in the Forties." *Film Quarterly*, 31:1 (Fall 1977), pp. 46–57. Continuation of the author's consideration of technological developments and production techniques for the decade of the '40s.

Sampson, Henry T. *Blacks in Black and White: A Source Book on Black Films*. Metuchen, NJ: Scarecrow Press, 1977. Excellent historical study of black film production, with brief credits and synopses for about 200 films, biographical sketches of personalities. Appendices include a filmography of all-black productions, black-cast film organizations, and credits for featured players. Index to names and titles.

Schumach, Murray. *The Face on the Cutting Room Floor: The Story of Movie and Television Censorship*. New York: William Morrow and Co., 1964. A broad discussion of censorship in American movies through anecdotes and vignettes, with appendices containing samples of foreign censorship and the Motion Picture Production Code. Index.

Steen, Mike. *Hollywood Speaks! An Oral History.* New York: G. P. Putnam's Sons, 1974. A series of interviews with persons representative of credit categories. Interviewees include Henry Fonda, Rosalind Russell, Agnes Moorehead, David Cannon, Stewart Stern, William A. Wellman, Pandro S. Berman, James Pratt, Hank Moonjean, Randell Henderson, James Wong Howe, Preston Ames, Arthur Krams, Edith Head, Perc Westmore, Nellie Manley, Arnold Gillespie, Busby Berkeley, Fred Y. Smith, Bernard Freericks, John Green, Catalina Lawrence, Ruth Burch, Hal Roach, Sr., and Albert McCleary.

Sterling, Christopher H., and Timothy R. Haight, eds. *The Mass Media: Aspen Guide to Communication Industry Trends.* New York: Praeger, 1977.

Steward, John. *Filmarama Vol. I, The Formidable Years, 1893–1919.* Metuchen, NJ: Scarecrow Press, 1975. Films listed for personalities involved; title index with casting key. 6 volumes projected.

Steward, John. *Filmarama: Volume II, The Flaming Years, 1920–1929.* Metuchen, NJ: Scarecrow Press, 1977. An extensive list of films arranged according to the names of the persons involved in the performance or production of them. Brief biographical sketches of Academy Award winners.

Thomason, David. *A Bibliographical Dictionary of Film.* New York: William Morrow, 1976.

Toeplitz, Jerzy. *Hollywood and After: The Changing Face of the American Cinema.* London: George Allen & Unwin, 1974. [transl. from the Polish by Boileslaw Sulik] A series of brief impressions of the contemporary film scene, divided into sections on recent changes, big budget movies, personnel changes, political emphases, violence and sex, the underground cinema, the impact of television, and new activities. Notes and indexes.

Trevelyan, John. *What the Censor Saw.* London: Michael Joseph, 1973. A member of the British Board of Film Censors discusses the development of the Board as a social institution and comments on the activities of other similar bodies. Appendices of various codes, subject index.

Truitt, Evelyn Mack. *Who Was Who On Screen: 1920–1971.* New York: R. R. Bowker, 1977. 2nd ed. Lists dates and places of birth and death (often lists cause) for about 9,000 performers active from 1905–1975, together with chronological lists of their films. Includes celebrity performances and those of animals.

Vizzard, Jack. *See No Evil: Life Inside a Hollywood Censor.* New York: Simon and Schuster, 1970. The anecdotal confessions of.

Wagner, Walter. *You Must Remember This.* New York: G. P. Putnam's Sons, 1975. A series of interviews with a broad range of people related to the film industry. The themes range from Jimmy Fidler on Hollywood gossip to writing the script for *The Ten Commandments.*

Directors

Canham, Kingsley. *The Hollywood Professionals: Vol. 1: Curtiz, Walsh, and Hathaway.* Cranbury, NJ: A. S. Barnes, 1973. Detailed essays on the directors, with filmographies and secondary sources.

Dawson, Bonnie, comp. *Women's Films in Print: An Annotated Guide to 800 Films by Women*. San Francisco: Booklegger Press, 1975. Lists the films of 370 film-makers with brief annotations. Identifies distributors and sources for further study. Title and subject indexes.

Geduld, Harry, ed. *Film Makers on Film Making*. Bloomington: Indiana University Press, 1967.

Hochman, Stanley, comp. *American Film Directors with Filmographies and Index of Critics and Films*. New York: Ungar, 1974. Compilation of excerpts from reviews and commentary on the work of 65 American directors, with filmographies and an index to critics and films.

Kantor, Bernard R., ed. *Directors at Work: Interviews with American Film Makers*. New York: Funk & Wagnalls, 1970. Interviews with Richard Brooks, George Cukor, Norman Jewison, Elia Kazan, Stanley Kramer, Richard Lester, Jerry Lewis, Elliot Silverstein, Robert Wise and William Wyler. Filmlists.

Koszarski, Richard, ed. *Hollywood Directors 1941–1976*. New York: Oxford University Press, 1977. A collection of fifty previously printed essays by directors, arranged in the order of the appearance of each director's initial essay. Index.

Parish, James Robert and Michael R. Pitts. *Film Directors: A Guide to Their American Films*. Metuchen, NJ: Scarecrow Press, 1974. Feature-length films (over 40 min.) listed with facts about director, production company, and date. No annotation or index.

Phillips, Gene D. *The Movie Makers: Artists in an Industry*. Chicago: Nelson-Hall, 1973. Essays covering the careers and individual films of American and British directors and cinematographer James Wong Howe. Filmographies, selected bibliography.

Renan, Sheldon. *An Introduction to the American Underground Film*. New York: Dutton, 1967. Contains a brief history, biographical sketches of directors and some performers, a chapter on theaters, and one on new directions. An appendix identifies distributors. Brief bibliography and index to names and titles.

Sarris, Andrew. *The American Cinema*. New York: E. P. Dutton, 1968. An adaptation of the auteur approach to a collection of selected filmographies and brief impressions of directors arranged alphabetically within sections titled "Pantheon Directors," "Fringe Benefits," "Expressive Esoterica," "Less Than Meets the Eye," "Lightly Likable," and other witty titles. A directorial chronology and index to films with directors and dates identified are included.

Schickel, Richard. *The Men Who Made the Movies: Interviews with Frank Capra, George Cukor, Howard Hawks, Alfred Hitchcock, Vincente Minnelli, King Vidor, Raoul Walsh, and William A. Wellman*. New York: Atheneum, 1975.

Schuster, Mel., comp. *Motion Picture Directors: A Bibliography of Magazine and Periodical Articles, 1900–1972*. Metuchen, NJ: Scarecrow Press, 1973. Index to articles on directors, independent film-makers, and animators from 340 magazines. Covers about 2,300 names.

Sherman, Eric. *Directing the Film: Film Directors on their Art*. Boston: Little, Brown and Co., 1976. [The American Film Institute Series] Based on interviews with some 86 film-makers, the volume attempts to cover opinions on all aspects of directors' involvement in film. Index to names and titles.

Thomas, Bob, ed. *Directors in Action*. Indianapolis: Bobbs-Merrill, 1973. Articles collected from *Action* (Directors Guild publication) include interviews, appreciations, and surveys of the work of new directors. Lists Directors Guild of America Awards, along with recipients of the D. W. Griffith Award.

Tuska, Jon, Vicki Piekarski, and Karl Thiede, eds. *Close Up: The Contract Director*. Metuchen, NJ: Scarecrow Press, 1976. A series of ten "career studies" of directors with filmographies and some interview material included. The directors are Walter Lang, H. Bruce Humberstone, William Dieterle, Joseph Kane, William Whitney, Lesley Selander, Yakima Canutt, Lewis Milestone, Edward Dmytryk, and Howard Hawks. The studies are contributions by various hands. Index to titles and names.

Tuska, Jon. *Close Up: The Hollywood Director*. Metuchen, NJ: Scarecrow Press, 1978. Career Studies of Billy Wilder, Frank Capra, William Wellman, William Wyler, John Huston, Alfred Hitchcock, Douglas Sirk, Henry King, and Spencer Gordon Bennett. Filmographies.

Screenwriters

Corliss, Richard. *Talking Pictures: Screenwriters in the American Cinema*. Harmondsworth, England: Penguin, 1975.

Enser, A. G. S. *Filmed Books and Plays: A List of Books and Plays from which Films Have Been Made, 1928–1974*. New York: Academic Press, 1974.

Froug, William. *The Screenwriter Looks at the Screenwriter*. New York: Dell, 1974. Interviews with Lewis John Carlino, William Bowers, Walter Brown Newman, Jonathon Axelrod, Ring Lardner, Jr., I. A. L. Diamond, Buck Henry, David Giler, Nunnally Johnson, Edward Anhalt, Stirling Silliphant, and Fay Kanin. Writers' credits and brief excerpts.

McCarty, Clifford. *Published Screenplays: A Checklist*. Kent, OH: Kent State University Press, 1971. Identifies the book and periodical sources for complete and excerpted screenplays for 388 films. Index to names and titles.

Rilla, Wolf. *The Writer and the Screen: on Writing for Film and Television*. New York: William Morrow, 1974 [British ed., 1973] Practical discussion of the problems and possibilities of writing for film and television. Three sections deal with general orientation, component parts, and writing non-fiction scripts. Index.

Salem, James M. *Guide to Critical Reviews, Pt. 4: The Screenplay from The Jazz Singer to Dr. Strangelove*. 2 Vols. Metuchen, NJ: Scarecrow Press, 1971.

Vale, Eugene. *The Techniques of Screenplay Writing: An Analysis of the Dramatic Structure of Motion Pictures*. New York: Grosset & Dunlap [The Universal Library, 1972, rev. ed.; first publ. 1944]. Straightforward discussion of writing and plotting in three parts: form, dramatic construction, and story. Index.

Performers

Aros, Andrew A. *An Actor Guide to the Talkies, 1965 through 1974*. Metuchen, NJ: Scarecrow Press, 1977. A continuation of the work of Richard Dimmitt. The volume identifies performers' roles according to film titles.

Barris, Alex. *Hollywood's Other Women*. New York: A. S. Barnes, 1975. Supporting actresses.

Baxter, John. *Stunt: The Story of the Great Movie Stunt Men*. Garden City, NY: Doubleday, 1974. An illustrated survey of the careers of these athletes of the film.

Dimmitt, Richard Bertrand. *An Actor Guide to the Talkies: A Comprehensive Listing of 8,000 Feature-length Films from January 1949 until December 1964*. Metuchen, NJ: Scarecrow Press, 1967–68. 2 vols. Arranged according to film titles, the guide identifies actors' roles in most American and European films. Covers some 30,000 actors.

Emmons, Carol A. *Famous People on Film*. Metuchen, NJ: Scarecrow Press, 1977. This is an international filmography of non-fiction films keyed to historical figures. Credits and annotations, with name, title, and subject indexes.

Griffith, Richard. *The Movie Stars*. New York: Doubleday, 1970.

Lahue, Kalton C., and Samuel Gill. *Clown Princes and Court Jesters*. South Brunswick, NY: A. S. Barnes, 1970. Illustrated biographies of several pages of fifty comics and comedy teams appearing in films from about 1915 to the late twenties.

Parish, James Robert. *Film Actors Guide: Western Europe*. New Rochelle, NY: Arlington House, 1976. Chronological list of credited films for the performers of many Western European countries.

Parish, James Robert, and William T. Leonard. *Hollywood Players, The Thirties*. New Rochelle, NY: Arlington House, 1976.

Pitts, Michael R., and Louis H. Harrison. *Hollywood on Record: The Film Stars' Discography*. Metuchen, NJ: Scarecrow Press, 1978.

Schickel, Richard. *His Picture in the Papers: A Speculation on Celebrity in America Based on the Life of Douglas Fairbanks, Sr.* New York: Charterhouse, 1974. Light, engaging exploration of Fairbanks' career and his relationship to his public, with provocative asides on contemporary stars.

Schickel, Richard. *The Stars*. New York: The Dial Press, 1962. An admittedly impressionistic and fragmentary history of stars through brief sketches and photos. Index to titles and names.

Schuster, Mel. *Motion Picture Performers: A Bibliography of Magazine and Periodical Articles 1900–1969*. Metuchen, NJ: Scarecrow Press, 1971. Supplement 1, 1970–1974. 1976. Lists magazine citations for performers.

Trent, Paul. *The Image Makers: Sixty Years of Hollywood Glamour*. New York: McGraw-Hill, 1972. Heavily illustrated survey of the stars.

Twomey, Alfred E., and Arthur F. McClure. *The Versatiles: A Study of Supporting Character Actors and Actresses in the American Motion Picture, 1930–1955*. South Brunswick, NJ: A. S. Barnes, 1969. A broad selection of supporting actors and actresses, identified in a still with birth dates, birth location where known, and brief biographical sketches for better-known performers. Selected filmographies are included for all performers.

HISTORY AND ANALYSIS

Andrew, Dudley J. *The Major Film Theories: An Introduction*. New York: Oxford University Press, 1976. Interpretations of the work of Munsterberg, Arnheim, Eisenstein, Balazs, Kracauer, Bazin, Mitry, Metz, Ayfre, and Agel. Notes, bibliography, and subject index.

Balshofer, Fred J., and Arthur C. Miller. *One Reel a Week*. Berkeley: University of California Press, 1967. Two cameramen reminisce about early days in film-making with the facts and impressions as they remember them. An important contribution to the understanding of silent film. Name and title index.

Baxter, John. *Hollywood in the Sixties.* New York: A. S. Barnes, 1972. Survey of the themes, trends, and major films of the decade.

————. *Hollywood in the Thirties.* New York: A. S. Barnes, 1968. Informal survey of the major films, trends and themes of the decade.

Bazin, Andre. *What Is Cinema?* Berkeley: University of California Press, 1967. (Selected and translated by Hugh Gray.) Influential essays on the ontology of the photographic image, myth of total cinema, evolution of film language, qualities of montage, mixed cinema, film and theater, stylistics of Robert Bresson, Charlie Chaplin, documentaries, and painting and film. Name and title index.

————. *What Is Cinema? Vol. 2.* Berkeley: University of California Press, 1971. (Essays selected and translated by Hugh Gray.) Influential essays on Italian realism, *La Terra Trema, Bicycle Thief, De Sica, Umberto D., Cabiria,* Rossellini, *Monsieur Verdoux, Limelight,* the Western, the American pin-up girl, *The Outlaw,* eroticism, and Jean Gabin. Name and title index.

Bergman, Andrew. *We're in the Money: Depression America and Its Films.* New York: New York University Press, 1971. Critical history of the films of the decade in relation to the social and economic milieu. Discusses genres, themes, and Hollywood production. Brief filmography, bibliography, index.

Bourget, Jean-Loup. "Social Implications of the Hollywood Genres." *Journal of Modern Language,* 3:2 (April 1973), pp. 191–200. Argues that conventional art forms imply a tension between the form and the artist that is essentially ironical, so that, in examining the pretexts leading to the final text, the critic unveils basic tensions in society. The implications of a number of popular genres are suggested.

Bowles, Stephen E. "*The Exorcist* and *Jaws:* Techniques of the New Suspense Film." *Literature/Film Quarterly,* 4:3 (Summer 1976), pp. 196–214. Discusses in some detail the changes made from novels to films that simplified the plots and removed moral implications, while substituting special effects to exploit the visual medium and maximize viceral effects on the audiences.

Braudy, Leo. *The World in a Frame: What We See in Films.* Garden City, New York: Anchor Press/Doubleday, 1976. Divided into three sections on visual coherence, genre, and acting and characterization, the study attempts to avoid mechanistic criticism and to provide a way of understanding film that goes beyond categorization. Film and subject indexes.

Buscombe, Edward. "The Idea of Genre in the American Cinema." *Screen,* 11:2 (March-April 1970), pp. 33–45. Identification of many of the icons and motifs associated with the Western, together with an argument for further examination of the relationships of genre to artistic creativity and social values.

Collins, Richard. "Genre: A Reply to Ed Buscombe." *Screen,* 11:4/5 (1970), pp. 66–75. Argues that Buscombe over-emphasizes the iconography of the Western at the expense of seeing the form as an arbitrary collection of situations, antimonies, and motifs related to the American frontier from 1860–1890 which are used by directors to make particular statements.

Conolly, L. W. "Pornography." *Dalhousie Review,* 54:4 (Winter 1974–5), pp. 698–709. Reviews recent investigations into the effects of pornography.

Cook, David A. "Some Structural Approaches to Cinema: A Survey of Models." *Cinema Journal*, 14:3 (Spring 1975), pp. 41–54. A useful analysis of the various structuralist and semiological perspectives on film, drawing on Frederic Jameson's work on literature. The survey touches on Sol Worth after discussion the Eisenstein and Bazin approaches and outlining the early development of semiology.

Dengler, Ralph, S. J. "The Language of Film Titles." *Journal of Communication*, 25:3 (Summer 1975), pp. 51–60. The author applied the General Inquirer computer program to 7,590 film titles culled from various sources for the period from 1900–1968. Semantic clusters are shown to be related to the industry and to the larger culture.

Durgnat, Raymond. *Films and Feelings*. London: Faber and Faber, 1967.

Eckert, Charles W. "The English Cine-Structuralists." *Film Comment*, 9:3 (May-June 1973).

Farber, Stephen. "The Power of Movie Critics." *American Scholar*, 45:3 (Summer 1976), pp. 419–23. Discusses the influence film critics may have in the success of films, with a critique of Pauline Kael's adventures in adulation and prophecy.

Geduld, Harry, ed. *Authors on Film*. Bloomington: Indiana University Press, 1972. Authors' comments on film, arranged into sections on silents, the medium, screenwriting, the Hollywood experience, and movie stars. Author notes and index.

Gow, Gordon. *Hollywood in the Fifties*. New York: A. S. Barnes, 1971. Informal illustrated survey of the themes, genres, and major films of the decade.

Grant, Barry K., ed. *Film Genre: Theory and Criticism*. Metuchen, NJ: Scarecrow Press, 1977. A collection of essays devoted to theoretical and critical perspectives and to individual genres including screwball comedy, disaster, epics, gangster, horror, musical, monster, sport, and westerns. Bibliography for genres, and index.

Greenberg, Harvey R. *The Movies on Your Mind*. New York: Saturday Review Press/E. P. Dutton and Co., 1975. A popularly written analysis of American movies by a psychoanalyst. Chapters on genres and themes.

Gubach, Thomas H. "Film and Cultural Pluralism." *Journal of Aesthetic Education*, 5:2 (April 1971), pp. 35–51.

Hanet, Kari. "Cinema Semiotics in English." *Screen*, 16:8 (Autumn 1975), pp. 125–28. Introduction and bibliography of "the most important works" on visual imagery.

Heath, Stephen. "Film and System: Terms of Analysis, Part 1." *Screen*, 16:1 (Spring 1975), pp. 7–77. Together with Part 2 (16:2, Summer 1975, pp. 91–113), this is an ambitious attempt to analyze the text of *A Touch of Evil* in structural terms.

Hendrix, Jerry, and James A. Wood. "The Rhetoric of Film: Toward Critical Methodology." *Southern Speech Communication Journal*, 34:2 (Winter 1973), pp. 105–122.

Higham, Charles, and Joel Greenberg. *Hollywood in the Forties*. New York: A. S. Barnes, 1968. Informal illustrated survey of the themes, trends and major films of the decade.

Isenberg, Michael T. "Toward an Historical Methodology for Film Scholarship." *Rocky Mountain Social Science Journal*, 12:1 (January 1975), pp. 45–57.

Jacobs, Lewis. *The Movies as Medium*. New York: Octagon Books, 1970. Strong collection of essays on the effects of the physical properties of films and their manifestation through imagery. Divided into sections on image, movement, time and space, color and sound; with short chapters on directors' comments, film expression, and the "plastic structure." This has been an influential volume. Bibliography and index to names.

————. *The Rise of the American Film, A Critical History; With an Essay: Experimental Cinema in America, 1921–1947*. New York: Teachers College Press, 1968. A standard history of film in the United States through 1939, with chapters on Porter, Griffith, Chaplin, and other directors; chapters on business, story development, and themes. Extensive bibliography and subject index.

Jarvie, I. C. *Movies and Society*. New York: Basic Books, 1970. (British: *Towards a Sociology of the Cinema*) Probably the best sociological study available. The volume contains a brief history, analysis of the audience, the experience of film genres (including Westerns, gangster films, spy films, and the musical), and the sociology of evaluation. Bibliography and indexes of subjects, names, and films.

————. *Movies as Social Criticism: Aspects of their Social Psychology*. Metuchen, NJ: Scarecrow Press, 1978. Analysis of film as an expression of collective behavior, with chapters on marriage films and images of blacks in films.

Journal of Aesthetic Education. Special Issue. "Film III: Film Morality and Media Criticism." 8:1 (January 1974).

Jowett, Garth. *Film: The Democratic Art*. Boston: Little, Brown and Company, 1976. The most useful general study of control over the content of film. Written for social historians and others, the volume touches on most issues of film and society. Chapters cover early history, development of the industry, attempts to control and censor films and film-makers, the war years, the impact of television on the film industry, the Hollywood image, declining control, contemporary issues, and other matters. Includes notes, tables, bibliography, index, and appendixes documenting industry policies and audience characteristics.

Kaminsky, Stuart M. *American Film Genres: Approaches to a Critical Theory of Popular Film*. Dayton, OH: Pflaum, 1974. An extremely useful collection of essays on film genres and methodologies. The author approaches each genre with a different methodology in order to demonstrate critical perspectives. Included are an analysis of *Little Caesar* within the gangster genre, a comparison of the Samurai and Western genres, the adaptation of Hemingway's *The Killers*, the theme of violence in the 1970s, various examples of the big caper film, the psychology of horror and science fiction, the musical as performance, historical development and individual expression in comedy, Don Siegel as a genre director, and John Ford's use of character types. Several filmographies and an index are included.

Karp, Ivan. "Good Marx for the Anthropologist: Structure and Anti-Structure in *Duck Soup*," in W. Arens and Susan P. Montague, eds., *The American Dimension*. Port Washington, NY: Alfred Publishing Co., 1976. A good application of Van Gennep's notion of the liminal to an understanding of the Marx Brothers' film.

Katz, John Stuart, ed. *Perspectives on the Study of Film*. Boston: Little, Brown and Company, 1971. A collection of essays reprinted for the volume by a wide range of contributors, arranged into sections on film study and education, the film as art and humanities, film as communications, environment and politics, and curriculum design and evaluation. Bibliography and index of names and titles.

Kauffmann, Stanley, ed. *American Film Criticism from the Beginnings to* Citizen Kane: *Reviews of Significant Films at the Time They First Appeared*. New York: Liveright, 1972.

Kowalski, Rosemary Ribich. *Women and Film: A Bibliography.* Metuchen, NJ: Scarecrow Press, 1976. Divided into four major sections on women as performers, as film-makers, as columnists and critics, and images of women, each section lists reference and historical works, catalogues, and "specific" works. The subject index is detailed.

Lacassin, Francis. "The Comic Strip and Film Language." *Film Quarterly,* 26:1 (Fall 1972), pp. 11–23. (Transl. from Pour un neuvieme art: la bande dessinée, Paris, Union Generale, 1971.) Discusses language, syntax, framing, and other devices, as well as developmental relationships.

Luhr, William, and Peter Lehman. *Authorship and Narrative in the Cinema: Issues in Contemporary Aesthetics and Criticism.* New York: Capricorn Books / G. P. Putnam's Sons, 1977. Based on the authors' dissertations, this volume provides an analysis of the Westerns of John Ford (with emphasis on *The Man Who Shot Liberty Valance* and *The Searchers*) and the narrative heritage of film (with emphasis on *The Strange Case of Dr. Jekyll and Mr. Hyde*). Selected Ford filmography and index.

McConnell, Frank D. *The Spoken Seen: Film and the Romantic Imagination.* Baltimore, MD: Johns Hopkins University Press, 1975. A significant contribution to the dialogue on the nature of the film experience, through a discussion of film forms and the basic "isomorphism between postromantic writing and film." Chapters on film reality, language, politics of the medium, genres, and film personas. Subject index.

McLuhan, Marshall. *Understanding Media: The Extensions of Man.* New York: McGraw-Hill, 1964.

Manvell, Roger. *Films and the Second World War.* South Brunswick, NJ: A. S. Barnes, 1974. An international survey of the films of the period.

Mast, Gerald, and Marshall Cohen. *Film Theory and Criticism: Introductory Readings.* New York: Oxford University Press, 1974; 2nd ed. 1979. Selections from the work of about 40 critics and scholars on reality and film, image and language, the medium, film and the other arts, genre, auteurs, and the audience. Brief bibliography.

Mayer, J. P. *Sociology of Film: Studies and Documents.* London: Faber and Faber, 1946. Interpretation of film's impact on children and adults, with testimonials from people on how films have affected them.

Monaco, James. *How to Read a Film: The Art, Technology, Language, History and Theory of Film and Media.* New York: Oxford University Press, 1977.

Monaco, Paul. *Cinema and Society: France and Germany During the Twenties.* New York: Elsevier, 1976. A valuable analysis of the relationships between popular films and society through the analogy of films and dreams. This Freudian approach is used to analyze the motifs with respect to the historical milieu.

Morrow, James, and Murray Suid. *Moviemaking Illustrated: The Comicbook Filmbook.* Rochelle Park, NJ: Hayden Book Co., 1973. A useful demonstration of film techniques through the use of comic imagery, this little volume is designed for beginning film-makers but is useful for demonstrating basic similarities between the two media.

Murray, Edward. *Nine American Film Critics: A Study of Theory and Practice.* New York: Ungar, 1975. Interpretative essays on James Agee, Robert Warshow, Andrew Sarris, Parker Tyler, John Simon, Pauline Kael, Stanley Kauffmann, Vernon Young, and Dwight MacDonald. Appendix includes brief responses by directors on critics. Index to titles and directors.

Nichols, Bill, ed. *Movies and Methods*. Berkeley: University of California Press, 1977. A generally strong collection of articles arranged according to critical perspective — political, genre, feminist, auteur, mise-en-scene criticism, and theoretical approach — film theory and structuralism-semiology. Glossary and general index.

Perkins, W. H. *Learning the Liveliest Arts: The Critical Enjoyment of Film and Television*. Hobart, Australia: Angus and Robertson, 1972.

Poague, Leland A. "The Semiology of Peter Wollen: A Reconsideration." *Literature/ Film Quarterly*, 3:4 (Fall 1975), pp. 309–15. Acknowledges Wollen's contributions to the understanding of auteur theory, but finds his semiology too mechanistic and fragmented, his references to Pierce and Levi-Strauss too glib and unsubtantiated. The author finds the ultimate weakness in Wollen's perspective to be a political one.

Potamkin, Harry Alan. *The Compound Cinema: The Film Writings of Harry Alan Potamkin*. New York: Teachers College Press, 1977. (Studies in Culture & Communication. Selected, Arranged, and Introduced by Lewis Jacobs.) Arranged into sections on aesthetics, technique, film and society, international features, political aspects, reviews. With bibliography and index.

Rohdie, Sam. "Who Shot Liberty Valance? Notes on Structures of Fabrication in Realist Film." *Salmagundi*, No. 29 (Spring 1975), pp. 159–71. Semiotic analysis of the levels of deception built into *Fort Apache* and *The Man Who Shot Liberty Valance*.

Roud, Richard, ed. *A Critical Dictionary of the Cinema*. New York: Viking Press, 1977.

Ryall, Tom. "The Notion of Genre." *Screen*, 11:2 (March-April 1970), pp. 22–32. Primarily a discussion of the Western, though with some references to the gangster film, the article is concerned with teaching the significance of genre imagery.

Screen. Special issue on Cinema Semiotics. (Spring/Summer 1973).

Sklar, Robert. *Movie-Made America: A Social History of American Movies*. New York: Random House, 1975. A broad cultural history of American film, from the beginnings through post-WW II, which draws on the technology of the medium, its audience, business organization, theaters, industry leaders, government policies, censors, and other matters. Divided into four major sections, the volume treats the emergence of movie culture, the mass cultural context, contributions of movies to mass culture, and the decline of movies as an influential medium. Individual chapters treat various subjects and personalities. Notes and general index.

Smith, Julian. *Looking Away: Hollywood and Vietnam*. New York: Charles Scribner's Sons, 1975. Essays on films during the Korean War and the Vietnam War and consideration of the relationship between the film industry and the wars of recent years. Appendices include an aborted scenario by a South Vietnamese, a list of films receiving Department of Defense support from 1950 to 1968, extracts from Department of Defense instructions on film policies; bibliography, name and title index.

Sobchack, Thomas. "Genre Film: A Classical Experience." *Literature/Film Quarterly*, 3:3 (Summer 1975), pp. 196–204. An essay relating the iconography and general conservatism of structure of the genre film to classical form that reinforces group solidarity. Contemporary film-makers who tamper with genres by changing them induce "in the audience a kind of irrational radicalism, as opposed to a reasonable conformism."

Solomon, Stanley J. *Beyond Formula: American Film Genres*. New York: Harcourt,

1976. Exploration of the Western, the musical, horror and science fiction, crime films, detective films and war films, through the discussion of major genre films. Bibliography and index.

Theall, Donald F. *The Medium Is the Rear View Mirror: Understanding McLuhan.* Montreal: McGill-Queen's University Press, 1971. A forceful critique of McLuhan as superficial and derivative.

Tudor, Andrew. "Genre: Theory and Mispractice in Film Criticism." *Screen,* 11:6 (Nov.-Dec. 1970), pp. 33–43. Using the Western as a point of departure, Tudor emphasizes the difficulty of identifying genre films without using *a priori* criteria and argues for the comparative use of the notion.

——. *Image and Influence: Studies in the Sociology of Film.* London: Allen and Unwin, 1974. Bibliography.

——. *Theories of Film.* New York: Viking Press, 1974. The author's interpretation of Eisenstein, Grierson, Bazin, Kracauer, auteur, and genre. Bibliography.

Wagner, Geoffrey. *The Novel and the Cinema.* Cranbury, NJ: Associated University Presses, 1975. Examination of literary "imagistic techniques and strategies" which contributed to the development of cinematic styles in European and American films. Bibliography and index.

Winston, Douglas Garrett. *The Screenplay as Literature.* Rutherford: Fairleigh Dickinson University Press, 1973. An introduction to the relationships between film and literature, with discussions of film language, narrative, dramatic aspects, standard screenplays, the portrayal of reality, literary adaptation, dream imagery, stream of consciousness, the anti-hero, psychoanalysis, "plotless" plots, the underground cinema. With notes, bibliography, information on film rentals, and an index.

Wollen, Peter. *Signs and Meaning in the Cinema.* Bloomington: Indiana University Press, 1972. An early attempt to bring film semiotics into respectability among critics. Divided into three sections dealing with Sergei Eisenstein's aesthetics, auteur theory through discussion of John Ford and Howard Hawks, and a semiology of film, the volume also contains a booklist of relevant works.

THEMES AND GENRES

Themes

Alloway, Lawrence. *Violent America: The Movies 1946–1964.* New York: The Museum of Modern Art, 1971. Based on a 1969 film series shown at the Museum, the illustrated essay examines "the transformations of meaning undergone by set figures and set situations, revealed by the forms of movie violence under the pressure of the contemporary world" as found in the formula films of the times. Appendix of the films cited, with credits and brief notes.

Atkins, Thomas R., ed. *Graphic Violence on the Screen.* New York: Monarch Press, 1976. Illustrated essays on the film noir, horror films from Hammer Studios, Kung Fu films and Italian westerns, massacre films, and a memoir about death in contemporary films. Brief bibliography.

——. *Sexuality in the Movies.* Bloomington: Indiana University Press, 1975.

Benson, Dennis C. *Electric Evangelism.* Nashville: Abingdon Press, 1973.

Bruno, Michael. *Venus in Hollywood: The Continental Enchantress from Garbo to*

Loren. New York: Lyle Stuart, 1970. A brief history of the stars, with appendices of the ten best films, the Production Code, name changes. Bibliography and indexes to titles, theaters, and personalities.

Butler, Ivan. *Religion in the Cinema*. New York: A. S. Barnes, 1969.

Cawelti, John G. "Myths of Violence in American Popular Culture." *Critical Inquiry,* 1:3 (March 1975), pp. 521–41. Discusses four ways in which Americans have tended to justify violence.

Deming, Barbara. *Running Away From Myself*. New York: Grossman, 1969. A portrait of America from the films of the Forties. Chapter 2, "I'm Not Fighting for Anything Any More—Except Myself," discusses the WW II war hero as portrayed in film, and Chapter 3, "I've Got to Bring Him Back Home Where He Belongs," concerns the theme of the returning soldier and the problems he encounters.

Dowdy, Andrew. *Movies Are Better Than Ever: Wide-Screen Memories of the Fifties*. New York: William Morrow and Company, 1973. A survey of themes, fetishes, and motifs in popular films of the decade. Chapters cover the decline of audiences, blacklisting, 3-D films, public fears in films, censorship, soft pornography, youthful rebellion, science fiction, stars, the breast fetish, adaptations, and the college audience. Name and film index.

Everson, William K. *The Bad Guys: A Pictorial History of the Movie Villain*. New York: Citadel Press, 1964.

Friar, Ralph E., and Natasha A. Friar. *The Only Good Indian. . . . : The Hollywood Gospel*. New York: Drama Book Specialists, 1972. An extensive critique of the depiction and use of native Americans in films, with some treatment of the literary and dramatic heritage also included. Appendices identify actors who have played Indians and provide a motif index to films dealing with characteristic plots involving Indian themes. Index.

Holtan, Orley I. "Individualism, Alienation and the Search for Community: Urban Imagery in Recent American Films." *Journal of Popular Culture* 4:4 (Spring 1971), pp. 933–42.

Lamb, Blaine P. "The Convenient Villain: The Early Cinema Views the Mexican-American." *Journal of the West* 14:4 (October 1975), pp. 75–81. Documented study of the stereotypes developed in American film before World War I.

Mapp, Edward. *Blacks in American Films: Today and Yesterday*. Metuchen, NJ: Scarecrow Press, 1971. History of the portrayal of blacks in films. Stills.

———. "Black Women in Films." *Black Scholar* 4:2 (March-April 1973).

Mellen, Joan. *Women and Their Sexuality in the New Film*. New York: Horizon Press, 1973. Analysis of the bourgeois woman, lesbianism, Bergman and women, sexual politics and Bertolucci's *Last Tango in Paris,* the moral psychology of Rohmer's Fu Manchu stories, Mae West, and other topics.

Merritt, R. L. "The Bashful Hero in American Films of the Nineteen Forties." *Quarterly Journal of Speech* 61:2 (April 1975), pp. 129–39. An interesting perspective on the characteristic hero represented by Bing Crosby, James Stewart, and others in the romantic comedies and light social dramas of the period.

Miller, Albert Jay, and Michael James Ari. *Death: A Bibliographical Guide*. Metuchen, NJ: Scarecrow Press, 1977. A checklist of 3,848 books, articles, and films arranged by discipline, with author and subject indexes.

Ogunbi, Adebayo, comp. *Blacks in Films: A Bibliography.* East Lansing: The Media Component, College of Urban Development, Michigan State University, 1974. Alphabetical checklist of books and articles about blacks in films.

Powers, Anne. *Blacks in American Movies: A Selected Bibliography.* Metuchen, NJ: Scarecrow Press, 1974.

Smith, Julian. *Looking Away: Hollywood and Vietnam.* New York: Scribners, 1975. Engaging essays on the Vietnam War and the homefront, with appendices that include an incomplete filmscript by Vinh Noan, a South Vietnamese, a list of films for which the Department of Defense rendered assistance, and an extract of the department's instructions for assistance to film-makers. Annotated bibliography, index.

Tyler, Parker. *Screening the Sexes: Homosexuality in the Movies.* New York: Holt, Rinehart and Winston, 1972. A sympathetic, perhaps affectionate, treatment of homosexual themes in film.

Walker, Alexander. *The Celluloid Sacrifice: Aspects of Sex in the Movies.* London: Michael Joseph, 1966. The emphasis in this volume is on the portrayal of women stars on the screen. Included in the discussion are Theda Bara, Clara Bow, Mary Pickford, Mae West, Marlene Dietrich, Greta Garbo, Jean Harlow, Marilyn Monroe, Elizabeth Taylor, and others. Chapters on British and American censorship and male leads conclude the volume. Index.

————. *Stardom: The Hollywood Phenomenon.* New York: Stein and Day, 1970. An exploration of the relationship between acting and the star image, with discussion in later chapters on the public qualities of the image. Roughly a history, the volume is divided into eleven parts: Innocence, Experience, Dedication, Extravagance, Servitude, Endurance, and Emancipation and After. Appendices, brief bibliography, name and title index.

Yacowar, Maurice. "Aspects of the Familiar: A Defense of Minority Stereotyping in the Popular Film." *Literature/Film Quarterly* 2:2 (Spring 1974), pp. 129–39. A defense of the use of popular stereotypes of women, Jews, blacks, and Indians. Such types are used as part of the popular iconography and should be considered in terms of their metaphorical appropriateness, rather than as realistic representatives of minority groups. The film-maker cannot be criticized for drawing on the pool of types in the popular imagination, but he also has a responsibility "to extend and to replenish the humanity from which he has drawn his metaphors, not to permit a human type to freeze formulaic."

Genres

Annan, David. *Movie Fantastic—Beyond the Dream Machine.* New York: Bounty/ Crown, 1975.

Barbour, Alan G. *Days of Thrills and Adventure.* New York: Collier-Macmillan, 1970. Illustrated history of the sound serial from 1930 to 1956. The appendix lists films with credits and chapter titles.

Barsam, Richard M. *Nonfiction Film: A Critical History.* New York: Dutton, 1973. International coverage of documentaries with emphasis on English language films. Chapters on Grierson, Flaherty, and World War II films. Appendices identify production facts and awards. Bibliography and index.

————. " 'This Is America': Documentaries for Theaters, 1942–1951." *Cinema Journal* 12:2 (Spring 1973), pp. 22–38.

Baxter, John. *The Gangster Film*. New York: A. S. Barnes, 1970. Illustrated career sketches of 225 personalities involved in gangster films, with a brief introduction to the genre. Film and name index.

————. *Science Fiction in the Cinema*. New York: A. S. Barnes, 1970. A good basic history of the science fiction feature, with a chapter on the serial, through about 1968. Selected filmography with credits and a checklist of criticism.

Bohn, Thomas William. *An Historical and Descriptive Analysis of the "Why We Fight" Series*. New York: Arno Press, 1977. (University of Wisconsin dissertation, 1968)

Borde, Raymond et Etienne Chaumeton. *Panorama du film noir américain: 1941– 1953*. Paris: Editions d'Aujourd'hui, 1975. The definition, background, major periods, stylistic sources and influence, together with filmographies of American and French films, and secondary bibliographies of the "dark film" popular from about 1940–1955.

Butler, Ivan. *The Horror Film*. New York: A. S. Barnes, 1967. A brief survey of horror films, which focuses on various classics. Includes a partially annotated chronology of best films, brief bibliography, and index.

————. *The War Film*. New York: A. S. Barnes, 1974. Photos, index.

Calder, Jenni. *There Must Be a Lone Ranger*. London: Hamish Hamilton, 1974. An extensive examination of the Western myth and its relationship to reality and the interpretation of the West through films. Notes, filmography, name and title index.

Cameron, Ian. *Adventure in the Movies*. New York: Crescent Books, 1973. Pictorial treatment of major themes in adventure films, including a section on the use of adventure for propaganda: confused. Index.

Cawelti, John G. *Adventure, Mystery, and Romance: Formula Stories as Art and Popular Culture*. Chicago: University of Chicago Press, 1976. The most thorough available study of three basic popular genres and a variety of formulas most pervasive in fiction, television, and film. Bibliographical notes and general index.

————. *The Six-Gun Mystique*. Bowling Green, OH: Bowling Green University Popular Press, 1971. Cawelti's is the first book-length study of the Western formula in fiction and film. Includes discussion of the importance of setting, complex of characters, types of situations and patterns of action, the dramatic structure of the Western and the relationships of formula to culture. Lists of titles in several media, bibliography.

Clarens, Carlos. *Horror Movies: An Illustrated History of the Horror Films*. New York: Putnam, 1967. Historical survey of early international contributions to the genre, with an examination of major themes in horror films. An appendix provides credits for about 400 films covered in the text. Index.

Clipper, Lawrence J. "Archetypal Figures in Early Film Comedy." *Western Humanities Review* 28:4 (Autumn 1974), pp. 353–66.

Daniels, Les. *Living in Fear: A History of Horror in the Mass Media*. New York: Charles Scribner's Sons, 1975. An affectionate collection of illustrations, photos, comics, cartoons, and stories, interspersed among an extensive essay. Though the study is not intended to be exhaustive, it does contain a sensible introduction to the interpretation of horror and much worthwhile historical information. Index.

Davis, Brian. *The Thriller*. London: Studio Vista, 1973. Illustrated survey of the detective, spy, and message thrillers, with chapters on the chase and the heist. Name and title index.

Druxman, Michael B. *One Good Film Deserves Another*. Cranbury, NJ: A. S. Barnes, 1977. A survey of movie remakes.

Durgnat, Raymond. *The Crazy Mirror: Hollywood Comedy and the American Image*. New York: Horizon Press, 1970.

Edelson, Edward. *Visions of Tomorrow: Great Science Fiction from the Movies*. Garden City, NY: Doubleday, 1975. A light treatment of science fiction films through the *Planet of the Apes* and *The Andromeda Strain,* with a chapter on television S-F.

Everson, William K. *Classics of the Horror Film*. Secaucus, NJ: Citadel Press, 1974. Photos.

————. *The Detective in Film*. Secaucus, NJ: Citadel Press, 1972.

Eyles, Allen. *American Comedy Since Sound*. New York: A. S. Barnes, 1969. An illustrated survey.

————. *The Western: An Illustrated Guide*. New York: A. S. Barnes, 1975. Career sketches and filmographies of 358 persons associated with Westerns. Index to films and names.

Farren, Jonathan. "Cinema et rock n'roll." *Cinema*. 200 (July/August 1975), pp. 18– 54. A collection of interviews, analyses and an extensive chronological filmography from 1956– 1975.

Fenin, George N., and William K. Everson. *The Western: From Silents to the Seventies*. New York: Grossman, 1973. "A New and Expanded Edition." A detailed history of the Western, with brief chapters on major directors, performers, films, and themes. Index to names and films.

Fielding, Raymond. *The American Newsreel, 1911–1967*. Norman, OK: University of Oklahoma Press, 1972.

————. *The March of Time, 1935– 1951*. New York: Oxford University Press, 1978. Excellent historical and technical study of the series through interviews, examination of the films, and secondary sources. Bibliography, filmography, and index.

French, Philip. *Westerns: Aspects of a Movie Genre*. New York: Viking Press, 1974; rev. ed. 1977. Useful exploration of the relationship between the Western and political and cultural values through analysis of the genre's iconology and characterization. Selected filmography and bibliography.

Gabree, John. *Gangsters: From Little Caesar to the Godfather*. New York: Pyramid, 1973. 160 pages, illustrated, b/w.

Glaessner, Verina. *Kung-Fu: Cinema of Vengeance*. New York: Bounty, 1973.

Gow, Gordon. *Suspense in the Cinema*. New York: Warner Paperback Library, 1971.

Grace, Harry A. "A Taxonomy of American Crime Film Themes." *Journal of Social Psychology* 42:1 (Jan.– July 1955), pp. 129– 36.

Haining, Peter, ed. *The Ghouls: Horror Stories That Became Great Films*. New York: Stein and Day, 1971.

Harmon, Jim, and Donald F. Glut. *The Great Movie Serials: Their Sound and Fury*. Garden City, NY: Doubleday, 1972.

Huss, Roy, and T. J. Ross, eds. *Focus on the Horror Film*. Englewood Cliffs, NJ: Prentice-Hall, 1972. Critical essays on the horror film, with a brief bibliography and selected filmography.

Jacobs, Lewis. *The Documentary Tradition, from Nanook to Woodstock.* New York: Hopkinson and Blake, 1971.

———. "World War II and the American Film." *Cinema Journal* 7:1 (Winter 1967–68), pp. 1–21. A key article on the movies of World War II and the war films. Broad coverage of numerous films from the late thirties through 1945.

Johnson, William, ed. *Focus on the Science Fiction Film.* Englewood Cliffs, NJ: Prentice-Hall, 1972. Essays on science fiction films covering the beginnings to the present, with several essays on the issues, together with brief responses by several authors and film-makers to questions about adaptations and production. Brief filmography and bibliography. Index to names and films.

Kagan, Norman. *The War Film.* New York: Pyramid, 1974. Edited by Ted Sennett, photos, index.

Karimi, A. M. *Toward a Definition of the American Film Noir (1941–1949).* New York: Arno Press, 1976. (University of Iowa dissertation, 1973.) Reprint of Karimi's dissertation, which includes a working definition, sources, pre- and postwar expression, and issues for further studies. The volume contains films listed according to directors, with an alphabetical list of films and review data, together with a bibliography.

Karpf, Stephen Louis. *The Gangster Film: Emergence, Variation, and Decay of a Genre, 1930–1940.* New York: Arno Press, 1973. A detailed examination of the films of the period, with critical apparatus.

Kitses, Jim. *Horizons West.* Bloomington: Indiana University Press, 1970. Illustrated studies of the Western films of Anthony Mann, Budd Boetticher, and Sam Peckinpah, with credited filmographies.

Lahue, Kalton D. *Continued Next Week: A History of the Moving Picture Serial.* Norman, OK: University of Oklahoma Press, 1964. An illustrated history of the silent serial from 1914 to 1930. The appendix lists serials from 1912–1930 and includes credits and chapter titles.

———. *World of Laughter: The Motion Picture Comedy Short, 1910–1930.* Norman, OK: University of Oklahoma Press, 1966.

Lee, Raymond, and B. C. Van Hecke. *Gangsters and Hoodlums: The Underworld in the Cinema.* Cranbury, NJ: A. S. Barnes, 1971.

Lee, Walt, and Bill Warren, eds. *Reference Guide to Fantastic Films, Science Fiction, Fantasy and Horror.* 3 volumes. Los Angeles: Chelsea Press, 1973. The most comprehensive filmography available.

Leyda, Jay. *Films Beget Films.* New York: Hill and Wang, 1964. A history and interpretation of compilation films.

London, Rose. *Cinema of Mystery.* New York: Crown, 1976.

Lovell, Alan, and Jim Hillier. *Studies in Documentary.* New York: Viking, 1972.

McArthur, Colin. *Underworld USA.* New York: Viking, 1972. An analysis of the gangster film and thriller from the early 1930s to about 1970. Chapters treat iconography, historical development, background, and individual directors, including Fritz Lang, John Huston, Jules Dassin, Robert Siodmak, Elia Kazan, Nicholas Ray, Samuel Fuller, Don Siegel, and Jean-Pierre Melville. Subject and film title indexes.

McCaffrey, Donald W. *The Golden Age of Sound Comedy: Comic Films and Comedians of the Thirties.* South Brunswick, NJ: A. S. Barnes, 1973.

McClure, Arthur. "Hollywood at War." *Journal of Popular Film* 1:2 (Spring 1972), pp. 123–35.

McVay, J. Douglas. *The Musical Film*. Cranbury, NJ: A. S. Barnes, 1967.

Mamber, Stephen. *Cinema Verité in America: Studies in Uncontrolled Documentary*. Cambridge, MA: The MIT Press, 1974. Essays on definition, style and film-makers, which are oriented to classroom use. Included is material on Drew Associates, the Maysles Brothers, D. A. Pennebaker, Richard Leacock, and Frederick Wiseman. Filmographies, rental sources, course schedule, bibliography, and index.

Maynard, Richard A., comp. *The American West on Film: Myth and Reality*. Rochelle Park, NJ: Hayden Book Co., 1974.

Menningen, Jürgen. *Filmbuch Science Fiction*. Köln, M. DuMont Schauberg, 1975.

Menville, Douglas Alver. *A Historical and Critical Survey of the Science of Fiction Film*. New York: Arno Press.

Nachbar, Jack. *Focus on the Western*. Englewood Cliffs, NJ: Prentice-Hall, 1974. Fourteen key essays on the origins, definition, cultural interpretation, and present state of the genre. Chronology of major films, annotated bibliography, and index to names and films.

———. *Western Films: An Annotated Critical Bibliography*. New York: Garland Publishing Co., 1975. An extensively annotated bibliography of sources, divided into sections on reference materials, pre-1950 criticism, specific films, performers, directors, history, theory, audience, comparative studies, teaching, and selected periodicals. Author and subject indexes.

Parish, James Robert, and Michael R. Pitts. *The Great Gangster Pictures*. Metuchen, NJ: Scarecrow Press, 1976. Includes information on detective, procedural, and other types, as well as gangster films. Production information; credits, usually with a plot summary and often some indication of the film's reception.

Parish, James Robert. *The Great Movie Series*. South Brunswick, NJ: A. S. Barnes, 1971. A useful illustrated survey of 25 series titles, including Andy Hardy, Blondie, Bomba, Boston Blackie, Bowery Boys, Charlie Chan, Crime Doctor, Dr. Christian, Dr. Kildare, Ellery Queen, The Falcon, Francis, Hopalong Cassidy, James Bond, Jungle Jim, Lone Wolf, Ma and Pa Kettle, Maizie, Matt Helm, Mr. Moto, Philo Vance, The Saint, Sherlock Holmes, and Tarzan.

Parish, James Robert, and Michael R. Pitts. *The Great Science Fiction Pictures*. Metuchen, NJ: Scarecrow Press, 1977. Synopses and credits for several hundred films, with brief lists of science fiction programs on radio and television. Brief bibliography of bibliographies, indexes, and checklists of works on science fiction.

———. *The Great Spy Pictures*. Metuchen, NJ: Scarecrow Press, 1974. This volume contains a brief history of the spy film, an excellent filmography of 463 films with credits and plot synopses; two weak lists of radio and television dramas; and a good selective checklist of spy novels and one of series novels by T. Allan Taylor.

———. *The Great Western Pictures*. Metuchen, NJ: Scarecrow Press, 1976. Brief history of the genre, with credits and plot synopses of 300 films.

Parish, James R., and Don E. Stanke. *The Swashbucklers*. New Rochelle, NY: Arlington House, 1975.

Porfirio, Robert G. "No Way Out: Existential Motifs in the Film Noir." *Sight and Sound* 45:4 (Autumn 1976), pp. 212–17. Perceptive essay on some of the themes and motifs in the film noir, with a discussion of the literary and philosophical background that pervades the form.

Rider, David. *The Great Movie Cartoon Parade.* New York: Crown, 1976.

Rovin, Jeff. *A Pictorial History of Science-Fiction Films.* Secaucus, NJ: Citadel Press, 1975.

Sennett, Ted. *Lunatics and Lovers: A Tribute to the Giddy and Glittering Era of the Screen's Screwball and Romantic Comedies.* New Rochelle, NY: Arlington House, 1973. A tribute to some 200 films and 100 performers in the genre.

Shadoian, Jack. *Dreams and Dead Ends: The American Gangster/Crime Film.* Cambridge, MA: The MIT Press, 1977. An insightful history and analysis of this complex genre through the detailed examination of representative films.

Shain, Russell Earl. *An Analysis of Motion Pictures about War Released by the American Film Industry, 1939–1970.* New York: Arno Press, 1976. (University of Illinois dissertation, 1971.)

Silver, Alain. *The Samurai Film.* South Brunswick, NJ: A. S. Barnes, 1977. A history of the genre that examines films of individual directors. Glossary, bibliography, and index to names and films.

Sontag, Susan. "The Imagination of Disaster." *Commentary* 40 (October 1965), pp. 42–48. Sees science fiction films as an imaginative mediator between man and his modern technological dilemma.

Spears, Jack. *Hollywood: The Golden Era.* South Brunswick, NJ: A. S. Barnes, 1971. Essays on World War I movies, early animation, baseball movies, the movie doctor, and the movie Indian; further essays on film personalities and collaborations.

Springer, John. *All Talking! All Singing! All Dancing!: A Pictorial History of the Movie Musical.* New York: Citadel Press, 1973.

Stedman, Raymond William. *The Serials.* Norman: University of Oklahoma Press, 1978, 2nd. rev. ed. The best available discussion of fiction serials in American film, radio, television, and comics, with appendices listing radio and television serials. Bibliography, index, photos.

Steinbrunner, Chris, and Bert Goldblatt. *Cinema of the Fantastic.* New York: Saturday Review Press, 1972. Discussions of a potpourri of science fiction and fantasy films from *A Trip to the Moon* to *Forbidden Planet.*

Steinbrunner, Chris, and Otto Penzler. *Encyclopedia of Mystery and Detection.* New York: McGraw-Hill Book Company, 1976.

Thomson, David. *America in the Dark: Hollywood and the Gift of Unreality.* New York: William Morrow and Company, 1977. See the chapter "Man and the Mean Street" for detective films; "Woman's Realm and Man's Castle" for images of women; and the chapter on *Citizen Kane.*

Turau, Kenneth, and Stephen F. Zito. *Sinema: American Pornographic Films and the People Who Make Them.* New York: Praeger, 1974.

Tuska, Jon. *The Filming of the West.* Garden City, NJ: Doubleday, 1976.

Vallance, Tom. *The American Musical.* South Brunswick, NJ: A. S. Barnes, 1970.

Whitney, John S. "A Filmography of Film Noir." *Journal of Popular Film* 5:3/4 (1976), pp. 321–71. Brief definition and extensive filmography, with credits and brief synopses, of the film noir. Index to performers, production, and literary sources.

Willis, Donald C. *Horror and Science Fiction Films: A Checklist.* Metuchen, NJ: Scarecrow Press, 1972.

Woll, Allen L. *Songs from Hollywood Musical Comedies, 1927 to the Present: A Dictionary.* Ref. Lib. in the Humanities, Vol. 44. New York: Garland, 1976. Index.

Wright, Will. *Sixguns and Society.* Berkeley: University of California Press, 1975. A structuralist examination of the Western as "a conceptual model for social action." Selective bibliography and index to names and titles.

Zinman, David H. *Saturday Afternoon at the Bijou.* New Rochelle, NY: Arlington House, 1973. Informal examination of 30 series film groups, with credited filmographies. Brief bibliography and index to names and films.

INDEX